Josyp Terelya WITNESS
to Apparitions and Persecution in the USSR

An Autobiography by
Josyp Terelya with Michael H. Brown

Edited and Published for
The Riehle Foundation by:

FAITH PUBLISHING COMPANY
P.O. BOX 237
MILFORD, OHIO 45150

Published for the Riehle Foundation by Faith Publishing Company.

For additional copies, write to: The Riehle Foundation
P.O. Box 7
Milford, OH 45150

"The God of our fathers has chosen you that you should know His will, and see the Just One, and hear the voice of His mouth. For you will be His witness to all men of what you have seen and heard." —*Acts* 22:14-15

Josyp Terelya

TABLE OF CONTENTS

DEDICATION

To the Mother of all humanity, and to the victims of persecution—that which has already occurred and that which is to come.

ACKNOWLEDGMENTS

This book could not have been done without the dedicated assistance of Father Roman Danylak, J.U.D., pastor of St. Joseph's Cathedral in Toronto. Father Danylak spent three months translating Josyp's version of events into English, which was then rendered into book format. His formidable talents as both a priest and a translator were indispensable. Other translators who assisted included Mychajlo Kobylecky of St. Catherines, Bohdan J. Swystun of Toronto, and Christine Swystun, a graduate of the University of Toronto who is pursuing further studies in journalism. The idea for this book originated largely through the efforts of Marie Leman, who runs the Medjugorje Peace Center at P.O. Box 923 in Williamsville, NY 14221 and produced a video interview with Josyp, "Apparitions of the Mother of God in the Ukraine," which is available by writing that address. Josyp's precious wife Olena, who was learning English, patiently translated on occasion and lent us use of their dining room, often to late hours. Also, thanks to the many who prayed, especially Harold and Rose Brown of Niagara Falls and Sue Flynn of Oyster Bay. Bill and Fran Reck of the Riehle Foundation showed great faith in taking on this project with little advance warning. Their dedication to Mary is a model for us all. May the Holy Spirit come upon everyone who helped, and everyone who reads the following pages.

PREFACE

The account you are about to read is the story of a mystic, a visionary, a suffering soul, a victim of Communism. It is the story of a nationalist, a rebel, a Catholic activist. It is the account of a man who spent much of his life behind bars because of his faith and evangelism.

It is also the story of extraordinary events—allegedly supernatural events—that are said to have occurred in the Soviet Union.

Josyp Jaromyr Terelya has fought for the cause of Christianity all his life and in the most hostile of circumstances. This is his autobiography, told through translators during his ongoing exile in Canada, a life story that reached a climax in 1987, when, according to Josyp and other Ukrainian Catholics, the Virgin Mary, as if in response to their suffering, appeared above an abandoned chapel in the Ukraine.

I say "alleged" because that and other events in this book are spectacular and controversial even by the standards of Marian phenomena. Did the Mother of God save Josyp from freezing to death in a prison cell during 1972? Could it be true that apparitions of Mary and Jesus have been witnessed by hundreds of thousands in the remote village called Hrushiv? And if so is there an apocalyptic warning in her messages—as Josyp claims—and was the outbreak of phenomena in 1987 connected in some transcendental way to the dramatic subsequent events in Eastern Europe and Russia?

These are all matters for the reader to discern for himself or herself. This is Josyp's book, and while a good number of facts have been verified, he was the sole source for the majority of names, places, and events. This is a memoir, not a journalistic pursuit, and as such the writing is often phrased the way it came through in translation. My job was to take what Josyp said and put it into organized format. At each turn I found Josyp's accounts amazing and confusing. Could a story this large and paranormal really be true?

Again, that's a question you the reader will have to decide. Josyp's detractors may claim that his story is simply a product of the folklore and superstition which have traditionally abounded in the Ukraine. The skeptics may also find refuge in the fact that Josyp spent years in Soviet psychiatric wards. Does he not possess a mercurial, even volatile personality? Was he not affected by the isolation of imprisonment? Could he not have simply concocted many of the stories for political and religious aims? Does he not possess powerful biases? His supporters will answer that political prisoners were routinely sent to psychiatric wards *not* because of actual mental disorders but simply as a way of discrediting and punishing them. They will also argue that his visions are very similar to apparitions witnessed elsewhere. One thing is for sure: aspects of his testimony have been taken seriously by Amnesty International, the Raoul Wallenberg Society, a Congressional subcommittee, international radio broadcasters, and the Vatican, which invited him to speak with Pope John Paul II in a private audience. Washington columnist Jack Anderson described Josyp as "another Alexander Solzhenitsyn" whose fingers had been broken for writing letters from prison and who was forced to drink water from a toilet bowl. The suffering was endless and went far beyond fractured fingers. Cleveland Mayor George V. Voinovich, in declaring January 11, 1988 "Josyp Terelya Day," explained that "this intolerable punishment was imposed on him because of his work for the freedom of the Church." Two decades in prison!

Never has there been a Marian "visionary" with such a tumultuous history. Those who accept Josyp's supernatural

experiences will probably compare them to Medjugorje—
the Yugoslavian village where it is said the Virgin has been
appearing since 1981. But the Ukrainian phenomena, especially the messages herein contained, should also be studied in light of LaSalette, which seems to have the most in
common with what Josyp and other Ukrainians experienced
in terms of prophecies.

The life story of Josyp Terelya defies the inventiveness of
even the poet, the novelist, the screenwriter. Is it all the product of an exceptional imagination? Is it a huge hallucination
induced by the psychological effects of incarceration? Is it
a hoax? Is it a counterfeit perpetrated by Satan? Or is it,
as many Catholics feel, another sign that events predicted
in the Book of Revelation are now upon us?

According to a front-page story in *The New York Times*
on October 13, 1987 ("Specter Haunts the Ukraine: The
Church That Isn't There"), a "series of miraculous visions
started in mid-May, in the small village of (Hrushiv) in the
Lvov region. A young girl, surprised at seeing a light in a
long-closed church, looked inside and saw a shining female
figure surrounded by radiant light and carrying a child."
According to another story in *The Catholic Register* (June
3, 1990), adult villagers soon saw the same apparition, and
pretty soon thousands of others witnessed Mary at Hrushiv—
prime among them Josyp Terelya.

Soon additional apparitions were observed at shrines,
monasteries, and various locations throughout the long-
oppressed Ukraine.

This is the story of those events in the context of Terelya's
life and prison sentences. His perseverance under the most
extreme inhumanity—his suffering for his beliefs—is itself
a story in some ways as spectacular as the subsequent
apparitions.

If what he recounts is true there occurred behind the Iron
Curtain a series of incidents the likes of which, in their political context, may be without precedent.

I have no reason to doubt what Terelya recounts, but neither did I have the capability of checking many crucial details.
I volunteered to help Josyp tell his story because I feel his
experiences lucidly portray the oppression of atheism. He
was a witness to the onslaught of anti-Christianity. He was

a witness to the brutality of godless Communism. He was witness to what he describes as supernatural interventions on our beleaguered planet, and in the end he is a witness to the resurrection of a Church that, against all odds and through the efforts of leaders like himself, survived the nightmare years of repression.

I don't necessarily share Josyp's political or philosophical views, which are often headstrong and controversial, but what I do share is his concern that atheists, egoists, and "humanists" have too often succeeded in suppressing spirituality. I also share his belief that God acts forcefully and often miraculously in our lives, when we let Him.

Michael H. Brown
Toronto and Niagara Falls

Chapter 1

QUEEN
OF FREEDOM

Word of the apparitions reached me soon after I was released from the Soviet prisons. I could hardly believe my ears. The Mother of God was appearing in Hrushiv, a village in the far western reaches of the USSR.

These things were not supposed to happen in the Soviet Union, where the official doctrine of atheism has no room for supernatural occurrences. Yet that's what a Basilian nun was telling me: that the Virgin Mary, messenger of Christ, was presenting herself to the world's foremost Communist country.

The nun, Sister Iryna, said people from across the Soviet Union were flocking to Hrushiv (pronounced *Hru-shoo*) to see for themselves. Thousands were gathering. As far as I know, it was the largest unsanctioned congregation since the establishment of Communism. It was even being mentioned—albeit mockingly—in the Soviet newspapers.

It was April 29, 1987. I didn't sleep that night. I was consumed by excitement and wonderment. The Virgin Mary, mother of our Savior and Redeemer, was intervening in a nation whose government had ruthlessly quashed Christianity and especially the Eastern Rite Catholic Church for most of the century.

I felt touched on a very personal level. It had been only three months since the Soviets, under pressure by such states-

1

men as President Ronald Reagan, had given me my freedom. I was 43 years old and had spent more than twenty
years—half my life in prisons, labor camps, and psychiatric
hospitals. My "crime"? Catholic activism. I was leader of
the Catholic underground. As you will read later, I was isolated, beaten, and tortured within a hairsbreadth of death.
I was forbidden from professing or even acknowledging my
deeply held Catholic beliefs. I was deprived of every form
of nourishment.

And now, in 1987, just months after my release, came
the most dramatic news conceivable—that Mother Mary was
extending her presence to a nation which had been horribly
oppressed since the days of Lenin. Moreover, she was appearing in my poor, beloved homeland, the Ukraine. It was a
part of the USSR that had struggled against all odds to maintain its faith, and it was suddenly home to an event that
was extraordinary even by the standards of Marian
apparitions.

Let us remember a few things before I proceed. It is true
that Gorbachev was in power during 1987, but it was still
a very precarious time for Christians in that vast empire
known as the Soviet Union. To this day it is extremely difficult to be a Catholic there. But at the time of the first apparitions, it was far worse. We had to worship in forests or
houses, hidden from the omnipresent eyes of the KGB. The
Catholic Church was totally suppressed and illegal. It was
viewed as the greatest single threat to the evil empire.

So in 1987 it was risky to go around proclaiming the
Blessed Virgin, or for that matter, even to be seen wearing
a crucifix. The forces of totalitarianism still exerted their
seemingly unbreakable hold. This was more than two years
before the liberation of Poland and Eastern Europe. The Catholic Church had been harassed since 1918 and actually out-
lawed in 1946, its churches, monasteries, and chapels
bulldozed out of existence or converted to Russian Orthodox. Can you blame me for being excited? The Mother of
God, in the godless Soviet Union!

From what I could gather, the story went like this: On
April 26, 1987, three days before Sister Iryna informed me
of it, a 12-year-old peasant girl, Marina Kizyn, was on her

way to school when she noticed a strange light. It was hovering over an ocher-colored chapel—the church of the Blessed Trinity (or Three Holy Ones). The church, which has a history of supernatural incidents, had been plundered and nailed shut by the Communists. It was named Blessed Trinity because during the last century people claimed to have seen three apparitional candles burning over a miraculous well there—a well whose waters were said to heal.

Marina lived nearby in a modest house. As she drew closer to the curious light she saw a woman with a baby cradled gently in her arms. The woman, clad in funereal black, was in the light over the church. She told Marina that the Ukrainians, by virtue of all their suffering, had been chosen to lead the Soviet Union back to Christianity.

Marina became very frightened and dashed back to tell her mother, Myroslawa, and her sister Halia.

Who can blame this young girl for experiencing fear and confusion? Her mother listened to her excited account and wondered if young Marina was making up a story to avoid going to school. But there were authentic emotions etched into the girl's face. Immediately Mrs. Kizyn walked out the door to see for herself.

It took only a minute or two to get to Blessed Trinity. The light was still there, over the balcony, and she saw what her daughter saw—the same lady holding the same infant. The incredible figure bowed to them.

Like her daughter, Mrs. Kizyn was overcome. She fell to her knees. "Marina," she said in what must have been a hushed, awe-filled tone, "this is the Virgin Mary. Kneel down and pray!"

I was struck by the date. April 26, 1987. It was the first anniversary of the most famous disaster in Ukrainian history, the accident at the nuclear plant in Chernobyl. The date was also significant in at least one other way. The Pope had declared 1987 a "Marian Year," and it was as if Heaven itself was acknowledging that proclamation. I am now convinced that this mysterious apparition, on the anniversary of Chernobyl, was a sign that the times prophesied in the Book of Revelation are approaching. Moreover, it was just before the millennial celebration of Christianity in the Soviet

Union. And where had that Christianity started? Along the Dnieper River in the Ukraine.

Within hours, hundreds and then thousands of faithful gathered around Blessed Trinity. It was word of mouth, the whole country can talk in one day of something so extraordinary as Marina's visions. The people felt touched mystically. They were coming from a thousand kilometers away. Naturally there were Ukrainians—Catholics and Orthodox alike—but they were joined by travelers from republics such as Georgia and Byelorussia, or from the Baltics. There were believers and non-believers, there were Jews and Moslems.

It was like Fatima and Lourdes. It was like what I have since heard about Medjugorje, in Yugoslavia. But there was an interesting difference between Hrushiv and those more famous sites. While the Blessed Virgin usually appears only to a small number of peasant children, in Hrushiv she was visible not just to Marina and her mother, but to the throngs who gathered around the church. Many, many people saw her. Many heard her incomparable voice. Many saw the huge, awesome lights that preceded her.

Immediately I pondered whether I should visit Hrushiv, which is about 35 miles southwest of L'viv (also spelled Lvov), not far from the Polish and Czechoslovakian borders. You won't find it on the map. It's almost 700 miles from Moscow.

To the south, not far from where I lived, was tyrannical Romania.

Hidden as it is behind the eastern bloc, Hrushiv was about as obscure and persecuted as anything to be found in the cold, dank corners of Communism. Should I go? Yes! No! Of course! Maybe! It wasn't fear that kept me back. I lost my fear—or most of it—due to an event that occurred in 1972, at a time when prison officials were trying to kill me. It wasn't fear. Though the KGB had threatened that the next time they arrested me I wouldn't get out of prison alive, I had spent the three months since my release organizing the underground church, working for the legalization of the Catholic faith, publishing a religious periodical, and evangelizing. As it was, individuals already had been sent with threats that they would bomb my house—all sorts of provocations.

It wasn't fear. It was concern. I was concerned that if I went to Hrushiv, I would be accused of fabricating the apparitions for the cause I was spearheading.

Soon there were newspaper items blaming me for Hrushiv. These accounts ranged from the sublime to the absurd. At one point the government-controlled press said that, in conjunction with the Vatican and CIA, I was using lasers or some kind of hitherto unknown projective device to create optical illusions.

Can you imagine this? Do they not know that if I had such technical expertise, I would have used it to make the prisons and camps disappear?

Still, the bishops felt I shouldn't go to Hrushiv because the Russians—and from now on you'll notice me draw a distinction between Ukrainians and Russians—were making their claim that we had set up some kind of an apparatus to create these apparitions of Our Lady. Besides, I was swamped as it was. Since my release people had been swarming all over my house. They believed I had mystical powers and I was beginning to get nervous about it. I never purported to be a man of miracles and yet people were bringing their sick children for me to bless. I was also busy with other matters. In addition to evangelization, I was preparing the May edition of Number 16 of the *Chronicles of the Catholic Church in Ukraine.*

And there was another factor that I considered, which was that as Catholics, we do not need or demand miracles. I don't need to see the Blessed Mother to keep my faith alive, and in fact those who spend too much time looking for miracles, or are overly skeptical, rarely find the spectacular events they are looking for. It is not up to God to prove Himself to us; it is for us to prove ourselves to Him. Our faith in Christ the King carries us through life. Our beliefs do not hinge on supernatural phenomena. But neither do we reject such signs from God once we are convinced the signs are authentic, edifying, and not a device or deception of Satan.

My home was in a tiny mountain hamlet called Dovhe. The nearest sizable town is Mukachiv, which is slightly closer to the Hungarian border than to Poland or Czechoslovakia. As I said, we were nestled between all the titans of

Communism. I went to see a friend of mine who is a priest, the provincial superior of the Basilians, an order named after St. Basil. I told him everything I had heard and we discussed the pros and cons. Our concern was that by going to Hrushiv, we would be implying that the apparitions were authentic and Church-sanctioned. That was not the case. It takes the Church years and even a decade or more before it renders a conclusion on supernatural manifestations. I did not want to interfere in that process. Then there was the matter of the KGB. I didn't want them to be able to use anything from a visit to Hrushiv as propaganda against our attempts at legitimizing the Catholic Church. Since my release from prison, I had been under constant surveillance.

For me the surveillance was expected but ominous. I was still hot stuff. I had been president of the Central Committee of the Ukrainian Catholics. While the Soviets, for reasons of public relations, didn't want to arrest me so soon after my release, it would be to their benefit if somehow I suddenly "vanished." Certain young officers with whom I had gone to school warned me that there were plans to kill me. They told me what the plans entailed and for me to avoid the forests. I knew who the assassins were to be.

At any rate, despite those warnings and my hectic schedule, I decided to go to Hrushiv on May 9, about two weeks after Marina had first sighted the celestial lady. As for the dangers, they would always be present. I simply had to watch behind my back. A detachment from the Ukrainian National Liberation Front would serve as bodyguards. There were five of us who got into one car— Vasyl Kobryn, who had helped me operate a defense league for believers, along with the driver and two young men who had served in Afghanistan.

In 1982, with people such as Vasyl, I had formed the Helsinki Group for the protection of the Ukrainian Catholic Church in the Soviet Union, also known as the Initiative Group to Defend the Rights of Believers and the Church in Ukraine. The Initiative Group was concerned with protecting the rights not just of Catholics, but of all the faithful— Moslems, Jews, Pentecostalists. You might think that formation of such a group was quite risky, and it was. I was constantly in and out of prison for such activities—mostly in. As you will read, I escaped from camps, hospitals, and prisons many times and, because of that, people got the idea I was kind of a super-hero. That is not true. When I tried to escape, when I faced barbed wire and bullets, I was very afraid. But there are moments in life when a force takes over and you can overcome many difficulties. I want to tell you from my own experiences that once a person is hesitant, he can not accomplish anything.

We came to Drohobych, which is about 80 miles from Mukachiv. There we dropped off Vasyl so he could circulate a petition there. Then we aimed the motorcar towards Hrushiv, which is about ten or 15 miles away.

As I am certain many of you know, the Mother of God has been appearing in many parts of the world during the past decade. People in the world have had much news from Heaven. This leads me to believe that we are in the end times. This is an apocalyptic nation, the Soviet Union. I believe that the current Soviet leader, Gorbachev, is also in the prophecies of John. He is the last ruler before the cataclysms. And I believe that Christianity will triumph in the end.

If momentous changes are about to occur throughout the world, you might ask, why doesn't the Virgin appear right in the Kremlin, or for that matter on network television? I want to say that the Mother of God only appears where people are very pious believers. She likes simplicity. She was herself a peasant girl, a peasant in Israel. The "sophisticated," cosmopolitan types—the "secular humanists" and masons—are not ready for her. They are not ready to change their lives. They are too caught up in the worship of sensuality, materialism, and science. They are still killing unborn infants, the greatest of all sins. They are still denying God. And they are not yet ready to hear about the colossal harm that is to come.

On the other hand, Hrushiv is the antithesis of sophistication, and the Ukraine in general has shown tremendous longsuffering. We are the only Church—the Uniate or Eastern Rite Ukrainian Catholics—which has endured 70 years of terror. We were the first nation—950 years ago—to consecrate itself to the Immaculate Heart of Mary. We lost count-

less millions during the government-engineered famine of
the 1930s. As the Virgin was telling pilgrims at Hrushiv,

> *Oh daughter of mine, Ukraine, I have come to*
> *you, for you have suffered the most and through*
> *all your sufferings you have maintained your faith*
> *in the Sacred Heart. I have come to you so that*
> *you will go and convert Russia. Pray for Russia.*
> *Pray for the lost Russian nation. For if Russia*
> *does not accept Christ the King, the Third World*
> *War cannot be averted.*

I believe Hrushiv is tied to Fatima and is connected with
the famous third secret. At Hrushiv the Mother of God said
the same things as at Fatima but more extensively.

Hrushiv! To this day the very name conjures in me a tingly,
uplifting sensation. There are perhaps 2,000 houses in
Hrushiv, and the people work on collective farms or at fac-
tories in larger towns like L'viv. They cultivate potatoes,
hay, peas, rye, barley, beets. Most of the farms are very
poor—cattle and swine for their own subsistence. The average wage of the collective worker is 18 or 20 rubles a month.
Those who drive tractors or have milk cows can make up
to 200 rubles—double the salary of a schoolteacher—but there
are no days off for them, and the rest of the people are poor,
living lives that few Westerners have known since the Great
Depression.

The area can best be described as a large tract of dusty
fields and woodland. Sparrows and crows kite above. There
is the clean, pungent aroma of manure and hay. As we
approached Hrushiv in the late morning of May 9, we saw
that the militia had set up a barrier on the road into town.
There were about 100 cars and light trucks lined on the
right side of the road, waiting to enter the obscure but beck-
oning village. I have no idea where I drew the courage,
but I told our driver to move into the left lane and drive
up to the police barrier.

A young militia officer approached. He was angry and
his face was twisted into a snarl. I got out of the car. I noticed
two men I had run into before, Major Tarakhonych of Uzhhorod, and Colonel Bogdanov from the L'viv detachment.
They were disguised in plain clothes but both were KGB.

I had a cap on my head and I removed it with a flourish. "Hi fellas," I said with preposterous cordiality. "What's happening?"

They didn't find me overly amusing. I noticed the first five cars were from Tbilisi, Georgia, which is on the other side of the Black Sea. After all that traveling they weren't being allowed to pass into Hrushiv. I heard one of the Georgians complaining. "I have the right to travel anywhere in the Soviet Union and there's no sign that I can't drive here," he scolded the militia. I too began to challenge them. "What's this provocation all about?" I asked. Because I had recently been released by the highest authorities at the Kremlin, the two KGB agents appeared uncertain of what to do with me. They departed.

The local police couldn't understand why the KGB had left and probably thought I was a prominent functionary. I called out to lift the barrier and let all the pilgrims through. A militiaman did as I said and the people headed for the church.

The traffic flowed smoothly. We were free to approach Blessed Trinity, the site of the apparitions.

What a sight greeted our eyes. I estimate there were more than 50,000 people there—an ocean of pious, praying people. It's hard to describe the enormity of the scene. According to *Svitlo,* a Ukrainian publication, 45,000 pilgrims were arriving daily. We put the figure higher, close to 80,000. Who knows. All we could do was count mementoes that were left there. Suffice it to say that a leaf could have fallen and not touched the ground.

To these people the message was that their liberation was at hand. After decades of living under regimes that placed no value on human life, after years of working for petty sums, after all this tyranny and deprivation, a new day seemed to be dawning. The sun was again shedding light. The century of Satan was nearing its conclusion.

But on the horizon were still many clouds. In its newspaper, the local Communist Party denounced the apparitions as a "political provocation by foreign clerical nationalist centers with the help of fanatics and extremists."

No doubt I was one of the "fanatics."

I've never seen more candles. So many had been lit near

the church since April 26 that there was a pool of wax a
foot or two deep. The faithful had also piled thousands of
embroidered religious scarfs near the church—an old Ukrain
ian custom—as well as flowers that were stacked knee-high.
I boldly walked forward, the crowd parting when they saw
me escorted by nuns. Many knew of me but didn't recognize my face. To them I was a news item on BBC or Voice
of America. I went up to the processional cross in front
of the church, a sermon swelling within me. What would
I say? I would let the Spirit speak through me.

All the area between the cross and chapel was laid out
in those embroidered scarves. There were also a few thousand loaves of bread—a custom those from the eastern part
of the Ukraine brought with them. And money. There was
a heap of rubles on the scarves and on subsequent days
people slipped money into a crack above a window. As I
mentioned, the church itself had been nailed shut by the
authorities. No one was inside except members of the militia, who went in to filch the offerings.

What greeted my eyes was inconceivable. Right away I
saw that something totally unusual was occurring. Above
and around the building was a soft, lambent glow. It's like
nothing that man creates. It was a surreal radiance. It was
like an aura.

That was the first visual phenomenon I observed, a dim
light enveloping the church.

But I was thinking about the money. It upset me. It choked
my voice. Christ never asked for money. Christianity isn't
about money. The Blessed Virgin isn't about money—that's
for the nattily dressed impostors who spend half their time
begging for funds on Western television. I turned to face
the people and raised my hands. "Brothers and sisters,"
I called in a hoarse voice. "Peace be unto you. Glory be
to God! But good people, what are you doing? It's a great
sin to throw down money. The Mother of God doesn't need
your money. She needs your prayers and humility. Do not
throw away money but instead rid yourselves of sin. The
Mother of God needs prayers and sincere repentance. Let's
pray for those in the prisons and the camps of Siberia and
Mordovia."

I broke into tears. I couldn't stand the thought of it, the thousands who are still imprisoned. Only 190 political prisoners were released from Soviet detention, and Gorbachev made politics out of us. I want to say that the majority of the sovietologists in the U.S. do not understand Gorbachev's policies, or if they do are covering them up. To this day Gorbachev has not announced amnesty for political detainees, and I am not allowed back into my homeland.

The KGB was photographing me. "Look, Josyp, you say your prayers fast, and get out, don't keep the people here," they had warned me. I knelt and started the Rosary. It's a shame that certain sects of Christianity don't understand our relationship with Mother Mary and haven't realized the power of the Rosary. We prayed for those in the prisons and camps. All the people fell to their knees. I would estimate there were about 200 KGB officers in civilian clothes, milling in this crush of solemn humanity. I recognized some of them by face. The militia was also standing around. There were even more of them than KGB. I was amazed to see the effect Hrushiv had on these agents and policemen. The officers took off their hats and fell to their knees. You heard me correctly. So intense was the atmosphere that *Communist policemen and KGB officers got down on their knees* like the rest of us. Later, some of them pretended they did so only because they were afraid if they remained standing they would anger the huge mob. Perhaps that's true in some instances. But I saw militiamen praying. During this time, and in fact through the day, people in the crowd were pointing to the cupola of the church, where, in that glow, they claimed to see the Virgin Mary.

They were pointing out the Virgin but I could not see her. What frustration! We prayed for four and a half hours and all of the people—KGB included—remained on their knees. I would speak to the people between prayers. I didn't want to leave the crowd. The people were my protection against assassination. A lot of our prayer consisted of the meditative Rosary. And after each Rosary I would speak. I couldn't believe how long I talked. It was as if the words came to me from somewhere outside of myself. I spoke about conversion, prayer, what we should do, what our goals and purposes should be. Especially I spoke about the need to legalize the Ukrainian Catholic Church. This was my greatest

cause. I want complete religious freedom and independence
for the Ukraine.

As if the apparitions weren't enough in and of themselves,
people were bandying about exaggerations and rumors. There
was one rumor I'll never forget. I have to smile when I think
of it. It was a rumor that my release from prison had been
a spectacular miracle. Don't misunderstand me. In some
ways it was. When I was sprung from the camp of Permska
Oblast, on February 5, I still had nine years left on my latest
sentence. But it was not a miracle in the way the people
were saying. Those from mountainous regions hadn't heard
the radio reports of my release in February. They began
spreading the rumor that the Mother of God personally carried me to Hrushiv from prison!

I felt I should leave because too many people were staying put instead of allowing other visitors to have a chance
to pray closer to the chapel. People were coming and going
in a constant stream. The KGB approached me and said they
were there to keep order. I went up to one of the officers,
the one named Tarakhonych, and said, "Misho, you're an
atheist. Why did you fall to your knees?"

"Listen," he said self-consciously, "everyone fell to their
knees and if we hadn't knelt the people would have torn
us apart."

The KGB wanted to call me out for further talk but I didn't
go. They wanted me to go quietly with them. Were they
crazy, after what I had learned about potential assassins?
I am many things but not crazy. The crowd was my insur-
ance. I refused and threatened to tell the multitude who
the two men were. I would call for help. They would be
in great trouble if they tried to haul me off, and they realized it. Bogdanov turned to Tarakhonych. "Let him alone,"
he said. "He is going to shout."

For the time being I was safe. I concentrated on prayer
and the presence of Mary. As dusk came, the light above
the church became stronger. I was truly moved because I
wanted to see the Mother of God. I still couldn't spot her.
Every once in a while people would cry out that she was
there, or they simply stared at the cupola, as if in spiritual
ecstasy. If you have ever seen this, the person has a shine
in their eyes and hardly blinks.

But for me, nothing. Just the light. I felt very strange. My pride welled up within me. I had a sacrilegious thought: *Here thousands are seeing the Mother of God and I don't, despite the years that I spent in prison because of my Catholic activism. Here I spent all that time in prison—two decades—and she is ignoring me!*

It didn't seem fair. Everyone but me.

Was I praying badly? Was my meditation off base?

Then I decided I wasn ι seeing her because of my sinfulness. I prayed and then went to a little hamlet nearby to rest and keep a healthy distance from the KGB. I can't say exactly where I stayed because I don't want the Soviet authorities to unleash any form of vengeance on those people. Although hopefully for not too much longer, I am currently living in exile in Canada.

At any rate, that night we all discussed the astonishing events of the day. Everyone had a story. There was a rumor that the peasant girl Marina, who hadn't been seen around the church, was taken off to a psychiatric ward. It wasn't true. She had been psychologically evaluated but remained at home, with the official warning not to go near Blessed Trinity. We also discussed reports that the Mother of God was appearing at other locations in the Ukraine. One of them was a May 5th apparition at a shrine in Zarvanystya. Eventually other villages and localities would report similar Marian phenomena.

After midnight we walked back to the chapel. By this time I had cast aside all my envy of those who saw the Mother of God. I stopped thinking of seeing her. I came back to pray and only to pray. I lit a candle for myself and my brother Borys, feeling peace pouring into me.

Tears began to flow down my cheeks. A deeper peace embraced me. I felt light and calm. Almost finished with a Rosary, I lifted my head in the direction of the belfry.

The glow around the chapel—the celestial aura—was now about two hundred meters high. The entire vicinity was swathed in a light that was clearly and breathtakingly celestial. It was like something between the silver glow of the moon and a fluorescent light. I don't know how else to describe it.

The chapel was enveloped in this luminosity and so was everything nearby. The leaves, the twigs, the people, the blades of grass, everyone and everything was phosphorescent, everything that was within that gargantuan field of light. On many leaves was a silver glow. This could also be seen around the hair, around the heads of many faithful.

There were people from Moscow and everyone made the same comment, that it was like they were in a living environment, as if the very air was alive and imbued with energy. Streams of light seemed to issue not only from the trees and grass but from our very fingertips, which were surrounded by aureoles.

No one could explain what or where the glow came from. This was not a reflection of the moon. The moon does not shine this way. The glow of the moon is silver but this was a different color, this was a very soft silver.

In the aura of light above Blessed Trinity was a smaller but more intense light—a globe of illumination. It was silver-lilac above the chapel—a fiery globe that moved back and forth. It was like there were tongues of fire coming out of it. This light continued to move inside the larger field of luminosity. It moved to the right—oscillating, shimmering, flitting sideways. Finally it lowered itself to the main cupola of the chapel.

My great dear Lord, I saw her! The Virgin Mary materialized in the globe of light, as if, like a vehicle, it had carried her into our reality. I can still picture the scene every time I close my eyes. There was no lightning or thunder, as I have since heard about other apparitions. It was as if the light was caused by a projector from quite a distance.

As the globe faded she became more distinct, like a living person above the church. Her face was there. It was not a mirage or anything of that sort, it was the face of a woman. I would like to say that in the first apparitions the figure of the woman was unnaturally large. The first time, what I saw was a woman in flaming robes. It was as if the robes were on fire and out of this only a face could be seen. These were not flames in our normal understanding of flames. She was garbed in a fiery light. I can only describe it as like putting alcohol on a shirt and setting it aflame. Holy God! Holy Mother!

I felt a great force behind my prayers. My dear great Lord! What could I do but pray all the prayers I knew by heart, the *Our Father*, the *Hail Mary*, the *Credo* and *Glory Be*— but with a new and remarkable power. Every word, every syllable, had fresh meaning. *Hail Mary, full of grace* . . . The Blessed Virgin said nothing. She stared directly into my eyes. It's a phenomenon unique to Hrushiv. Everyone who saw her said she was staring into his or her eyes. They felt she was paying personal attention to them. They said she was looking at them individually. How can the atheistic psychologists possibly explain so many people seeing and experiencing the same thing?

There she was, a woman of 18 to 21, with gold and flaring red garments. I can never relate the feelings I felt. Her face was clear and bright, and I thought how beautiful and celestial she was, but at the same time how real and close. She smiled, but through tears. She was crying. I felt she was there to warn us and comfort us and encourage us, to lead us back to her Son. She is His forerunner. She was at His first coming and is preceding His second coming. My entire body was electrified. It was the tingling I still occasionally experience when I talk about these events. To understand the way I felt, it was like going to my grandmother when I was in distress—going to my grandmother for a soothing caress. Almost everyone who saw her was crying.

At the time, however, I was hardly aware of my surroundings, only of Our Blessed Mother. I had similar mystical experiences in prison, including two apparitions, but nothing as visually spectacular as Hrushiv and never with other people to witness a vision with me. All I could see was her. All I could hear was the gurgling of a creek and the wind brushing against the grass—as if nature was whispering to us. Those who came only to pray saw her while many of those who were just curious onlookers did not share the entire encounter. Did any KGB, militiamen, or reporters see her? Yes. I'll discuss that later. Some of the children saw only angels, and some women saw a celestial being who described itself as "the Guardian Angel of the Ukraine." There have been reports of this angel since 1943, and while many people are skeptical about this, let me assure you that nations have guardian angels just as individual people do.

To me the fact that some of the older children saw only angels and not the Mother of God implied that they may have been tainted by sin. The younger, purer children seemed to see both the angels and Virgin. There were other phenomena as well. Many people saw a massive gleaming cross in the sky and in the cross Jesus would appear. I didn't see Him. I was still entranced in the extraordinary Virgin.

People often ask me what her face and countenance were like. I must admit that after a while I grow a little weary of this. How she looked is not important. The fact that she appeared, asking for prayer and penance, is what's important. But let me endeavor to describe her once and for all. It's no problem for me to remember her beloved and loving face. I witnessed her for an entire unforgettable hour.

Let all those who have sought me out—the Church authorities, the devoted, the Marian scholars—take note of the following details. First of all, she was the most beautiful woman I have ever seen. There is no such earthly beauty. She was not beautiful like a Hollywood star, but beautiful in another sense, in her overwhelming and precious simplicity. She exuded a sense of goodness and peace. Her face was extremely pleasant, like an older sister. She had a normal nose, gentle features, and dark blue eyes. In 1990, a friend showed me a picture of the Virgin of Guadalupe, and I must say that there were resemblances to that picture, especially in the aspect of simplicity. When I saw Mary, her head was covered by a light blue veil.

I was drawn to her skin. She had an extremely clear complexion. Old people say that from a face like this you can drink water. Her skin was healthy and glowing. It was like our skin and yet it was totally unlike our skin. She was shining. But not shining with light. She was shining with immense goodness. Since my arrival in the West I have followed all the sightings of the Mother of God but no one says what immense strength is in her. This strength is passed on to people who see her. She looked like a living person except for the fiery garb. I can't put the image into words. It was like I see you. She was a live woman, a young woman. A living mother. Her eyes were warm and kind. Under their gaze I felt like a small child. She was like an older sister showing compassion in a time of crisis. In her right hand was a Rosary and in her left arm the infant Jesus. The Rosary sticks out in my mind. The Hail Mary beads were azure and the Our Fathers were *burshtyn,* or amber. But the colors really were not of this earth.

My hands tingle when I think of these details, and afterwards I have strange dreams. Following my own vision, I spoke with many people and they all described her the same way. Kind. Pleasant. Everyone who saw her lost all sense of fear. Who cared about the KGB? We were all filled with goodness and courage. There was no sense of hostility to anyone.

During the apparition there was dead silence. You could have heard a mosquito flying. There was a fragrance that reminded me of milk, reminded me of how my dear grandmother, who raised me and taught me my faith, smelled when she returned from milking the cows. The Virgin's garb changed colors and undulated in the wind. Her garb was so delicate I felt I could reach out and crumple it in my hand. Her body was not transparent but her raiment was. There was a bright white light coming through her apparel. Let me assure you that this was no projection from the Vatican or CIA. It was a projection from the Holy Spirit.

She would extend her arm over the crowd and occasionally look to Heaven.

When she looked upward I believe she was communicating with Jesus.

She wore no jewels or embellishments and she kept smiling through her tears. She was at once gentle and severe. She seemed huge—huge like the luminosity—and yet normal size. Again, how can one use worldly words and dimensions to describe the supernatural? As I said, she stayed before my tearful eyes for an hour and when she left it was as if she faded back into the light or into a mist...

It was something how the Soviets soon initiated a campaign to discredit everything. Eventually they threw me out of the country and stripped me of Soviet citizenship. They assured me that no one in the West would believe me.

But all my sufferings in prison, all my loneliness, all my humiliations and in the end the trauma of exile were worth that single hour in the presence of the Mother of God. She was silent that night but not in subsequent days. She relayed encouragement to me, along with certain predictions and secrets. Later in this book I will have more to report about equally interesting occurrences at Hrushiv in the following days. I saw her five more times there and while she said nothing to me that first night, later she said many important things. I was given some very long messages, and shown certain unusual visions. The apparitions were especially intense for three or four weeks and still occur to some pilgrims, especially young untainted children. All told as many as 400,000 to 500,000 people probably have caught glimpse of her at Hrushiv, along with her spectacular light.

I suppose, in view of the subsequent events in Russia and Eastern Europe, that Our Lady of Hrushiv might be called the Queen of Freedom. Within two years of that appearance the Iron Curtain came down. Actually there is a long way to go before my people are truly free, and as I will explain, if there isn't freedom, there will be disaster. But still, it was obviously a momentous visitation, and the light from Our Lady split the blackness of Communism.

It also poured light into the blackness of my own life, a life spent in bondage to totalitarianism.

The Queen of Light. The Queen of Freedom.

But before I show you more of her light, I must show you the darkness.

Chapter 2

DARKEST CLOUDS

I was born in the Carpathian Ukraine on October 27, 1943. It was the middle of that enormous calamity known as World War II. The leader of Russia was Josyp Vissarionovich Stalin.

My mother gave birth to me while escaping to the home of my Auntie Maria Terelya in the village Kelechyn. She was on the run from Nazis. My father, Michael Pojda, had already been caught. He was being detained in a concentration camp at Graz, Austria. When I was two months old he escaped and fled to Yugoslavia, where he joined Tito's partisans, known as the International Brigade.

At the time of my birth, Stalin had been in power for 20 years. To him killing had become as automatic as eating or shaving. He was every bit as bad as his enemy, Hitler. Stalin had just hosted a visit by Churchill to Moscow—highlighting his ascent to international stature—and he was a man who had forgotten what it was like to have an order disobeyed.

Stalin caused disasters and defeats without precedent in Russian history. On the Soviet front, Sevastopol had fallen after nearly a year-long siege, and the Nazis were forging deep into the Caucasus, aiming for Stalingrad.

While most of my family was profoundly Catholic—with cousins and uncles who were religious or priests—my own

19

parents were ardent Communists. And they attained rather
prominent rank. To give you an idea, my father eventually
was in charge of collectivization in parts of the Western
Ukraine. He was made head of the governing assembly in
the Volovets district, with the authorization of the Ukrainian Central Committee to quash nationalism. Sometimes my
father was hard to figure out; he read the Bible but didn't
believe in God. He believed *every* man could become a god.
He believed in the power of nature. My nickname was
"Myhailovich," which meant "son of Michael." My mother,
for her part, was connected to the Central Party in Moscow,
powerful enough to make the local Communist functionaries tremble.

I wasn't raised by my parents. I didn't even know they
were my parents until I was ten or 12. It was my grand-
mothers who took care of me. In the Ukraine, at that time,
it wasn't unusual for grandparents to raise the children,
and my parents were obviously preoccupied. My father never
said just what position he held in Tito's brigade, but it must
have been a high rank because later, when he had troubles
with Moscow, Tito personally spoke on his behalf.

In 1944, the International Brigade was defeated by the
SS. Only 15 or so members survived. My father was very
seriously wounded and captured again by the Nazis. He was
placed in the concentration camp known as Baaden-Baaden.
Unlike my father, who had been a Communist since 1933,
I identified most closely not with the atheistic Soviets but
with the dear Catholics of the Ukraine. Located exactly in
the middle of Europe, the Ukraine, which means "borderland," now forms the southwestern part of the Soviet Union
but considers itself a separate nation. It is a lush area, the
soil black with fertile humus, the mines full of iron and
coal, and it has been like a fine quilt tugged apart by its
many neighbors. Everyone wanted those natural resources.
While it is currently under the domination of its northern
neighbor, Russia, and has yielded to Russian spheres of
influence for centuries, the Ukraine, during this century
alone, has been encroached upon by the Polish, Czechs,
Romanians, Hungarians, and at the time of my birth, the
Germans.

Despite occupation by these powerful forces, the Ukraine has always possessed a strong streak of independence. As far back as Ivan's reign, the region had been settled by Cossacks who fought with the Poles and in effect established a separate nation. I am talking about a period of time about four centuries ago. From then on independence became a constant theme and this theme is currently reaching another crescendo, as my homeland again seeks to detach itself from Soviet Russia.

The turmoil caused by Germany and Russia was prophesied long ago at Hrushiv, where the Mother of God had appeared in 1914—long before the subsequent apparitions of 1987. At Hrushiv, 22 peasants mowing hay in a field near Blessed Trinity had spotted the Virgin and heard her warn that there would be war and horrible persecution if Russia did not turn to her Son. While the 1914 apparition was not nearly as spectacular as what would happen at the same chapel much later, her message was startlingly similar to what the three Portuguese children would hear three years later at Fatima. In 1917, the Mother of God told the Fatima visionaries that if the world did not stop offending God, a great war would erupt during the reign of Pius XI. One of the Fatima visionaries, Lucia Abobora, was also told that this punishment upon mankind would include hunger and religious persecutions, and that if Russia was not converted, its errors would spread throughout the world and the good would be martyred.

Lucia, who is now a nun in Coimbra, was told that the sign indicating arrival of God's punishment would take the form of an inexplicable light in the night sky. Large portions of the world spotted such a light—which newspapers tried to explain as an unusual reflection of the aurora borealis—on the night of January 25, 1938. Less than a year later Stalin signed a pact with Hitler that many blame for leading to the worst war mankind has so far encountered.

The great persecution began the same year as the Fatima apparitions—1917. That was the year Vladimir Lenin succeeded in his momentous "revolution." He and his henchmen established the Marxist philosophy of Communism and decided to eradicate religion. When Stalin took over in the 1920s, he persecuted religion with the same vengeance.

Stalin allowed only one denomination to remain, the Russian Orthodox Church, and only because he was able to infiltrate and control it. The Russian Orthodox had long ago severed relations with Rome. While the Eastern Rite Catholics conducted Mass in a way that was very similar to the Orthodox, we believed that Christianity was established in the Ukraine by two missionaries, Cyril and Methodius, who, while importing the Byzantine or Orthodox rite, were aligned with the Pope. In other words, while practicing the Eastern (or "Orthodox") rite, we remained loyal to the Vatican and proclaimed ourselves Catholics.

Throughout the Ukraine, especially in the capital city of Kiev, were magnificent churches and monasteries. Few places in the world had churches as ornate. These buildings carried a distinct Byzantine flavor—domes, round arches, splendid mosaics. Stalin began to plunder them unmercifully. First it was the independent or autocephalous Ukrainian Orthodox Church that was desecrated, and later, in an even more brutal fashion, the Eastern Rite Catholic Church—my Church, my grandmother's Church, the Church I would spend the rest of my life defending.

Although this ruination did not reach its full force until after my birth, as early as 1935, in Kiev, the gorgeous, gold-filled Monastery of St. Michael, built in 1108, was demolished by Stalinists. St. Michael is of course the great archangel who cast Satan from Heaven, and that a monastery dedicated to the magnificent Michael had been torn to the ground was startling testimony that the devil's time had come.

The doctrine of Communism was a grand, egotistical scheme devised by Satan. What greater goal does the devil have than crushing belief in God and instituting sadism? Besides St. Michael's, the Communists desecrated the Desiatyna Church erected by Vladimir the Great; a famous cemetery called Askold Tomb; and the Cathedral of St. Nicholas. Starting in 1939, all Uniate Catholic monasteries and convents, church schools, and lay organizations were suppressed. Within two years, 28 priests in the L'viv area alone disappeared without a trace.

While they were beginning to destroy our religion, the Soviets likewise embarked on a campaign to destroy our livelihoods. In the aftermath of the Revolution of 1917 and the break-up of the Austro-Hungarian Empire in October 1918, the Ukrainians, having failed in an attempt to set up an independent state, found themselves in the midst of horrible, man-made famines. The Ukraine is the Soviet Union's breadbasket and under normal conditions produces more than enough grain for itself; yet starting in the 1920s, and reaching a peak in 1933, my homeland was suddenly without food. Why? Because Stalin had begun hauling all its grain to Russia. So bad was the situation that Ukrainians had to steal shirts from corpses and trade them for a loaf of bread. There were so many dead that the Russians made regular nightly runs to remove bodies from our streets and alleys. It is estimated that up to 12 million Ukrainians starved to death or died as a complication of malnutrition in the 1930s.

They stole our food. They stole our culture. They stole our spirit. Those Ukrainains who owned land or a private business were arrested and their wealth confiscated by the Soviets. All rights to any enterprise suddenly belonged solely to the government. Russia's secret police, which had its origins back in the days of the Czars, was greatly expanded and strengthened. We Ukrainians became impoverished serfs. No longer could you hear laughter and bells in the tiny mountain hamlets.

One of the early founders of Soviet Communism once said that Communists had to know how to hate because "only through hatred will we be able to conquer the world." They certainly hated Ukrainians. So did neighboring countries. The southern part of the nation, known as Carpathian Ukraine, attempted independence again in 1938, but again it didn't last. On March 15, 1939, 11 Hungarian divisions attacked this part of the Ukraine in a very unequal war and Polish legions attacked from behind. They killed peasants, destroyed roads, and exploded bridges. I have a macabre photograph from 1939 showing Hungarians laughing and smiling gleefully as they execute Ukrainian nationalist soldiers.

Then, from 1941 to 1944, the Ukraine was occupied by the Germans, who held on almost to the conclusion of World War II, when they were defeated by the combined forces of Russia and the Allies. This paved the way for the Communists to "rescue"—or rather invade—all parts of the Ukraine. Nazis were replaced by Communists.

The tragedies of World War II were always readily witnessed close to home. Five people from my family were shot by Hungarian occupiers. On my grandparents' farm, three Jews were found hidden in the hay and as a result my Aunt Olena and cousin Oleska were both shot under the crab apple tree in the garden. It was no better by the end of the war when the Russians returned. More in my family were killed simply because they loved their land and deliberately took part in the Ukrainian movement.

Nazism and Communism were of the same evil spirit. Like demons in Hell, they fought among each other for control and power. I am not using metaphors here nor am I using the words with fantasy or anger. When I say evil, I mean evil. Communism is a total negation of the Catholic Church, and the mission the Soviets had in mind, when they assumed control over the Ukraine, was, like the Nazis, cancellation of justice, human rights, and personal freedom. As such, Communism must always be resisted. You cannot be a Christian and a Communist. You cannot enter into *detente* with the devil. Was supernatural evil really at work? It is interesting to note how Lenin, the father of Russian Communism, met his death. Some of these details I get from the Swiss newspaper, *Schweizerisches Katholisches Sonntagsblat*. His death had a seemingly diabolical nature. A whimpering and crying Lenin was confined for weeks to his bed or wheelchair, his body decaying, his mind lapsing into insanity as he unsuccessfully fought a fatal sclerotic disease—hidden away in a Gorki castle. At the end, ironically, it was only nuns who would care for him—nuns from a cloister outside of Moscow that had not yet been liquidated—and what they saw and heard must have been ghastly. During the night such horrible howling could be heard from his room that it antagonized the watchdogs to the point where they too began to howl. Even dogs in neighboring villages joined in.

But of course Lenin's demise was no impediment to the spread of Communism. His protege, Stalin, carried it forth with great vigor. I won't bog you down with much more history, but you must get a sense of the tumultuous past. The Ukraine was not really independent. It was controlled by a regime that had us in a stranglehold and would end up rivaling and perhaps surpassing the Nazis for brutality. If it wasn't the Communists, it was the Fascists, and if it wasn't the Fascists it was the Communists.

I was too young to observe this dizzying path towards annihilation. While my parents were becoming dedicated Communists, I was in the hands, thank God, of Catholic grandparents. Except for my parents and a few other relatives, our family was deeply faithful. My very godfather, who was later murdered, was a priest. And the Terelyas had been patrons for a monastery in the Carpathians back when it belonged to the authentic Church established by St. Cyril and Methodius.

Although my father's surname was Pojda, I was given my paternal grandmother's maiden name of Terelya in order to continue that lineage. There were no male descendants on her side of the family. Her ancestry was more or less an aristocratic one that dated to the 13th century. During the time of King Danylo, my forefathers were settled on the border between Hungary and Ukraine—settled there to defend that border.

Thus you can see the long history in my family of both Catholicism and nationalism. The family emblem was blue and gold. On the blue background was a silver horseshoe. And on the gold background was a raspberry-colored bear.

I am now the head of the lineage of Terelyas. This is very important in the Ukraine. When I was baptized, I had 32 godmothers. I was of Boyco peasant stock, but people in the area were also very aware of my aristocratic lineage.

My paternal grandmother died in 1944 and I was taken into the home of my maternal grandmother, Anna Sophia Fales. I wasn't quite a year old. There I lived until I was 13—a place known as Svalyava, again in the Carpathians. I called my grandparents "mother" and "father" because my grandmother didn't tell me I had other parents. My grandfather, Ivan, had been in charge of a notary office when the Czechs controlled the region, and he quit to become a gentleman farmer. Like my paternal relatives, the Faleses were also descended from ancient aristocracy and they were likewise nationalists. My grandmother Fales was highly traditional and totally anti-Communist. She was at odds with her own children—including, of course, my biological mother, Marie Margerita Pojda, who quickly assimilated into Communism.

While the Communists were intent on destroying our churches or handing them over to the Russian Orthodox, the destruction of Eastern Rite Catholicism was a gradual and tortuous process. By 1944, when I was one, it was still possible to attend regular Mass. Despite the religious repression, there was a special fund devised by the faithful to aid the Eastern Rite Catholics. People were very active in a Marian movement and in what was called the Missionary Society of the Sacred Heart of Jesus. There were two key churches in the Ukraine, us Catholics and the Orthodox. As I explained, the Orthodox Church, which shared most of our Byzantine rites, had no allegiance, however, to the Pope. It had broken away from Rome in 1054—the "Great Schism"—and while the Orthodox too suffered terrible persecution, along with the Baptists and Evangelicals, the Communists were more tolerant towards the Russian Orthodox because they made important concessions to Moscow, and did not answer to the feared and detested Holy Father.

In September of 1944, while I was still cradled in the arms of my grandmother Fales, the Holy See appointed Theodore G. Romzha as the bishop of our diocese. He was based in the nearby city of Mukachiv. At this time there was still fierce fighting between the German and Russian armies. There were grenades and bombs exploding everywhere. The German command issued an order for the complete evacuation of the Carpathian Ukraine. They wanted to move everyone to Germany. Who knew what fate would have awaited us all there? Bishop Romzha came to our rescue. He reached an agreement with the Germans to rescind this order.

The following month the Hungarian-German armies left Uzhhorod, the provincial capital of Carpathian Ukraine. I keep referring to "Carpathian Ukraine" because it was the hotbed of Catholicism—there were no Orthodox churches until the Czechs forcibly introduced them in the 1920s—and it is like a state within the Ukraine. When the Germans were retreating, they destroyed all the bridges and airports, and on October 27, 1944, my first birthday, new occupiers entered: the Russian army.

It entered Uzhhorod and the people welcomed the Russians with silence. Representatives of the Soviet government reassured my people that the only reason they were there was to defeat the Hungarian-German forces. But immediately the NKVD and NKGB—forerunners of the interior police and KGB—started to arrest people.

There were nationalists hiding in the woods and resisting the Communists as best they could. But Russia moved into the Carpathian Ukraine with brutal determination. Military command in the region was assumed by Colonel Tulpanov and General Colonel Mekhlis. As soon as these two commanders arrived, they searched for people who would help in annexing Carpathian Ukraine to the Soviet Union. They pretended to allow us independence but never were we more suppressed.

Around this time certain past atrocities were coming to light, soon to be overshadowed by new ones. In the city of Vynnytsia, a number of graves were opened up, revealing 9,432 corpses. Under both Stalin and the Nazis thousands had been shot, especially the simple, humble, and greatly despised peasants. On the site of this particular burial ground what did our "saviors" the Communists erect? Something called the "Park of Culture and Rest"—with facilities for dancing and merriment! Let me assure you that there were many other such graves.

On November 6, 1944, an ominous-looking sedan arrived at Bishop Romzha's residence. It was Colonel Tulpanov with his bodyguards. They surrounded the palace with automatic weapons. Accompanied by his adjutant, Tulpanov went to visit the beloved bishop. "I wish to speak with Bishop Romzha," he said brusquely. "Send a message that I wish to speak with him. Tell him that I am the colonel of the Soviet army."

The monks led him to the office of the bishop and Colonel Tulpanov immediately invited Bishop Romzha to attend a solemn celebration commemorating the return of the region to Russians. The bishop answered that he couldn't leave just then. He didn't want to promote the Communists. There was a commotion and Tulpanov insisted that the bishop had to go. Said the colonel: "You will officially welcome the Soviet army for the liberation of the Carpathian Ukraine. And you will thank us. And at the same time you will make an appeal to the youth to join the army and ask Stalin personally if the Carpathian Ukraine can officially join the Soviet Union and fulfill the perennial desires of the Carpathian people."

What a farce, and Bishop Romzha realized it. He replied, "I can only thank God Almighty that the war is ending, and ask Him for peace on earth."

Tulpanov didn't much like that answer. "Are you refusing? I hope not. You have to go. Otherwise there will be repressions."

The "celebration" was at a theater. There were a few hundred people there. They escorted the bishop in and when the people saw him, there was silence. From what I understand, the silence was very oppressive. The crowd felt fatalistic and depressed. The building was surrounded by Soviet soldiers armed to the teeth. Bishop Romzha was brought to the microphone. He welcomed those present and thanked God that the war was ending without any greater sacrifices. A murmur spread through the hall. And in the end the bishop, under duress, also thanked Stalin for the successful conclusion of the war and consolidation with the Soviet Union.

Chapter 3

DEATH BY INJECTION

While the Eastern Rite Catholic Church was not immediately destroyed, such was clearly the goal of Stalin and his thugs in Moscow. To help achieve that goal, the Kremlin sent an administrator named Nikita Khrushchev.

Khrushchev arrived in April of 1945 and his attitude was clear. Already he had induced a dozen or so Ukrainian poets to write a collective poem, *To the Great Stalin from the Ukrainian People*. It was a bogus petition that sought to deify the dictator. "Today and forever, O Stalin be praised," was part of one blasphemous stanza. "Thou art the heart of the people, the truth and the faith. We're thankful to Thee for the sun Thou has lit!"

If people were going to pray, Khrushchev was going to make them pray to Stalin.

Let me give you another quick inkling of Khrushchev's affinity for religion. He objected to architecture in Moscow that even vaguely resembled spires and cupolas, and he once derided the central spire at Moscow State University for resembling a cross. He found that especially distasteful.

At his disposal were officers of the regular Russian army as well as the NKVD and NKGB—secret police who evolved into the MGB and then the horrific KGB. What terror the secret police began to wreak! Villagers couldn't trust anyone anymore. They didn't know who was associated with the MGB. Arrests and trials were a daily event throughout the Carpathian Ukraine. The Communists had incarcerated the first president of Carpathian Ukraine, Monsignor Augustine Voloshin, who was taken to Moscow by plane, thrown into the main MGB prison of Lefortovo (where I too was later held) and evidently executed for having refused to sign an official declaration of union with the Soviets.

With his death, Moscow began its talks with the president of Czechoslovakia about the fate of Carpathia. In actuality our fate had been predetermined. At the end of August 1945, the governments of Czechoslovakia and the USSR signed a treaty by which the Czechs resigned their claims to the northeastern lands of the Carpathian Ukraine, and officially relinquished the land to the Soviet Union. The southwest fell to Czechoslovakia. Another part of the Ukraine was ceded to Romania.

These were the last days of our independence. The northeastern lands were renamed the Transcarpathian Province, an integral part of the USSR. We ceased to exist even on the maps of Europe. My people finally realized that this was no temporary occupation but a permanent oppression. The Soviets began to impose their Russian culture, nationalizing schools, mandating instruction of the Russian language, and forbidding teachers to attend church or speak of religion. Atheism was the new doctrine in this previously pious land.

While it's true, as far as language, that there are similarities between Ukrainian and Russian, there are huge differences as well. If you showed a Ukrainian 50 Russian words, he might be able to identify only 20 of them. One example: the same word that means "charming" in Ukrainian means "ugly" in the Russian language.

So you can see how, religiously and culturally, we were quashed. The indoctrination began. And those who had been blind to it began to see the satanic designs. Those who a short while before didn't consider themselves as Ukrainians, very quickly began to understand the implications of dissolving the Ukrainian nation, and they became converts to the idea of national liberty. Among those who abandoned any form of accommodation with the Soviets was Bishop Romzha, who had begun supporting the underground.

In 1945, the Soviets initiated the first legal proceedings against "the enemies of the people," which meant us Christians and especially our clergy. On April 11, the entire Eastern Rite Catholic hierarchy in the Western Ukraine, including Metropolitan Josyf Slipyi, was arrested by the NKVD. The next month a Soviet-sponsored "Action Group," seeking reunification of Eastern Rite Catholics with Russian Orthodox, suddenly appeared on the scene. The Soviets demanded the names of clergymen who refused to submit to the "Action Group" while Orthodox leaders, including Metropolitan Ioan Sokolav, issued pleas for Catholics to break away from Rome. Those clergymen who resisted reunification with the Russian Orthodox were handed over to the NKVD, and if that kind of persuasion failed, the clerics were sentenced to an average of ten years in the camps. In December of 1945, a priest named Father Peter Demjanovich was arrested and five months later shot to death. This information I later learned from the confidential archives of my own father. The reason I'm bringing it out is that many historians indicate that these repressions of the clergy began in 1949. It's not true. It was earlier.

I have more names from my father's files. Father Eugene Pasulko, arrested in the village of Trebushany; Father Steven Chyzmar, in the village of Noyeselo; Father Stefan Egreshy in Bógdan. The arrests took place in the dark of night. They didn't use the local sycophants, they used the regular Soviet army. Drunken officers killed two brothers, one a monk, one a priest, for example, in the village of Zatyshne. They barged into the priest's home and began demanding alcohol. The priest gave them the bottle of wine he was keeping for Mass, but sometime later these Russian drunkards came back and were enraged to find that the priest had no booze left. In their furor they killed both men, and if that wasn't enough, they sexually mutilated the victims. When the people learned of this, they were understandably enraged. They began proclaiming that the Russians were more cruel than the Hungarians and Germans.

There was another incident that was particularly important. This was the arrest of Father Fedor Durnevych in the village of Zniatyn. It was another signal that the Communists were determined to confiscate Ukrainian Catholic churches

and hand them over to the less threatening Russian Orthodox Church, which also suffered persecution (eventually losing more than half its churches), but not to the extent of
the other Christian denominations. The independent or
autocephalous Orthodox Church in the Ukraine, which was
not aligned with the Russian Orthodox, had already been
all but eradicated. Afraid to go too far too fast, Moscow
was going to allow Russian Orthodoxy to remain in existence, but that existence would be greatly diminished—
more a delusion than anything else. The secret police had
already infiltrated the Orthodox leadership and that
"Church" was under the control of government officials.
Meanwhile the children were schooled in atheism.

By 1946, talks were being held concerning unification
of the Carpathian Orthodox Church with the Orthodox
Church in Moscow. The head of these talks on behalf of
the Carpathians was an Orthodox "priest," Father Teofan
Sabov, who was given the rank of major superior by the
Communists in Moscow! When he returned to Carpathia,
he began persecuting Catholics in the Khust area. The Soviet
press was publishing tirades against Catholics and other
Christian faiths, which was an especially ominous signal.
The clergy were called "fascists" and "reactionaries." The
lies were evident. The real fascists—yesterday's Black
Shirts—were serving with the Communists in Moscow.

Beginning in March of 1946, those bishops who still refused
to publicly detach themselves from Rome were indicted in
Kiev for "traitorous activities." The threat of imprisonment
led 264 priests to "reunite" with the Russian Orthodox.
Hundreds of others refused and were imprisoned, deported,
or forced into hiding while nearly 300 others remained at
large, refusing to inject themselves into an alien, anti-Catholic
denomination. That same March, there was a fake *sobor* or
synod in L'viv, at which the Eastern Rite Catholics supposedly decided to liquidate their institution and officially join
the Russian Orthodox. It was all staged by the Soviets; Ukrainian Catholic bishops neither convened the "synod" nor par-
ticipated in it. But the net effect was that the Ukrainian
Catholic Church was declared illegal.

The Soviets did not even bother to stage a similar synod
in Carpathia. All they needed to do there was take Bishop

Romzha out of the picture. Plans to do just that were in the making.

Bishop Romzha's nationalistic activities had begun in 1945, only a year after that coerced speech at the Soviet "celebration." His humility before God and courage against Satan could fill an entire volume. Romzha rose in opposition when he saw the Communists chasing away all schoolteachers who believed in God and luring youth from church by organizing sporting events, hikes, and theatrical presentations on Sundays. Bishop Romzha also directly challenged the Communists when they began encouraging the use of alcohol. Most of the goods had disappeared from the stores and in the place of healthy food was vodka. The booze was brought in from demoralized Russia and sold very cheaply. The goal was plain. They were alcoholizing the youth! The brave bishop turned to his priests, exhorting them to intensify the religious instruction of children and prevent them from becoming enslaved drunkards.

That did not sit well with Communists. The authorities began to threaten the bishop with exile to Siberia. Romzha understood his days were counted and that the Russians had come with only one purpose: to destroy us as a people. He realized their goal was not to make us Communists, but rather our total assimilation and destruction. Bad news was arriving from other parts of the Ukraine like Galicia. The arrests of Ukrainian bishops caused a great wave of opposition to the Russians, and Catholic youth began to gather at large rallies and services with priests delivering eloquent and courageous sermons to them. It was our death rattle. Though the Ukrainians maintained their fidelity, they were up against pure tyranny. Our churches were given to the so-called Orthodox (who became the eyes and ears of the Communists), and the repression continued to spread.

On the Feast of the Assumption of Mary, to whom Ukrainians long have had a special and intimate devotion, many people gathered in Mukachiv at a revered monastery known as the Hill of the Monks. It was something like a mass demonstration in support of Bishop Romzha. The feeling of enthusiasm was so intense that even some Orthodox took part in this pilgrimage. Over 93,000 faithful were there. No one knew that this would be the last legal holiday on the

Hill of the Monks—that the decision had already been made
to hand over the monastery to the Russian Orthodox.

Colonel Tulpanov and his adjutant were furious. By decree
of the local Communist council, they fined the diocese 21,000
rubles and each priest 1,000 for the massive rally. That is
quite a sum in a country where, at the time, a farmworker
made at the most three or four rubles a day. The Communists
also began writing cruel articles against the Marian associa-
tions; the Mission of the Sacred Heart of Jesus; and another
organization known as the Apostolate of Prayer. The secret
police questioned, threatened, and arrested more Catholics.

Bishop Romzha watched through tears as the Soviet brass
traveled from village to village trying to convince our priests
to turn Orthodox. They promised a comfortable life and
ecclesiastical honors if the clergy agreed, prison if they did
not. The Russians also began a specific campaign against
the Basilian order. The people loved the Basilians and the
Russian propaganda met with little success. But it was the
Soviets who owned all the military power. They summoned
the superior of the Basilians, Father Anthony Mondyk,
together with the superior of the monastery, Ivan Satmarji,
to the provincial council.

Before going to the meeting these two priests prayed before
the stations of the cross. Then they went to see what awaited
them. Two trucks were in the courtyard when they arrived—
the type used to transport prisoners. There were also automatic weapons.

A Major Kulchytsky was in the vestibule together with
an unknown civilian. Without greeting them, they led the
priests to the third floor, where Colonel Tulpanov, along
with Colonel Boyko, who headed the provincial NKVD,
waited impatiently.

Tulpanov laid it out bluntly. "We with our associates have
decided that the time has come to speak with you on behalf
of the authorities. Comrade Stalin is disturbed by the fate
of Carpathian Ukraine. And this is why you must make your
choice between the Pope and the native Russian Church.
We can't permit capitalists and agents of the Vatican to have
any influence on our socialist structures. You have to sign
this document."

Two declarations were on the table and they concerned

the transition of Catholicism to the tainted Russian Orthodox Church. Father Satmarji would have none of it. He
declared that he was ready to go to prison. That firmness
and boldness caught the NKVD off guard. They released
the priests but told them the matter was not yet over.

And it wasn't. On March 24, the monastery at Hill of the
Monks was surrounded by NKVD agents and the local gar-
rison. Major Kulchytsky and a Captain Viktorov entered the
dining room. The monks and the priests silently stood up.
Father Satmarji asked what the visitors wanted. Kulchytsky
ordered the priests separated from the brothers and then
he turned to them and advised them to "voluntarily" join
the Russian Orthodox Church. Should the priests and monks
not sign the declaration, said Kulchytsky, their monastery
would be leveled to the ground and the priests sent to Siberia.
The monks were faced with two equally odious options.
What would they decide? Father Satmarji faced the brothers
and said, "Do as your conscience dictates. God is witness
and God is with you."
The monks were incredibly brave. No one signed the declaration. That infuriated the NKVD. They ordered the resil-
ient, stouthearted priests to go with them and take nothing
but their clothes. Out they headed for prison trucks while
the occupiers entered the monastery.
A Russian Orthodox monk, who had accompanied the
Communists, approached Father Satmarji and said, "We are
not driving you out. Who wants to remain with us can."
But no one wanted to stay and become Orthodox. By morning all 30 monks, along with their superior, were deported
to the village of Imstychevo. The loss of the Basilian monastery at Hill of the Monks was a heavy blow to our Church,
which gradually began to descend into the catacombs.
But in the Carpathians, Catholicism still tried to cling to
its public existence. At the end of October in 1947, Bishop
Romzha went by horse and carriage to the village of Lok-
hovo. There were two theologians and a priest with him.
They were to consecrate a church in the village.
After the consecration they went to the neighboring village and the bishop remained for the night. That same
evening a military car entered the village and soldiers were
seen about. This was October 27—again, my birthday. I had

just turned four years old. Anyway, Monday morning the bishop and his companions left by a village road and soon approached a rail line.

Suddenly, a military lorry with Red Army soldiers materialized and smashed into the carrige at full speed, destroying the vehicle, killing the horses, and sending Bishop Romzha and his associates sprawling into a ditch, bleeding and unconscious.

Eventually the bishop came to and groggily arose. There was a gravel truck with soldiers in it and they were watching. Seeing Romzha and his companions reviving, they jumped down with automatics and began smashing their heads. That evening the villagers found Bishop Romzha and brought him to the hospital. He was in a coma but, miraculously, he was still alive. Within days he regained consciousness and asked for someone to hear his confession. After confession he asked for a razor and to everyone's amazement began to shave.

News of this incredible recovery spread throughout the city. People from all of Carpathia began arriving at the hospital.

But the Communists, as you will see time and again, are very persistent. Two days after the bishop's recovery, a new surgical nurse appeared at the hospital. No one knew who this person was—a secret and sly woman known only to her bosses. On November 1, accompanied by the chief surgeon, who was a Jew, the nurse entered Bishop Romzha's room carrying a tray with a syringe on it. The dearly beloved bishop died a few moments after the injection.

Chapter 4

YOUNG AND CATHOLIC

Diabolical! Can you think of a better word for it? Remember, these are only a few snippets of the agony.

After Bishop Romzha's death, the Eastern Rite Church in Carpathia was forced into the Russian Orthodox fold. During the summer of 1949, the Soviets placed one of their own agents as secretary of the Mukachiv diocese.

Of course, as I pointed out, I was only a boy of four at the time of Romzha's murder. My grandmother Fales was schooling me in the Catholic faith, but I was oblivious to the mayhem swirling about me. For me life was still a spree. Ah, the Ukraine. Snow-capped mountains to climb, caves to explore, wildlife to observe. There were eagles, owls, deer. And resounding waterfalls. The name for the area translates into "between the hills" and I used to climb the cliffs and inhale the mountain air. Often it carried the scent of apple blossoms. As the sun set on the alpine-like valleys, the sunflowers yearned upward and stands of pine looked almost purple and turquoise.

As a youngster I would pick giant mushrooms or tend to the few livestock my grandparents had. You see, they were left with very little because they refused to join a collective farm. It was a simple humble life. When I was young we plowed with horses and got water from a well. My grandfather, a good innovator, made a trench to channel the water closer to our house. He had geese, poultry, a cow and ram. It was mining and logging country—the Ukraine has the richest and most accessible mines in the Soviet Union— and the inefficiency of Communism could be evidenced even in the logging pulleys. The pulleys had been built by Americans when we were under Czech control and when such mechanisms broke down the Communists were unable to fix them.

So too were the collective farms a disaster. Who wants to work when your eggs, milk, and grain go to the government and you are left to scratch together a meal?

This, as far as I'm concerned, is Marxism. Scratching together a meal even though you live amid lush farmland. It is not an altruistic or viable system, and those intellectuals who believe it is, are spiritually blinded. There were always rumors that Marx had dabbled in Satanism—yes, actual black masses—and whether or not that is true, as a youth he wrote a rhapsodical and surreal poem in which he talked about being handed a "sword" from the "prince of darkness."

That sword was pressed into the throats of my people for the next five decades. We were turned into serfs. We were expected to relinquish our land, tractors, combines, cattle, and plows to the government. Besides forcing us to hand over our farms, the Soviets rubbed vinegar into the wound by levying burdensome taxes.

In many cases every family member had to work in order to squeeze out the barest livelihood, and the work lasted ten to 14 hours a day. A worker on a collective farm *(kolkhoz)* might earn a daily wage of three pounds of grain, a couple pounds of potatoes, and two to five rubles. This wasn't very much when a good suit of clothes cost 700 to 800 rubles. Taxes and loans ate up 25 percent of the income. Individuals were allowed to maintain a limited amount of personal livestock, but if you owned a cow you might have to pay the government 150 quarts of milk a year, or if it was a pig, 18 pounds of meat. The cow or pig couldn't be slaughtered except by written permission.

And to think: my own father, who I still didn't know, was one of the bureaucrats converting Carpathian farms to collectivization. My father's activities got him in a lot of trouble with the farmers, including his own relatives. In October of 1949 he was wounded by a Ukrainian nationalist group for organizing the first Soviet-imposed farm in the area. As I heard the story, he was returning to his office when the nationalists—led by my cousin Vasyl and my father's own brother Mykola!—ambushed and captured him. My uncle told my father, "Pray, Misha, death is near." And Mykola said, "Who are you, instructing him to pray? He is a Communist. Kill him and that's the end of it." He was shot in the side but due to his heft, which acted like a buffer, he managed to survive.

It was like a civil war. My cousin and uncle had shown no mercy. They had shot my father and left him for dead.

Neither was my mother very popular. She was a confirmed atheist who was unable to show affection. I saw her on occasion—she would enter the house and pat me on the head like a dog—but I didn't realize she was my mother. I wasn't told who my parents were until later. My grandmother didn't want her around. She called her own daughter "a woman of Babylon." It was my grandmother's description for all female Communists.

By this time my mother had finished her higher education in the Central Committee of the Ukrainian Communist Party. She was preparing for special detachments. There was an ideological department and she ended up in its anti-religious bureau. My mother was headed for a career of destroying Christianity. Her job, eventually, was to squelch people like my grandmother, people who went to church on Sunday and taught their children to pray.

At school, the teachers mentioned a Communist leader named Lunacharasky who always said: "God is my personal enemy." They taught us to rebel against God. They made spiritual invalids out of us and created a hero out of one 12-year-old boy who turned his parents into the Soviets for some kind of infraction.

They drove love, loyalty, and God from the hearts of the young.

How my parents and so many others could be swept into such a heartless system is what philosophers call a *mysterium tremendum*. It's hard to explain with logic. They were oppressing not only their own people but also themselves. It was ludicrous. It was mysterious. Do you think they were safe because they were ranking Communists? Think again. In 1945, after my father was freed by the American army, he had returned to Carpathian Ukraine and found himself a *persona non grata.* The Stalinists didn't trust him because, after his emancipation, he had served a short while as an interpreter for the Americans. Despite his denunciation of Americans, he was asked to give up his Party card and, to repeat what I said previously, was spared prison only after intervention by Tito of Yugoslavia.

There were constant purges in the paranoic Communist Party.

Soon my father was back in good Soviet graces and climbing the bureaucratic ladder. He had the authorization of the Politburo and Central Committee of the Ukrainian Party to destroy the Ukrainian nationalist bourgeois—the middle class. But even while he was carrying out such duties, there were tensions with the Kremlin. If Stalin thought you were failing him, it could mean your head. An example came when Stalin called in my father and the secretaries of several other districts, such as L'viv and Drohobych, to report on their progress. My father was to present a report on the formation of collective farms in the Carpathians.

They traveled to Moscow with an intense military guard and each of them was very disturbed at what they were going to tell Stalin. They hadn't yet succeeded in destroying the Ukrainian Insurgent Army, known as the UPA. Not that they weren't trying: In Drohobych there had been daily hangings.

When they arrived in Moscow, my father and his companions were led to Stalin's residence in the Kremlin. The MGB separated them so that they couldn't talk among themselves, and then the MGB escorted in one of my father's friends. After his chat with Stalin this man was led away and no one was quite sure what became of him. Next was my father. When he entered, there was Stalin, short, dark, and pock-faced, standing behind his desk. His left arm was shorter than his right because of a bone malady that had never healed properly. Stalin's attaches were sitting, waiting. My father saluted Stalin and Stalin saluted him. "How is it going, Hutsul?" Stalin asked.

My father was a bold man. "I'm not a Hutsul," he said. "I'm a Boyco." He was referring to types of peasantry.

But the dictator laughed. "What, are you daring to contradict me? If I call you a Migrel or a Svan, what would you say?"

What would any sane man say? They would agree. They would agree if Stalin said the moon was green. He told my father to sit down and asked if he wanted cognac or tea. My father wanted the cognac. "Tell me how things are going with you," Stalin repeated pointedly.

"The struggle is continuing and we don't know when it will finish," my father said.

"I gave you six months to finish with the Banderites," said Stalin, referring to the nationalist guerrillas who had been led by Stefan Bandera.

My father was very impulsive. (It's another trait we share.) He said to Stalin, "If I was here as you are, and you were in my place, what would you say?"

The audacious but candid response apparently pleased the usually implacable dictator. "Everyone is coming here and telling me lies. At least you're not." The point was that there was still a huge problem with the partisan guerrillas. Stalin accepted the assessment and waved my father off. What a sigh of relief. The wrong answer got you a trip to Siberia.

My father was then led to a private room for a discussion with a lieutenant colonel who told my father to write a report and in the report to ask for all the military and financial help that he needed.

My father filled out this summary, presented it, and asked to be given until 1949 to organize the collective farms. It was that year, on the way back from Huklyvv, that he was shot by his relatives.

Does it all seem too strange? The Soviet Union was and is a very strange place. Our cow had to be fed along the road because my grandparents refused to join the collective and were thus denied rights to pasture. It made it even worse to be actively Christian. The Soviets were closely monitoring religious activities. They had a roster of those who went to Orthodox services and those who went to the Roman Catholic ones. The Eastern Rite had been formally disbanded in 1946, but a few Roman churches still functioned. The children of Catholics were often thrown out of school, made to work at a young age in the fields, and deprived of milk rations. We ate a lot of homemade black bread. On the other hand, those who went to the Orthodox Church got their fair share of milk and had no problem pasturing their cattle. Sundays, the government procurator went house to house to see who was listening to Vatican Radio.

My people saw the Orthodox as agents of the state and deeply resented their takeover of Eastern Rite churches. Among the confiscated property was St. George's Cathedral in L'viv, which was given to the Russian Orthodox in 1946. We Catholics were the scum of the earth, official state "enemies." There were no Catholics in the higher government positions, and the mountain villages were composed mainly of women and children, for many of the men had either died during the war or were imprisoned in camps, working in mines, or hiding in the forestland as nationalist guerrillas. Like me, many children were abandoned or being raised by their grandparents.

It was in the summer of 1949 that the Soviets set out to liquidate the Ukrainian Catholic Church once and for all. At the time, in the Carpathian region of the Ukraine, there were 700,000 Eastern Rite Catholics, 459 churches and chapels, 281 parishes, and 359 priests. The figures come from my father's government archives. There were 35 monks of the Basilian order in five monasteries and 50 nuns in three monasteries. There were also 12 Vincentian sisters, nine sisters of St. Joseph, and 32 sister-servants. Again, this is only for the mountainous southern part of the Ukraine. Taken as a whole, the Ukrainian Catholic Church, before 1946, had 2,772 parishes and more than four million faithful.

The arrests and trials did not stop. By night they would haul off the priests and the priests would never be seen again. I ran into some of them later, in the bottomless pit of the Soviet prison system. The Catholics were often accused of abetting the nationalistic movement, and cars came for those who were formally charged. Horror stories abounded.

The most visible manifestation of this extermination was the closure or outright destruction of church buildings. Perhaps never before in history has destruction or transferral of Christian edifices occurred on such a massive scale. For some reason, the full reality of it never reached Christians in Western Europe and America. The Western press, dominated as it is by non-believers, secular humanists, or those of a masonic bent, has still never told the English-speaking world of my country's—and Christianity's—full tribulation. Yet there was plenty of suffering to report. Church steeples were toppled, artwork was pillaged, icons were ruined, and bells were smashed—not just in the Ukraine but throughout the Soviet Union. Picture in your mind a wrecking crane knocking the cross off the top of a church.

Picture a baroque belfry collapsing into a heap of dust. Picture the authorities clamping chains and padlocks across the front doors.

It was around this time that the venerated chapel at Hrushiv was closed to worshippers. Hrushiv, and nearby L'viv, were special targets because they were strongholds of the Eastern Rite Church.

So, just as I was learning its precious teachings, Catholicism was being torn down all around me. Worshippers had to hide their prayer like a criminal hides his smuggling. Among the saddest memories was the day—Sunday, August 28, 1949—that there was no longer a Ukrainian Catholic Church to go to. Late that night, after my grandmother milked the cows, neighbors began congregating in the house. Then more distant relatives came. I remember them whispering among themselves. We children were huddled in a corner. I heard one of the neighbors say, "He'll come after midnight. Do not light any lights in your house and seal the windows."

I wanted to sleep, but I also wanted to know who it was who would be coming after midnight. Tired, I drifted off. But soon I awoke to the sound of singing. Catholic hymns and songs. The visitor was a Basilian priest, Father Dionysius Drybidko, who was my mother's uncle. Thus it was in our house that one of the very first underground liturgies was being celebrated.

For children this was something exciting and for the adults an utter tragedy. It was naturally a special tragedy for the priests. Each night they had to stay with a different family, hiding like fugitives. The people left our house one by one, so as not to draw undue attention from Communist sympathizers. The priest slept on a bed of hay.

From then on we would gather in the woods to celebrate the divine liturgy. Or, people sometimes secretly opened up a closed church, singing vespers, molebens, and parts of the liturgy. Occasionally they might also participate in a Mass said by an Orthodox priest they trusted. Many Orthodox priests quietly maintained their Catholicism.

In the evenings the adults talked both politics and religion— careful who they were conversing with. Others read the biblical prophets and believed the trouble was destined to last into the foreseeable future. The Book of Revelation may be pertinent here, especially Chapter 12. One wonders what or who the "red dragon" is, and one notes the role of the "woman clothed with the sun." Time periods are rarely clear or specified in prophetic utterances, but they imply long waits of "a time and times and half a time," according to John's famous prophecy.

We had a prophet in the Ukraine named Pelagia, whose mysticism coincided with the messages of Fatima and Hrushiv. She was a remarkable woman who, when she was in a supernatural state, could read Latin and Greek. Yet, normally she was illiterate. She foretold the future of both Germany and the Ukraine. She called on Ukrainians to repent and stated that the root of atheism is egocentrism. She also warned that fanatical nationalism was a product of egoism. When the Ukraine purified itself, she said, it would rise again. Pelagia was killed during the 1930s.

We were going to have to wait for purification, and for the most part, to wait in silence. The Red Army was on the march and the betrayals began. To curry favor, or escape punishment themselves, people turned into informants against neighbors, friends, and even relatives. At the back of your mind were always the horrible stories about prison.

Once a week my mother would stop at my grandmother's and bring sweets and cakes. Sometimes she also brought clothes for me. I still didn't realize who she was. She was a strong-featured but refined woman, very well coutered, and I thought her name was "Babylon," since that's what my grandmother was always calling her. I was told not to let anyone into the house if grandmother wasn't there but

I was very greedy for the sweets. My mother would enter the house and say very little. She wouldn't kiss or hug me. I was seven and in grade two, very poorly clothed; my grandmother's only income was selling milk to the officers. Still, she didn't want me taking any of the clothes my mother brought or eating any of the chocolates.

I recall one visit in particular. My mother stopped by and I put the chocolates on the table. Then, like a hungry cat, I paced around and around this packet of sweets from Babylon. Finally I broke off a piece of chocolate, silently hoping my grandmother would think a mouse had been nibbling at it. Then I ate more. There was no way I could blame it on a mouse, and when my grandmother found out she embraced me and began to cry. "Never take anything from her," she said. "If you eat this, Jesus will never love you. It comes from very evil hands. The people who make this chocolate do not like Christians. I'll give you something much better than chocolates." And with that my dear humble grandmother fetched me a basket of dried pears.

My grandfather died in 1951 when I was in grade three. That left the entire burden of caring for me on my grandmother, who raised me in an ascetic environment. I didn't normally eat sugar or chocolate, and never drank or smoked. The children of Catholic families stuck together. We never mentioned that we belonged to the Catholic Church. We hid this from the other youngsters, but we knew each other because at night we'd attend secret prayer gatherings. In a way it was a happy time. There was such strong faith. Although I had not yet developed the deep, active faith that would later fill me, as I grew older I acquired a great affinity for the richness and traditions of the Catholic Church— Christ's own Church, built on the rock of Peter.

When you denigrate that Church, you risk personal catastrophe. I have catalogued any number of instances in which events of a seemingly supernatural nature sent strong warnings to disbelievers. In the L'viv province was a man named Stojko who was in charge of the village Holohory. One day in 1952, Stojko was standing at the chapel near a figure of Jesus. For no particular reason he took a hammer and started to break the statue apart. "Where's that God?" he shouted to the villagers who watched him. "Why is He not punishing me? This is a piece of rock. You are all fools!''

That evening there was a local Communist celebration and his wife had made *pierogies* that were very hot. Stojko stuffed himself on the spicy food and a blockage developed in his intestines. By the time they got him to the hospital it was too late.

There was also a stigmatist named Stepan Novrotsky, who was being interrogated and beaten by an NKGB officer. This had happened way back on April 16, 1939. The Soviet agent challenged him to prove there was a God by telling him about his own family. Stepan remained silent and asked God to send him an answer. Then Stepan got an impression of the officer's wife, who was pregnant. "At the moment you were striking me, your wife died in labor," said Stepan, who knew nothing about the agent's family. And it was true. It happened in Kiev. They released Stepan but rearrested him later and put him in a psychiatric prison.

I'm convinced God gives and takes away His grace on an individual basis. Pedantic Christians tend to be dried up. They lack grace because they lack living belief. God is waiting for them to assert their faith. To simply concentrate on surface etiquette (dressing properly, singing loudly, making the sign of the cross at the appropriate time) is not nearly enough. One has to follow the living spirit of Jesus. One has to be willing to forsake everything for Him. One has to operate with love and knowing.

Take the example of my aunt, who had been married to a count in Hungary. In 1945 her husband died and grandmother had brought her home to Carpathia. She was a very proper Catholic but once her husband died and she no longer possessed wealth and prestige, she found it immensely difficult to live as an ordinary citizen. She had been forced to sell all her gold and jewelry, but she never wanted to give up her lifestyle.

Is there anyone reading this who does not have a smiliar form of pride? Think about it. Watch yourself throughout the day. Notice all the circumstances in which you crave attention, get aggravated with others, want to have a better car than the neighbor, or experience envy, egoism, or jealousy. Are you overly self-satisfied? Do you think you deserve better than you have? Do you see a man on a street and think to yourself: "I am holier than he is, poor soul"! That is the worst form of pride, spiritual pride. Pride inhibits the flow of grace and is often very difficult to unmask and realize.

I mention my aunt not in judgment but as an example of how religiosity can replace true faith and Christianity. She was such a proper Catholic that when I wasn't praying right, she'd give me a prod or pull my hair. But not once did I see her help someone in need, someone who was suffering. She lived with grandmother and all the sisters disliked her. Maybe this was why my grandmother had compassion for her. Her name was also Anna, but when she came back she no longer used her Ukrainian name. My grandmother would ask, "Why are you so stiff? You have a wooden heart. It's not enough to pray. You have to do something. You must make acts of faith and love." She criticized my aunt for never laughing or crying.

My aunt was convinced that the Americans would drive the Russians from Carpathian Ukraine, and the people would be given back their property. My grandmother told her the Soviets would never leave. She told her to accept the fact that she was no longer a countess, which my aunt found very hard to do. She needed to exercise authority. She was a pharmacologist by profession but a disciplinarian by avocation—my own personal disciplinarian. She never yelled; she just twisted my ears; and sometimes I couldn't blame her. I was a dervish. On Sundays, when possible, I went to church, but at first, like any kid, I didn't like it. It wasn't as if I immediately appreciated the depth of Christianity. I went to church only because I liked to play with the other children before the service.

We played in the church garden and when the bell rang for the service, each parent would take a child by the hand and we would stand like soldiers in a special area set aside for the children. Under the cupola there was an area where a balcony ran circularly inside and we would walk around and spit at the people below. They thought the roof must be leaking. There were forty of us up there, bending down and hiding, but eventually we were caught. My aunt whipped us with nettles, a plant with stinging hairs.

Wow! Did it burn! Everything was on fire. We began

*Photos of Josyp Terelya
During the Time of First Arrests—1962*

Borys Terelya (Brother To Josyp)—1982

screaming. Somebody thought of cold water but when we entered the water it just made it worse.

The next few months we behaved ourselves, but we had long memories and one day we decided to exact our revenge. On Pentecost, we had dinner in the orchard. There was a narrow path to the old church, with tall grass around it. The adults were going through there and so we took telephone wire, stretched it across the path, and in the evening when they returned, some of the adults tripped and fell into a ditch of water. My aunt was the first one.

Naturally we were afraid to go home after that stunt, but if we ran away, we'd all be severely punished. So we began to look for volunteers who would take the blame. The choice fell on me and a boy who was the son of a local teacher.

We knelt down, prayed the *Our Father* and *Hail Mary*, and then the two of us went to the house. To my surprise my aunt didn't immediately start yelling at me but that night, at prayer, she turned to my grandmother and told her I would never be an aristocrat, that I was scum. My grandmother was my friend. I told her they beat us with this stinging nettles and we wanted to get even with them. I told her about the telephone wire. My grandmother laughed and kissed me.

I was always in trouble. Once I let the ram named Beck out and he butted my aunt in the rear end when she was bent over hoeing potatoes. There was another incident where, as a prank, I covered over the eyes of a statue of St. Nicholas. Yet at the same time, I used to pray to stay out of trouble! This was around grade five. We had a new teacher, a Russian, and I must have forgotten that I had just prayed to stay out of trouble. This Russian teacher came to the classroom and we wanted to make her remember the first day in school. I took garlic and rubbed it on the blackboard so she couldn't write on it. The whole room smelled like *kovbasa*.

Next, I caught two mice, locked them in the teacher's desk, and threw away the blackboard chalk.

When she went feeling in the drawer for another piece of chalk what she felt were those furry rodents.

I say this as proof that I was no candidate for sainthood.

But it wasn't all fun and games. Those teachers were trying to "Russify" us—taking away our culture and forbidding anything to do with God—and they would go to the church and take note of everyone who attended the Roman Masses. The children of Communists also made it difficult; they were very officious and arrogant. They would go home, talk to their parents, and get people into trouble. Those who belonged to the Party had all sorts of comparative luxuries. They had good food and they rode in automobiles.

Stalin died in 1953, but the brutality and oppression remained, at first lifting a bit but other times becoming severe again. Stalin was succeeded by Georgi M. Malenkov, who became premier, and Nikita Khrushchev, who my father knew well and who had long terrorized my people as chief of the Ukrainian Communist Party. Khrushchev became the new First Secretary.

My father was nearly executed in 1951 for not exiling all the people Stalin wanted exiled, but he survived again with the intervention of Tito, who heard about my father's latest travails from a cousin who was second secretary of the Ukrainian Communist Party. My father was made director of mineral deposits for Carpathia and later director of resorts. They had taken his Party card from him and when they offered to return it, he refused.

In grade five or so, I discovered that the woman who brought the sweets was my mother. She and my father lived in the mountains about thirty kilometers from us. Occasionally I'd go to stay with them, but I always returned to grandmother. In 1953, as the son of a high Communist Party functionary, I was sent to a sanitorium in Yaremche under the pretext of having tuberculosis. I spent two months there, and one day I heard rapid gunfire from the direction of Dora. The next day we children were taken by a man in uniform to see several "bandits" (really nationalists) who had been executed. They were just young lads, and we were interrogated as to whether we recognized any of them. We closed our eyes at the sight. Another man in civilian clothes swore at us and, referring to our group, said in Russian, "They will soon be like them. They should all be executed."

Executed?
I swore on the bodies of our heroes that when I grew up I would fight the Russian occupiers as long as I lived. They

were horrible. They would send actual criminals—thugs and thieves—to pillage our villages and rape the women. Yet they couldn't extinguish our nationalistic feelings and our Catholicism. The nationalism surfaced even in Communists like my father. "Do you see these hills?" he once asked me. "They are ours and only ours. Remember to love truth, as all people have their own truth and liberty, their own unique lifestyle."

I had two brothers and a sister who lived with my parents. The closest was my brother Borys. My other brother, Sergius, died as a young child. When I was ten and he was eight, Borys set fire to hay at a collective farm. It was the way Borys expressed his nationalistic impulses.

I used to steal hay from the collective for my grandparents, hauling it back in a blanket. Throughout the Ukraine, peasants were sabotaging farm equipment, slaughtering collective cows, and on occasion attacking Russian officials. Certain Ukrainians who couldn't deal with the way they were living committed suicide. And across the Soviet Union, people were being scooped up and thrown into prison. In one four-year period, a million had perished at a single location alone—the Dalstroy concentration camp in Siberia. Of the 31 students who attended grades eight and nine with me, 19 ended up in labor camps or prisons. The kids who went to prison were the active ones who got the best marks. The duller children, who got good marks only in class behavior, became the Communists.

The greatest trauma of my life occurred in July of 1956. That summer, my grandmother—my political ally, the one who taught me to love God—found her way into eternity. It was a very turbulent time for me. The woman who raised me as a mother was dead. I was going to have to live with my real parents, this time for good.

It was time to say goodbye to my home turf and go live with Babylon.

Chapter 5

SOLDIER FOR CHRIST

Suddenly I was in the house of a woman whose job it was to destroy Ukrainian Christianity. I wanted to die and follow in the footsteps of my grandmother. I ran away from home for days at a time. Where my grandmother prayed with me in the mornings and where my daily routine had always included errands or something at the church, my mother wanted nothing to do with those things. I was forbidden to pray at home and my mother grabbed my cross from me.

My father's attitude was to let me be for the time being. He figured that sooner or later I would come to my senses. But my mother, Maria Margareta, was a strict Communist. There were Party gatherings at our house and I learned the truth about Communist psychology. They aren't really idealists. They aren't really for the common people. I never once heard the Communist elite speak about the fate of the peasants. All they talked about was money and *dachas*—weekend homes where they could go and enjoy life. Devoid of spirit, Communists, along with other atheists, are the ultimate materialists.

Had I chosen the Communist path, all doors would have been open to me. During the next seven years I would see a parade of Soviet luminaries—generals, ministers—welcomed into our living room. When he was a Ukrainian official Khrushchev spent a whole weekend at my parents' *dacha*. My father's cousin became secretary of the Provincial Party and I also saw people like Kosygin. Meanwhile, the local Party functionaries knocked themselves silly proving to my mother that they were dedicated atheists working feverishly to liquidate the Church.

Here I wanted to become a monk and was surrounded by espionage types. The corruption and treachery were at both a personal and political level. I remember one story about how my father and other regional officials fixed Khrushchev up with a Hungarian prostitute named Magda. She became his mistress and influenced some of Khrushchev's official policies. This is why I always preach that if a person has a morally corrupt personal life, that person cannot be trusted at a political level. My father loved me very much and I was good in school, but I don't think my mother really loved us children. She wasn't the Communist she pretended to be, but she knew the structure of the bureaucratic machine and she knew how to provoke enemies and play them off against each other.

It was not a life of peace or bliss. My parents had some serious spats. At one point my father got agitated and said something to the effect that my mother should start staying home, that he didn't need a "Communist in a skirt" in the house. She began denouncing him, saying he couldn't be trusted. Although my father was not a believer, he kept an icon in his room and mother reported it back to the Party. When my father beat her black and blue, the officials in Kiev and Moscow turned a deaf ear. They knew what she was like. And the KGB, which had compassion for my father (and realized he knew too much about their own scandals), explained away her bruises as the result of an accident.

Let me give you another idea of how farcical and degenerate Communism was and still is. In 1951 my father received a directive from Moscow to find three candidates for Lenin awards—an exceptional swine herder, an exceptional beet collector, and an exceptional cow milker. It was like the Pulitzer Prize of agriculture. But finding someone who was truly dedicated to a *kolkhoz* was quite a task. We didn't even have a *kolkhoz* in the area. The young people were resisting the collective system and no one was weeding the beets or tending to the hogs.

Undaunted, my father went looking for anyone who could be fashioned into a prize-winner. At a high school in Bukivets, he spotted a very pretty girl named Anna Slychko. He spoke to her and told her she was about to become a famous swiner. They took her to the regional office and the procurator fell in love with her. The Russian secretary also fell in love with her. And my father fell in love with her. She slept with all three. Although there was no collective farm in the village—at least none with swine—they fabricated a list of accomplishments and she was awarded the red banner.

It must have been some resumé they concocted for her. The next thing anyone knew, Kiev called Anna to receive a still higher honor. Then the worst thing possible happened: Khrushchev was so impressed that he decided to stop in the village and pay a personal visit to Anna's famous pig farm.

The problem, of course, was that no such farm existed. My father was nervous. It was one thing for Moscow to glide over his personal indiscretions, but failing Khrushchev at a public level was another matter. The press was trumpeting Anna as a young hero of the Soviet Union and Khrushchev was coming in three days! It's impossible to build a farm in three days, yet that's what my father had to do—scramble like mad gathering building materials and the best pigs from throughout the area.

They took Khrushchev to the "farm" and he was overwhelmed. The pigs were not only huge but clean. There wasn't even an odor. What a beautiful farm!

Where did they find such good, large pigs? From the private farms. But Khrushchev didn't know that and Anna received the "Order of Lenin."

With such chicanery, is it any surprise I utterly rejected the system? My loyalty was to the Church and the anti-Soviet nationalists. These partisans were heroes. Their lives were brave, exciting, and romantic to us. At this time, there were new battalions in the underground, preparing for the Hungarian revolution. In May of that year, a number of political prisoners who received amnesty after Stalin's death began returning home to form a new political front.

One day Borys and I were struggling in the dense thicket along a stream to a secret glen where we had constructed a treehouse. We planned to camp in it over the weekend. There was a stockpile of food, first-aid supplies, and weapons. In those days there were a lot of weapons in the Carpathians.

We prepared to fry bacon, building a fire with dry twigs, when all of a sudden we heard the cry of a magpie. That meant something large—animal or man—was approaching us. The whir of a helicopter split the air and we quickly doused the fire. Then we heard shooting. Machine guns. The explosion of grenades. We climbed back into the treehouse and remained perfectly silent.

Nothing more happened. Borys went down for water and I dozed off. But suddenly he shook me awake and told me to look down. There was a group of armed men standing by the fire we had put out.

We didn't know if they were just woodsmen or from the Soviet army. One of them was wounded and we listened to them talk. Three were speaking in a Carpathian dialect and two with a Galician accent. We heard them saying how nice a place the glen was to hide from the Russians. These men were the good guys. That meant they were partisans.

But we were still apprehensive. Eventually I snuck down to relieve myself—stepping within 15 meters of them—and when they heard me snap a branch as I started to climb back up to the treehouse, the men turned silent and all I heard was the clicking of guns.

That can be the loudest noise in the world, cocking a gun. I crept back to the stream and crouched out of view. I was sweating profusely and suddenly as I bent over to wash my face, I heard someone behind me. Before I knew it he had a gun to my neck. I didn't say a thing. The man searched me and found a pistol in my belt. He asked me what kind of bandit I was and I told him I was from Volovets. "Who're your parents?" he wanted to know. I gave them the surname of my grandmother: Terelya. I wasn't about to utter my father's name.

The nationalists brought me to their camp and there I saw the man who had been wounded. They had already dressed his sore but blood was coming through the tourniquet. Another of them I recognized as a man I once had seen pasturing sheep. He knew of my tendency to run away and spend time alone in the hills. The leader of the group was a well-known partisan named Michael Shtayer.

Borys and I, with famous nationalists! My brother came down from the treehouse and we gave them iodine and cotton for a better bandage. As it happened they knew my parents were Communists but it was obvious by how we spoke that our affinity was for the Nationalists and they knew a cousin of mine who was a partisan. Borys also brought down some potatoes, bacon, and sausage. We prepared dinner.

But then we heard a dog bark and scrambled to pour water on the fire again. After that, a volley of shooting. We were forced to remain hiding until Sunday.

Our concern was the injured guerilla, whose wound was becoming inflamed. He needed antibiotics and Shtayer asked if we could go home and get them medicine, honey, and flour. We agreed and began the five-hour walk back to our house.

My father was on duty (he was often out of town), but my mother was there. As luck would have it, however, one of her friends—Brekhova, the wife of a militia commandant—came dashing into the house asking my mother to go to the theatre with her. My mother left, and that gave us the opportunity we needed: there were medical supplies in the house, supplies that weren't available in the public pharmacy.

We found the needed medical supplies, and while we were putting together those supplies we came across a weapons cache. It was my father's secret little arsenal, concealed in the wall: bullets, grenades, and an automatic. We gathered some bullets and stuffed them in with the medical supplies. A doctor had been staying with us and she was also at the theatre. I took a key and went into her room. There was a valise under her bed and I found two rolls of bandages and the specific medication we were looking for.

We put it all into our knapsacks and that night, after mother tucked us in, we stole out of the house back into the woodland, there to hand the supplies to the nationalists.

My brother Borys himself later became a well-known partisan. It was quite a contrast, Borys and I gravitating to the underground while my mother was responsible for atheistic propaganda and collaborated with the KGB.

Meanwhile my father was friends with a secret operative who had helped organize destruction of the Romanian Church.

Where Borys became immersed in political issues, I was to become increasingly involved with the religious side of the underground in later teen years. I was especially committed to a group called Catholic Action. We used to copy Scripture onto wax mimeograph paper and print selections from the Bible. To hide what they were, we bound them between covers of the *Communist Manifesto*. In addition to Catholic Action, there was an organization called the Apostolate of Prayer. Its main purpose was the deepening of devotion to the Eucharist. The annual feast of the Holy Eucharist, which was especially big among the Boyco peasants, was celebrated with special solemnity in Verchni Vorota. At the end of the village were five large linden trees and a chapel and cross. It was in this chapel that we celebrated the feast. We informed the people of where and when the secret celebrations were to take place by wandering down village streets pretending we were playing a game called roll-the-hoop. What we were really doing was giving the Catholic peasants instructions on how to rendezvous. On feast days like the Holy Eucharist, people from distant villages would start wending their way in the early night and arrive by morning. The army and KGB tried everything but couldn't prevent us from coming to celebrate.

Yet another of our duties was to conduct debates with Jehovah's Witnesses and Pentecostalists. The Soviets financed certain underground Protestant groups to antagonize and demoralize us.

But the Apostolate was growing into a very powerful group and some of us were also members of the Ukrainian National Organization. I joined in 1959. We were looking for new ways of resisting the Communists because their pogroms were just awful. We had contacts with the Romanian Catholic underground, which was being persecuted even worse than we were. They were the ones who taught us to bind passages from Scripture under the disguise of the *Manifesto*. As for the children, we organized them into groups of fifty or a hundred and took them into the woods for prayer and instruction. This was the "Church of the Forest" and the children found it exciting. The youngsters pretended to be faithful Communists, wearing red scarves and carrying banners. So convincing were they that they even got the local collective to allocate them grain as Soviet "pioneers." The Communists didn't know what we were up to and it worked so well, these secret celebrations in the woods, that later, in the 1970s, Baptists followed our initiative.

My piety was rising from the depths of my being. I prayed everywhere and grew to love God more and more. When I was younger my parents had often been summoned to school, where I was lectured and punished, but my father always said that this rebelliousness was my own choice and I should do as I saw fit. What I saw fit was to resist the Soviets at every turn. People talk a lot about the catacombs, and what they envision are the Masses said among the pines or rosaries recited out there in the snow. But it wasn't just a matter of coming secretly to pray. The Church also conducted an active operation. Catholic Action had ties with similar groups in Hungary and Romania. Even though we are called Greek, Byzantine, or Eastern Rite Uniate Catholics, with distinct liturgical differences and priests who are allowed to marry, we always worked as one with Roman Catholics. After all, we are both loyal to the Vatican, and the Roman churches, especially in the late 1950s, were also being destroyed. The Roman Catholics were often Czechs or Germans and although they were not decimated to the extent we were, their activity was severely limited. Some of the underground gatherings would take place in Roman churches that were still open, and during Mass we would hand out sheets with information on where the next Eastern Rite meeting would take place.

During these Masses, our priests would be on the balconies hearing confessions while we young people stood on the lookout for the KGB or anyone who seemed suspicious. If someone strange was spotted, the priests would fold their stoles, put them in their pockets, and act like the ordinary faithful. The only people who had access to the underground were those who belonged to old Catholic families. It was handed down from generation to generation. The older we got the more the Church trusted us. It was a life of intrigue.

The name of the woman who cleaned and ironed the priests' clothes was a big secret and so was where we kept the vestments. We generally knew an Eastern Rite priest would be coming on the first Friday of the month to hear confessions. Confession was important not only as a sacrament but also as a way of mobilizing the people and detecting possible infiltrators. We would observe each other going to confession and if there was a Catholic who missed confession, we had less trust in that person and wouldn't share as many secrets with him. We developed a strong nucleus. We lived only through the Church, secretly proclaiming and preaching to others. It was this nucleus that printed prayer books and underground literature. When I was 14 or 15, I had beautiful handwriting. We would copy gospels or a psalter by hand and then bind them. We got away with that for five years but in the end, as happened time and again, someone betrayed us and told the KGB.

The struggle between the Church and the Communists was a never-ending one. The youths of Catholic Action campaigned against alcohol and strove for purity. Few among us took the easy way through life, few among us succumbed to the sensual temptations, and few among us headed, in short, for the wide gate of Hell. This was how the Communists could spot us, by our habits—or I should say, by our lack of bad habits. In the late 1950s, the KGB would go to the senior grades in high school and hand us questionnaires. Do you drink? Do you smoke? Do you believe in God? That way they could narrow down the field and ferret out the Christians. When asked if we believed in God, we had little option but to write down, "no." We didn't want to blow our effective cover. And if school or university officials found out we were secret Catholics, they would suspend scholarships or throw us out of school.

I was blessed with certain traits that served me well as an underground leader. I was bold, unyielding, and inventive, I had a high threshold for pain and fear, and I was absolutely dedicated to the peasantry. Whoever has felt with his own heart the love of ordinary workers and peasants knows that he lives for a cause. I loved my hills, my people, the streams, those fir trees. And I was increasingly ready to lay down my life for belief in the Almighty. Besides the boldness I inherited from my father, I was physically durable and strong. My legs were very muscular, and I became quite adept at the sport of boxing. I started in 1958. I was fast with both hands, and I knew that to win I had to strike first and with full force.

One advantage to living at my parents' was that they had an immense library. I was a voracious reader. I enjoyed the world classics, especially the poetry of Victor Hugo. I developed a large library of religious literature. I read Pascal. And we had the books of Dietrich Bonhoeffer, who wrote of satanism. Not only were there indications of a hidden religious streak in my father, but also a subtle distaste for Communism. He was an administrative official but was disgusted with the atrocities supervised by my mother and was disturbed at the destruction of Ukrainian culture. His circle of friends congregated to view Christian artwork that wasn't allowed for public view, and while they repeated Communist slogans in public, privately they began to form a quiet intellectual opposition to Moscow.

In grade ten, I went to a vocational school, training in carpentry, furniture-making, and wood-working technologies. Then I attended an institute in Kiev. When I completed studies at the institute I began work in the big city. There I met a woman named Olena who was a student in the second course at a medical school. We became friends—two students striving to pave careers. But what I was, really, was a Catholic militant. I became outright defiant. What right did the Reds have, chasing away our priests, killing bishops, destroying our chapels and shrines? The older children whose parents were in the underground Church became involved with the liberation groups. It's hard to say whether this was wise or not, but the natural tendency was to associate with the partisans and divorce ourselves from the Russians.

Think how you would feel if your government prevented you from worshipping. You too would gravitate to anti-Soviet groups. In 1961 Khrushchev gave the order to destroy all the churches and for that matter any sign of religion. This was to be accomplished by 1965. In short order all such symbols, especially roadside crosses, were taken down throughout the region. There wasn't one wayside cross between Prague and Moscow.

Two or three kilometers from the village of Otynevychi, in the province of L'viv, was a nice chapel with a fine statue of our Blessed Mother. Both the Roman and Greek Catholics loved this statue. During Khrushchev's renewed campaign against the Church, the decision was made to demolish this chapel. The leader of the Communist youths in the village went to the chapel with two friends and tore the statue down, breaking it with hammers. They each got something like a hundred rubles for the job. It was July of 1961. They went out afterwards and got drunk with the money. They were driving a motorcycle with a sidecar and they were having fun motoring around at very high speeds. But when they returned, the motorcycle hit the ruined pedestal and the motorcycle overturned, killing one of them immediately.

That same year I first initiated celebration of the Last Supper following the Eucharist at our catacomb services. What was this celebration like? The service would begin around midnight on a Friday. We would cover the windows, light candles, and begin worship. After Mass, the ladies would set the tables with baked bread, stewed prunes, and cabbage rolls stuffed with mushrooms. We would never cut the bread but instead break it, as Christ did. And we would cook beans and pour sunflower oil over this. One of the elders would lead in prayer, and after prayer we would eat. When we were finished we would begin our discussions, and during these conversations we would decide where it would be best to meet next. We were tightly locked in with each other and would rarely accept an outsider. Each prayer group would pray only with each other. Each group had its own underground priests who baptized and heard confessions. Sometimes another priest would come from a distant area but they had to be extremely careful. Priests in the Soviet Union were known to receive three years imprisonment for giving religious instruction to children, or 18 months for praying at a sickbed. They could also get 15 years for criticizing the regime.

The activist element was growing and the bishops took us very seriously. Out of our Apostolate came some of our best underground priests and bishops. Those who had been praying together since childhood remained lifelong friends, remembering fondly the first clandestine Masses, or the good deeds we did, the times we would go and mow the grass for a widow and not even let her know we'd done it. Such experiences bind one person to another and we never severed our ties. Instead, we continued to build an intricate underground. We had our own little defense system and even people working for us in the KGB.

This was my type of activity in the early 1960s. We supported churches in danger of destruction. We tried to refurbish broken relics and monuments. But the destruction continued. On June 22, 1961, in a small town called Drachyno, not far from Svalyava, five cars carrying local militia and civilian Communists arrived at midnight to begin destruction of a Roman Catholic church. Word spread rapidly, and the villagers surrounded them. People stood in three lines around the church, arm to arm, elbows locked, several of the women inside ringing the bells. The people brandished sickles and wash paddles as weaponry. The police saw that they wouldn't be able to do anything and they left. But two days later the KGB drove into the village and stopped outside the house of the woman who kept the church key. They took her to the town hall but she refused to give them the key. That didn't deter them. Quickly they made their way back to the church, broke down the door, and proceeded to tear down the icons and embroidery. They also vandalized the altar and removed the Mass books.

One of the villagers noticed the commotion and again the people surrounded the church. Several women ran up to the KGB officers and swung at them with rolling pins. The people were able to drive the KGB outside village boundaries—throwing some of them in a ditch—but there was no way a small band of religious peasants was going to deter the regime of Nikita Khrushchev, who had vowed to rid the nation of all Christianity by 1964. In the morning, four tanks, two jeeps armed with machine guns, and five other military vehicles rumbled into the village. Yet again the people locked arms around the church, remaining there for three days. But eventually the Soviet soldiers were able to pull down the tower with their tanks.

In the city of Mukachiv, an official named Holovnych gave the order to demolish a monastery on a hill called Chernecha Hora. It was a convent. They had turned it into a

Russian Orthodox building. It was a holy place and the villagers were very angry. The Catholics in town prayed for
three days and nights—didn't eat or sleep. And the Orthodox prayed with them. There was no confrontation—they
prayed together. The local official planned to destroy the
monastery on the third evening, but that night he had a
row with his wife, who told him to go hang himself. He
did! In an incredible turn of events, the official, despon-
dent over her leaving him, got drunk and hung himself.

We never gave up. We fought with dedication and
patience. We didn't just preach, we tried to replace what
was in ruins. There was a very strong young man, Vasyl
Bohovych, who lived in the hills and was paralyzed. But
despite this disability, he set to work carving a crucifix that
was six and a half meters high and made out of granite.
It took him a year. He even carved a fine likeness of Christ.
One day after he finished, he got out of his bed and for
the first time in years was able to walk.

With the destruction of the churches in 1961 and 1962,
a deep despondency fell upon the faithful. Some people
might think we prayed only when we had the opportunity
to use a church, but that's not so; we would gather at the
ruined crosses and demolished monasteries. When the local
Communists learned of us, they went on another blind ram-
page. They committed themselves to the wholesale destruction of everything that was religious. The local Communists
were trying to prove themselves to Khrushchev. All the Christian peasantry were doubly outraged. Some people gathered
with axes to defend their churches, and in the air was what
the Soviets feared more than anything else: a general upris-
ing in the precious, mineral-rich Ukraine.

Faced with such a threat, the Central Committee demanded
in July of 1962 that the local Party chiefs see to the Church's
total liquidation. The regional offices sent in reports to the
effect that all forms of Christianity—not only us but also
the independent Orthodox and Baptists—were being rooted
out. They also trashed mosques and synagogues. On paper,
Christianity was through. More baroque belfries came tumbling down. More crosses were smashed. Satan was having
a field day.

The KGB was pulling every string it could, especially in

the Russian Orthodox Church. Just before the 1960 pogroms, the Soviets replaced the Orthodox Metropolitan Nikolaj (who retained a sense of morality) with Metropolitan Nikodim. According to former KGB agent Peter Deriarin, the new Orthodox official was really a KGB officer named Viryukin, who had served in the emigre department and had been working against churchmen abroad before he was disguised and inserted into the Orthodox hierarchy. In 1978, Nikodim died suddenly during a meeting in Rome—right at the feet of Pope John Paul I.

That seemed like another sign of divine retribution. There were other such remarkable indications as well. In the village of Dovhe was a beautiful wood crucifix. It had been carved in 1803. The cross was broken with hammers by three people working, again, for the Communists. A week later these three went to Khust to pick up a new gravel truck. They got into the truck but despite the fact that it was new, the vehicle stalled in the middle of the road. The man who did most of the cross-breaking was in the cab of the truck while the other two went to look under the hood. Suddenly the motor caught fire and the man in the cab was burned alive.

Ironically, the reports from regional Communists claiming victory in liquidating Christianity worked to their later disadvantage. Because they had assured Khrushchev that the Church was destroyed or under dismantlement, they had their hands tied in dealing with the prayer groups who persisted in visiting the fallen monuments and congregating in large numbers. What were the authorities to do: make a big scene and let Moscow see that they had failed in their mission?

So this helped us to a certain extent, and for the next 17 years the underground Church held clandestine services. We were hard to catch and convict. The only thing they could convict us of was nationalism.

In the 1960s, I was a very popular boxer in the sports club known as Truduvy Rezervy. It was during my enrollment at the building college. I had been boxing for a couple years and had appeared at the Palace of Culture. In 1959, a trainer saw how I boxed and signed me up. The next year, I began preparing for the regional competitions. There were strong boxers in these matches and as a newcomer, I wasn't too sure of myself. They were like black belts and I second-class. My technique wasn't all that polished.

But, as I said, I had good physical power, very strong legs, and I could jump from one corner of the ring to the other, very light on my toes. And that's how I won, by quickly delivering the first blow. I started fighting right at the gong. I would jump into the ring and smash my opponent. My left hand was stronger than my right. I hit my opponent in the forehead, and that was usually the end of it. If the man was stunned, I gained the victory.

Twice, in 1960 and 1961, I was middleweight champion for the entire Ukraine.

When I entered the ring, young boys would go crazy. And when I came out they would grab for my trunks. I came to understand this was all vanity and emptiness—not to mention an exhausting, brutal sport—and my last match was December 14, 1961. I left the ring, bowed down to the youngsters, and said, ''The Lord has given me much strength and I am going to use it in another arena. Forgive me, but who wants to follow me, come.''

No matter the consequences, I was going to evangelize.

My mother was really agonizing over me. Imagine how embarrassing this was for her. During regional Communist meetings she would explain that I wasn't balanced, that I should be sent to a psychiatric clinic. But the people knew me, knew that I was active in the community and a member of a folk dance group. They knew I wasn't off my rocker, despite my mother's insistence otherwise.

At that time I was especially at odds with her because I was one of those who had tried to halt destruction of that church in the town near Svalyava. I was working in Kiev and returned to Transcarpathia precisely for that event. My mother told me I had disgraced the family and that she would never forgive me. At that time, 24 people had been arrested and sentenced for the incident near Svalyava, and I was also supposed to be put on trial but was released because my mother was a high-ranking Communist official. She maintained that if they sentenced me, I would come out of prison with even stronger convictions, so she urged them to send me to a psychiatric institution, where they could destroy my very thought process.

Had she looked close enough, with an objective eye, my mother would have seen the metaphysical battle that surrounded us. While those who defended the places of worship were compensated with healings and other miraculous rewards, those who did the destruction met with mysterious calamities.

Another instance: in the village of Chernyk, the head of a collective farm and a member of my mother's committee ordered two large, granite crucifixes torn down. He hired three former soldiers to do it. They were tractor drivers on the collective and he told them to take the crosses at night and throw them into a river. They received money and liquor for the job.

The villagers were disturbed the next morning when they saw their cherished monuments gone. They were very angry. They called a factory strike as a protest. It wasn't an organized strike. It was spontaneous. People simply didn't go to work.

That day it started to rain severely. For a month there were downpours of torrential strength. Everything rotted in the fields and people were terrified because we had never had such heavy rainfall. And the head of the collective farm in Chernyk—the man who originally gave the orders—suddenly became paralyzed and couldn't speak.

The man rapidly wasted away from the incurable disease. His wife, a teacher who was also a Communist Party member, started going to the fortune tellers looking for herbs to save him. And one older lady, a Hungarian in the adjacent region, told the woman to have her husband go and recover what he had thrown into the river. The woman, who hadn't been told about the crosses, didn't know what she was talking about. This woman came straight to my mother's—they were good friends—and told my mother what had transpired with the Hungarian clairvoyant. And my mother told the woman she would send a car to take the fortune teller to a psychiatric ward.

Still bothered, the woman went home and told her husband about the mysterious advice the clairvoyant had given her. He certainly got the message, and he summoned the three tractor drivers to do just what the seer said, recover the crosses. Within two days the rains ceased across Transcarpathia and within a week he could sit and speak. Then he went to the regional offices and surrendered his Communist card. He wanted nothing further to do with the Party.

My mother thought he too was ready for a mental ward.

In 1961, in the village of Pnjatyn, there was a man named Ivan Kryvyj who also tore down a cross. It was another little hint of God's wrath. Three days after he destroyed the cross, his ten-year-old son died from an impacted tooth.

Coincidence? Folklore? Some of it might be, but don't underestimate the extraordinary events that were occurring on that horrible spiritual battlefield called the Soviet Union. I don't claim to be a historian. Occassionally, dates, times, and names may be off. I do the best I can from notes, archives, and what I saw and heard. Naturally, what I know best was what happened in my own life, and the year 1962 was a monumental one for me. While my mother and her cohorts were destroying the chapels, the shrines, and the churches throughout all Ukraine, I was putting on my poor garb and attending services. My parents were shocked. My mother continued to say I was stubborn and should be locked up in a psychiatric institution. I was 19 and drafted in the Soviet Army. I refused. And you receive a sentence for this in the Soviet Union. I woke up the last day available for enlistment and told my parents I was going to sign up for the army. They were very happy. They said, "We knew that sooner or later you would rid yourself of your folly and come to your senses."

I went to my room, put a knapsack on my back, took two icons with me, an embroidered scarf, a catechism, and the Bible, and went to the registration center. The authorities who knew me called the procurator to take me off to the local prison. They thought that I came to make a public act of defiance. How surprised they were when they heard me say that I had thought it over and was going to enter the army.

They didn't know what to do with themselves. One of the officers asked, "What has happened to you?"

I said I had reconsidered and decided to enlist.

He said, "What do you have in the bag?"

I replied, "Books that I want to read in the army."

"In the army we have so many books you don't have to

take any with you," he responded.

"But I have my own books and I want to take my own books with me," I insisted.

"Show us what you have."

I showed them the books.

"What's this for?" they asked, staring at the Bible and catechism. Some of the officers thought I was involved in a religious sect. "What is this?" they asked again.

My reply: "I've come to evangelize the Soviet army."

Chapter 6

BOWELS OF
THE BEAST

The Soviet atheists were not ready for an answer like that. To them it wasn't an answer. It was a challenge. Yet I wasn't being smart-mouthed. I meant it. No one was in more need of evangelization than the young boys who might be shipped out to battle on Moscow's behalf.

The officials couldn't make a case against me on the basis of my religious activism because they were already supposed to have liquidated the Eastern Rite Catholics. How could I be an activist when all the activism had supposedly been pulverized? Instead they charged me with nationalism. I was arrested on September 4, 1962, along with my brother Borys. They accused me of possessing weapons. During the search they found four bullets belonging to a small caliber pistol. Although we had acquired weapons for self-defense, along with a hidden cache of a thousand Bibles, initially they didn't discover these. The bullets they "found" had been planted by the investigators. For each bullet I was sentenced to a year in prison. Four years. It was a daunting thought.

The Soviets had developed a network of prisons and labor camps that was unmatched in history. They stretched from the southern corners of the Ukraine to Mordovia and Siberia. No one could count the numbers who died in them. But the figure was in the *many millions*. And accounts of life behind bars were entirely depressing. The Soviets were known to treat their prisoners as subhuman creatures. Those incarcerated found themselves herded like cattle, cramped into cells where there was room enough only to stand. They existed on very little bread, were denied anything to read, were strictly forbidden to pray, and were thrown into isolation cells at the slightest infraction. The prisons were too hot or too cold. The floors of some cells were earth and water. Mold grew on bread between breakfast and lunch, and they made prisoners sleep in damp beds. By comparison the worst Western penitentiaries are like country clubs. Then there were the routine beatings and torture. The Soviets invented every conceivable way of breaking the spirit.

We took some sound beatings for about a week after our arrest, and then on September 12 were hauled off to the prison in Uzhhorod, which is near the border with Czechoslovakia. At Uzhhorod you could get thrown into solitary confinement for praying. We would be interrogated for ten days in one place, then ten days somewhere else. Occasionally I was flown to Kiev.

They continued to drive us around to various centers of interrogation. My mother had been present at one such interrogation of my brother, who at 17 was the youngest in the group arrested with me. When the interrogator left the room, Borys took his file of documents—the evidence against him—and shoved it into a lit stove. They began to beat us even harder. I laughed it off. But it was difficult. At one point, a sub-officer named Horokh, who was known to have killed quite a number of people in the 1940s, hit my brother over the head with a huge latchkey. For two months we weren't allowed to shower or bathe. Then the KGB in Kiev assigned another group of interrogators and began to talk to us in a more delicate fashion. They were trying to use the "carrot" after failing with the stick.

The interrogations took place in Svalyava. They gave us blankets and my mother brought us food from home. The authorities also allowed us sufficient water to drink. But it didn't work. I wanted nothing to do with the Soviets. They tried everything to scare us into confession. At one point my brother found himself in what's called a *boksyk,* a special cell that was a yard wide, like a small closet with a little bench. They shaved our heads, stripped us of all jewelry (including crosses, of course), and put me on the third floor in the 34th cell with nine other people.

I entered the cell and quickly discovered that my cell mates were not political prisoners but criminals. There was one huge inmate—built like a mountain—who had covered his entire body with tattoos. When he stood up, stretching his two meters of physique, I was very scared and intimidated. Around his left breast was a portrait of Lenin and on the right, a portrayal of Stalin. Meanwhile, his back was covered with a large tattoo of a church with Karl Marx's head in the middle. Another man was a pimp. All the criminals claimed to be anti-Communist, and I asked if that was so why the big guy had the tattoos of Communist leaders. He told me it was because he figured if he was ever brought before a firing squad, the executioners wouldn't have the nerve to shoot into the portraits of Lenin and Stalin.

It wasn't too bad in this prison. Our relations with the other people were very good because they had a sympathy for our cause. As for the guards, we got away without further beatings. During interrogations they would shine a light into our eyes but never beat us.

After some time—I think December—they took me for yet another interrogation. The KGB had found an old Banderite who had been in hiding for 25 years. His leader, the exiled nationalist Stefan Bandera, had been killed by the KGB in Munich three years before—shot in the face with an ampul of prussic acid.

They took me to see the Banderite and determine if we knew each other. They were interrogating him at the KGB center in L'viv. When I entered the room they forced me to put my hands behind my head, my forehead to the wall, and spread my legs. Then I heard the door open and someone came into the room.

It was the Banderite. They grilled him on whether he knew me, mentioning my underground alias, which had been "Voron." I heard them name Majdan, the village where my grandfather lived. The old Banderite told the interrogators that he had never been there. They asked him if "Voron" was really "Terelya." The man said he didn't know me and had never seen me. They told me to turn around, and

I recognized the Banderite. I was scared. I had a feeling they saw from the expression on my face, that I knew him.

I started fidgeting and my hands became very wet. It's easy to mentally plan how one would act and what one should say in such situations, but quite another matter, in actual circumstances, to carry it off. My body was reacting to the possibility that my silence and denials would result in torture. They told me to sit on a stool and they clamped my legs and arms to it. I noticed an electrical wire leading to the arm rest. The officials ordered me to take a closer look at the Banderite. Did I know him? I shrugged my shoulders: "No."

One of the officers paced around me and hit me in the back of the head with a hard tube. The pain wasn't exactly excruciating but neither was it pleasant. I was frightened. I started yelling and screaming. He punched me in the chest and said he was going to beat my kidneys if I kept shouting. It's not hard to intimidate a 19-year-old man. "I haven't hit you yet," he snarled. "I just stroked you. And if you don't cooperate then I'll really start to beat you." They wheeled up a small table similar to what a dentist would use, and on it were several items that caused me to cringe. There were hooks, wires, and other dental instruments. But this was no dental office. They pulled the table next to me and said, "You should tell us everything right now. If you don't we'll proceed with this interrogation in such a fashion that you'll sing everything out to us."

It was all a psychological game. By the grace of God, I was able to avoid the tooth torture and at the same time to reveal nothing. I got hit once more but was not seriously injured. Still, my mind was paralyzed with fear and my clothes were soaked with sweat. After a while they unclamped me and brought me back to the cellblock.

The rules state that in order to torture prisoners, the interrogators need an affidavit of permission from the local procurator. As they do so often in the Soviet Union, the officials found ways around their own regulations. If they want to get to you they simply put you in a cell with inmates who have agreed to work with the KGB.

The next day they brought me into the same interrogation room. There was a wooden table there and I was discomforted to note that it was splattered with something that looked like blood. The table was bolted to the floor. They told me to sit on it and two officers entered, dressed in civilian clothes. That indicated to me they were KGB. "Who gave you permission to sit?" one of them shouted. "Lay down on that table and take off your clothes."

They had me strip except for my undershorts. Then they began a good cop, bad cop routine. One of them said to the other, "Josyp, he's a good guy. We won't have to do this. He'll tell us everything."

His friend replied, "What, are you crazy? We have to beat this fellow. The government taught him everything, gave him schooling, and now he's trying to overthrow the government that gave him so much. We should beat him."

Suddenly the other agreed. "Put your clothes on," I was now ordered.

I prayed very quickly and put my clothes on. As I bent to tie my shoelaces, I saw one wink to the other, so I knew they were playing games. I sat on the table and they made sure I saw that they had a file on me. They began the interrogation, wanting me to give them information on the Banderite and promising that no one would find out that I talked. When that didn't work they tried to make me believe the old nationalist had squealed on me and had confirmed that my underground name was Voron. I told them I wanted to hear the Banderite say it in person. But they were fairly convincing. I believed them—that maybe he had testified against me.

But still I wanted to read a sheet of paper that supposedly contained his testimony. They glanced at each other and then gave it to me. It was garbage. There was a phrase that cued me—a phrase that he would never have used.

I told them, "Kill me, I don't know this man." I became hysterical and ripped my shirt open. "Beat me or do what you want," I said, "I don't know this man." They told me to settle down. All they wanted to know was where the treasury for our Apostolate was hidden. I told them I had no dealings with the money. I should have phrased my answer differently, because while it was a denial of my own involvement with the treasury, it indicated that such a reserve of money did indeed exist. They were trying to use me to get to the heart of the Catholic underground.

They patted me on the back and said that it was okay for me to go back to my cell and relax. It was lunchtime and that meant a watery soup with bits of fish and cabbage. They gave us the bare minimum, enough just to keep us alive. My head was aching from hunger and I grabbed a spoon for some of the "soup" when a guard growled through the little slot on my cell door. "Have your things ready within five minutes." They were obviously planning to take me somewhere.

I quickly drank the soup and dressed as fast as I could. I hadn't the time to pull all my belongings together when they opened the door and someone said, "Come on. You're going."

There was a group of KGB, waiting to take me back to the prison at Uzhhorod. It was a five-hour trip, and when we got there it was back into an interrogation room. This time they had a new ploy. They had searched places I was known to frequent and had come up with a sack of my belongings—a ball, a few trinkets, intimate souvenirs from my childhood. That may seem innocent enough, but in that sack I had also kept funds for the Catholic movement and a list of donors.

Fortunately I had used only the initials of those donors. They also said they'd found a prayer in my handwriting that denounced Satan. Actually, "Bolsheviks" was how it was phrased. In our Church, the term "Bolsheviks" was synonymous with "Babylon" or "Satan." I didn't know what to say. But I had already learned the previous day that when being interrogated it was best to say nothing. I knelt down in front of the interrogators, made the sign of the cross, and began to pray aloud—*Credos, Our Fathers, Hail Marys.* I prayed and wouldn't stop.

For some reason—perhaps to humor me and get a confession—the officials let me go on, watching quietly. One man was smoking nervously. They asked if I was going to pray for very long. I told them I had just started. I prayed for almost four hours. They kept looking at their watches. They were very impatient but they waited it out. Then a major, Tymko, came in. I didn't look up. I was praying with my head in my hands. The major hit me in the back of the head and I fell to the ground. He told the others to leave.

When they did he turned to me, called me a "God-mongerer," and began to threaten me. "I won't be as patient as they were, and starting tomorrow, I'm in charge of the interrogation," he said, adding: "If you say another word about God I'm going to kill you."

It was past midnight. They took me into my cell. They gave me two or three hours to sleep but I lay awake in fear of the next day's interrogation. Giving up the idea of sleep, I washed my head and the back of my neck and then was given a breakfast that was so salty I couldn't eat it. It was basically boiled water. They took me to the interrogation room and proceeded to go through my whole life, most of their questions innocuous ones and none of them eliciting any kind of real information. But they did get my voice on a hidden recorder. This they could play to my friends. It would make them think I was squealing and in this way they managed to obtain a good number of documents against me.

Suffice it to say, I was facing a solid four years in confinement, and right away I began devising plans for something I later became famous for: *escape.* I was never one to sit still. In all, I would spend time in more than thirty prisons, camps, and hospitals and would escape nine times. That number does not take into account the smaller incidents of breaking free from guards and doing something like diving through an open window or climbing up a wall.

I was bold, determined, infuriated. In the outside world all the indications were that Christianity would be totally eliminated while the Red Dragon tightened its hold. The Eastern Rite Catholics were already decimated—4,119 of our churches and chapels liquidated or taken over by the Russian Orthodox Church—and Khrushchev's anti-religious campaign was still in progress against the Roman Catholics. The overwhelming majority of Roman churches were now closed and the few remaining parishes were without a bishop. So relentless were the Soviets, and so hateful of anything at all that was related to God, that they were even going after the one denomination they had sanctioned, the Russian Orthodox, which lost 10,000 churches by the mid-1960s and had only 7,500 left open.

On January 4, 1963, I succeeded in my first major escape. I am not able to give you the details for a number of private reasons. Let's just say it was an extremely foggy day—people outside were mere silhouettes—and there were four of us who fled from imprisonment. No one had ever escaped from this prison, neither under the Czechs nor the Hungarians. The prison had been built by French engineers in 1934. It was a technical escape. These escapes were always well-planned. But I was caught and in deeper trouble. There were many ways to be spotted after escapes, including by underground priests who served as informants to the KGB. Life was treacherous. When they caught me they tied my arms behind my back and led me back behind the barbed wire. They sentenced me to an additional five years.

My mother was furious. She and my father had nearly arranged for my release, and now I had a new term because of my impatience. "You're going to severe regime," she said. "Be very careful. In half a year you'll be home."

I was shipped to a special concentration camp where they kept high-risk prisoners. It was known as P-JA-128-42, in Manevychi, the northern Ukrainian lake region. The camp was in the middle of muddy land—lakes and bogs, like an island, the only road a series of wooden planks. I was the youngest prisoner. There were many men who had been sentenced to 25 years and hadn't seen their families in a long time. The older men were protective of me on account of my youth, and not one guard dared do anything because they were afraid the other prisoners would look after me. In one block there were 220 prisoners and overall more than 5,000 in this one camp. Unlike a prison, which was often one big block of cement, the camps tended to resemble barracks and we were able to intermingle with many others at work or in the yards.

There was no way you could dig a tunnel to escape from P-JA-128-42 because of all the mudland and bogs. I started to look for alternate ways out. I could see a way of hiding materials that would be necessary for an escape in compartments of machinery we used at our jobs, but it would be impossible to escape as a group. It seemed to me that the best way out would be on high-tension electrical lines that crossed the camp. They were 41 meters high and it was about 300 meters from pole to pole. If I could get to the wires and somehow make my way to the next pole, I would be outside the barriers. The next pole was across some water on a small island.

I set to the task of collecting the necessary materials. I stole a pair of rubber gloves, carefully concealing them. We did logging work at this camp, and we used rollers to move the logs. I stole some of these, too. It was an inventive, perhaps even eccentric escape, but, no, I didn't get the idea from any movie. It was a simple matter of observation. I knew I could touch the wires and not get electrocuted as long as my feet weren't grounded. I had noticed this simply from watching birds perch on the electrical lines. What I did was weld the rollers to a handle, fashion a harness with a belt, and wait for a good electrical storm. Why a storm? Because during intense lightning, much of the electricity is discharged from high-tension wires.

The storm came on May 18, 1963, and I made my way up to the wires, connecting my contraption to the power cables. Then, dangling like a ski lift, I let myself go and there I was rolling down the power line towards freedom.

There was a strong wind and I stopped near the next tower but couldn't get any further. It took me an hour to work my way to the pole. I was totally exhausted. I lowered myself, discarded the rollers in the water so no one knew how I had escaped, and decided I was going to have to swim from the prison island.

It was a 200-meter swim, and the lake ended in bulrush and bogs. There were snakes, but I had no choice but to swim by them. Dawn was soon arriving, and when the fog rose the helicopters would come.

It was a nightmare. I had to make sure my feet didn't touch the mud because it was quicksand. And I had to avoid the slithering, quick-darting snakes. They were called "European mud serpents" and from what I understood they were plenty poisonous. They were swimming all around me.

I was praying constantly, of course, and God granted that not one snake touched me. You had to be there and see the number of snakes to know this was something of a miracle. I arrived at a solid island and was so exhausted I collapsed and slept until noon. The snakes were still an issue. There were hundreds of them on the island, weaving through the mud. Whether they crawled over me while I slept, I don't know. I started wondering how I would get out of there. I could hear dogs barking in the distance, and warning shots. But the helicopters weren't flying over the island.

I suppose they figured no one would head into that marsh. On this little island there were small trees with ductile twigs and I had a knife which I had surreptitiously fashioned in camp. Out of these flexible branches I wove something like snowshoes so I could walk across the mud. I cut the belt I had in two, tied the "snowshoes" to my feet, and began to walk across the quagmire.

I had to step millimeter by millimeter in order not to sink. All told, it took three days to get out of that swamp. But the length of time was all to my benefit. They were searching for me further away, yet I was still within one kilometer of the camp.

I got out of the bog, arrived at some train tracks, and kept a very low profile. They had the regular army, the KGB, and the guards looking everywhere for me. But God was with me; He was directing my thoughts. I realized there was no sense heading to the train station. Instead I decided to hide under a railcar. They were old-styled trains, and under each wagon was an area where they kept supplies in sort of an undercarriage around the axle. I climbed into one such box, and while it wasn't very comfortable, it was fairly safe. Whenever they stopped to check the trains no one thought to look there. I arrived in the Carpathians and while it was wonderful to be back in my native land, the trip grew all the more dangerous because the train was passing through tunnels and they were all under guard, with dogs that can sniff out a hidden passenger. I climbed out of the small undercarriage and went by foot into the mountains.

I managed to remain free for about a month before I was spotted by a KGB officer, getting on a bus. The bus got me to Mukachiv, and here the dogs were out waiting for me. Everybody got out and I remained inside. One of my father's friends, a major, boarded the bus and asked me how I had escaped. The Soviets are obsessed with plugging any holes in the prison system. I said nothing.

I found myself in a number of prisons during 1963 and 1964, including one at Vynnytsya. I was there a month, restricted to my cell. No exercise. No nothing. I thought they were going to put me on trial and sentence me by the end of December 1963 for my escape. Instead, from Kiev, the head honchos came down to see me, including a colonel of the Ukrainian Republic KGB, a well-known man named Lysenko, who was in charge of all operations against the Catholics and Protestants. They came directly to my cell, which was highly unusual. Only under special circumstances do they go directly into a cell and bring apples or a chocolate bar to try to get information from an inmate. That's how it turned out with me—he brought white bread, chocolate, and an apple, put them on a table beside me, and started laughing. "How the hell did you escape from there?" he wanted to know. The colonel assured me he wasn't from the branch of the KGB that operated with terrorism. "I just want to know how you escaped."

I told him I escaped and that's the end of it. He said, "You're a young fellow with a lot of talent and it's a shame you have to sit here. We could use your talent for the Motherland."

I told him, "Well, what do you suggest I do? They won't give me a job or anything. I'm blacklisted."

He said, "Don't be a pessimist. Why don't you join us and help us?"

I tried to act as if I didn't realize that what he wanted was for me to become an informant. But of course I knew. That's the only work they had for people in prison. "What kind of rank will I have?" I played along. "Will I be an officer?"

"You don't understand," he replied. "At first you have to sit in your cell and keep your ears open and tell us anything you hear."

I knew I couldn't joke with the KGB for very long. If you fool with them you are in for a terrible beating. I stood up and told them in a very direct fashion to leave. I wasn't cooperating.

He continued to joke and told me not to jump to conclusions. Then he pulled out his notebook and told me he wanted to ask a few questions. "If you wish to answer, fine, if not that's fine too. Take a look around. You have nothing to fear. I have no instruments, no tape recorder."

I was hardly going to fall for that. "You know yourself that all cells are bugged and everything is controlled," I said.

He tried to assure me that this wasn't the case. The KGB couldn't afford to bug every cell. I was defiant. I told him to prove I wasn't in a specially outfitted cell. He got a little huffy. "If that's the way you feel, we can talk on a strictly official basis. I'll take you to the cabinet room and interrogate you. We don't have to be friendly."

He was trying to pull information from me because they were under great pressure to explain each escape. They were also under serious pressure to eliminate any lingering Christianity. He mentioned the name of an underground bishop, Pavlo Wasylyk. I said I didn't know him. He pulled out a photo of the bishop and barked. "Here, take a look. You and your aunt in 1959, when Wasylyk was released from prison, you came to a place of retreat, called Zarvanystya."

It was my Aunt Olena who had also been an activist and indeed had hidden some of my belongings. I told him I had nothing to talk about. "I've got my sentencing. I have nothing else to add."

He said, "Fine, I'll note you know nothing of him."

I told him to write whatever he felt like writing. He was just trying to entrap me. He also wanted to know where the underground Church's treasury was. He was very clever, making it seem he had more information than he actually did. "We want to trust you," he said. "We've already gotten the treasury and arrested everyone but want to see if you're truly a Christian because Christians don't lie."

I told him I didn't have anything further to say. "I'm not a Babylonian. It makes no sense to spread pearls in front of pigs, Christ said, and I want nothing to do with you."

Lysenko was irritated. "Here I have been so nice to you and you call me a 'pig.'"

"I didn't call you a pig," I retorted. "I said that Christ preached we should not spread pearls in front of pigs, but once you say you're a pig, you are one."

"I'm stopping the questions," he said threateningly.

I told him if he had made so many arrests, he had all the information he needed and there was no use going on. "If you want to talk about my escapes, go ahead, but otherwise I haven't done anything."

Lysenko said he wanted to ask one more question before

talking about the escapes. Really it was another series of questions about the ties between the Ukrainian underground and the underground in neighboring Romania. He wanted to know how information crossed the border, which the Soviets thought was air-tight. I told him I didn't live at the border and didn't know. He became very agitated at me and raised his voice, saying, "Who do you think you are? We've closed the whole border so even a fly can't get in. You must tell us."

I told him that if the border was so well-controlled, then it must be that nothing did get through. It was a cocky answer. He stood and lit a cigarette. I challenged his need to smoke, saying that I thought Leninists had nerves of steel. As you can see, I was very defiant. I didn't believe in any form of compromise with the devil's own crusaders. He threatened to take me into a more "official" interrogation room and then told me I'd be leaving Vynnytsya the next day and taken to Kharkiv, which was in the northern reaches of the Ukraine, near the Russian border. I didn't really have much faith in the fellow. Our discussions didn't get anywhere and I knew they weren't through with me. They already had a plan. What they were going to do was put me into a cell with an undercover KGB agent who would then try to milk information from me.

They took me to Kharkiv, and I saw something fishy right off the bat, because they were treating me with such kid gloves. They didn't even make me wait in line to use the wash area. They checked for lice and placed me in a cell for two people. I saw that my cell mate was an intellectual type. "Glory be to Jesus Christ," I said, greeting him.

He looked at me over the top of his glasses, then took his spectacles off. "Glory to Jesus Christ," he answered.

This automatically made me sympathetic towards him. He called himself Dmytro. We got to be friends and he told me he had been employed as a professor in a military academy. He came into conflict with the authorities for one reason or another and had been given 15 years. This is what he told me, anyway. We got to talking and I told him that I had escaped from the prison camp and they were now moving me to another area. When I started talking about my escape, his attitude seemed to shift and I started to feel that something was amiss. We sat together for a whole week in the cell.

Then one day—I don't know the exact date, it was the end of January 1964—they took both of us to a concentration camp in the Donbas Komisarovka region. It was known as PJA-128-22. I attended a meeting at which I was denounced as a "God-prayer" and Banderite. Dmytro came to my defense, telling them not to treat me so harshly, and for that the head of the concentration camp, Major Vykhrov, and his assistant, Captain Lemeshko, sentenced him to 20 days of solitary confinement.

I felt badly. Solitary was a grueling ordeal. It meant being pent up in a closet of a room with no window and water dripping everywhere. They put salt on the wall to retain the moisture. There was just a single light bulb and it was very cold. It also meant a reduction in diet. Solitary prisoners got food only once a day: two cups of water, 400 grams of bread, and 63 grams fish. A person in solitary gets so hungry he is prone to lick the salt off the very walls. Along with the cold, the intake of salt causes a prisoner's body to swell painfully.

I decided I had to get some additional food to my "friend" Dmytro. Bread. I would somehow smuggle him some bread. But how?

I knew that once a week they would come by and clean out his toilet bucket. They went with him to dump the wastes and there was a fence there where I wedged a little packet of food, along with some notes. They caught me and took me to the administrator's office. Trouble. Big trouble. The administrator said, "You just got here and you're already breaking the rules of the camp, and to top it off, you present yourself as a faithful person, a Christian. If you were to pass only bread we would understand, but you also passed on some notes. You're young and we have to punish you for what you did. But you come from a Communist family and perhaps we can come to some kind of agreement."

I told them I didn't know how I would be able to help them. They replied that I could be very helpful indeed. They told me the other prisoners held me in high esteem because of my daring escapes, and that I would be able to use that esteem to help the administration.

If I cooperated, they said, I would get an early release. Again they were tying to set me up as an informant. No one would know about it, they said, and I played with them for a while but in the end I announced that I wanted nothing to do with them.

The administrator pulled out a blue document. "Well," he intoned, "if that's the way you're going to be, here's a decree for 15 days in solitary confinement."

I didn't say anything. He wanted me to sign the document, an acknowledgement that I'd done something wrong. I told him I would sign nothing. He pressed a button and two men built like gorillas came and grabbed me under the arms, dragging me to a cell across the hall from Dmytro.

My room, however, was a bit larger than his. There were several others in there, criminals who were drunks or who'd been involved with narcotics. We called them "narcs," and they were known to cooperate with the administration in return for special favors, including supplies of narcotics. After two days, they brought Dmytro into the cell with us. Soon an argument erupted and one of the narcs began to speak in a very unflattering way about the Banderites and other Ukrainian partisans. They were working on me psychologically. At that time I was still in boxing shape and wasn't afraid of many inmates. I told the one instigator to shut up but he continued on. Suddenly Dmytro hit him flat-handed over the face and a brawl erupted. Us against them. The walls were covered with blood and we were lying on the floor on top of each other.

They had us removed and taken to the regular cells so I didn't complete the 15 days in solitary. Instead they arranged for us to do the worst work, a job that involved grinding and packaging caustic soda. The guards never came into this area because, with the chemicals flying around, it would just about gag you.

It came to a point, in the fall of 1964, where there was a horrible prison strike. None of us went out for work. There were 5,000 inmates, mostly young men like myself, and we beat up all of the informants. It was a matter of survival. More than forty people were fatally beaten and two men were doused with gas and set afire. I survived three such camp uprisings and let me tell you, it's something unbelievable.

Most of the people in the camp were there for minor offenses—hitting a wife, stealing from a collective farm. After that group of prisoners, the next largest number consisted of people like myself who refused to serve in the army because of their Christian beliefs. Another group of religious prisoners included evangelists. Then there were the nationalists and dissidents. Lastly were the outright criminals: mafia types, the upper echelons of Russian organized crime. This was a smaller group but they controlled the prison. They would have a game of cards and the loser would have to kill whomever the mafia had most recently targeted.

Then there were miscellaneous prisoners like homosexuals, who had been sent to prison as a means of disposal.

The racketeers didn't have to work; everyone had to work for *them*. They had control over all the people who composed the support staff. There was a high school in the camp, and some of the teachers were married to various camp officials. One of the wives, who taught English, was turned into a whore by a mafia type who acted as her pimp. I just want you to see the milieu of evil into which I was thrown. Prisoners went to school and there was a special room set aside for trysts with her. In order to get by in this environment of lust, one had to be very spiritually strong.

While wives sold their bodies, the administrators stole from their own prison or sold narcotics.

So there I was, exposed to every conceivable evil at an age which, in a place like North America, was too young to qualify me to purchase beer or liquor. I silently prayed *Our Father* after *Our Father,* countless *Hail Marys,* innumerable *Creeds.* It was those prayers that let me see beyond the corruption and temptations to the Kingdom of our heavenly Father, who must have looked upon the mess in the Soviet Union with a frown that was larger than the cosmos.

I was in the bowels of the beast. Satan was unleashed in full fury. If you look back to 1884, that was when it is said that Pope Leo XIII had an awful vision in which he heard Satan vowing that he could destroy the Church if he was given enough time to do so. Pope Leo was so troubled he immediately composed the famous prayer to Saint Michael, a prayer that used to be said after each low Mass and now has fallen into tragic disuse. It is said that Satan was granted a century to attempt his diabolical goal. A hundred years. And look what has happened since then: toxic chemicals, radioactivity, huge wars and the threat of larger wars, the occult, drugs, abortion, humanism, wanton sex, and theories of godless evolution. Church pews emptied while theatres showing pornographic and violent films filled.

But there was a catch in God's granting Satan that period of time. If Satan did not succeed in destroying the Church, then Satan himself would suffer a crushing and humiliating defeat. We are on the verge of the end of that era. The big denouement has arrived. In prison I was granted visions pertaining to this. As I hinted in the first chapter, I saw the Mother of God while I was incarcerated, long before Hrushiv. But I'm jumping ahead of the story. Let me continue to show you what life was like under the claws of Satan.

Back to the uprisings: I saw one instance where emotions were so high that all it took to set off a riot was a guard killing a crow that we had adopted as a pet. (The bird, which sat on our shoulders, was taken in when it was found to have a broken wing.) Other of the uprisings were instigated by the prison administrators, who wanted sections of the camp destroyed, especially the warehouses, in order to cover up their stealing. If that isn't enough to give you a sense of hopelessness, I don't know what is. From February 1964 to August 1964, I counted 240 people who saw no way out and attempted suicide. Of these, 154 died. Some cut their wrists, or they would puncture their stomachs, hang themselves, poison their bodies with gas. Or, they would thrust their hands into high-voltage equipment. Sadly, these people were among the most morally upright individuals in the prison. Many of them were trying to make a statement by their deaths, a statement pleading for the officials to change the draconian system. They wrote suicide notes to this effect, but no improvements were made because the prisons were simply a reflection of the entire Soviet system.

There were 210 concentration camps and 36 prisons in the Ukraine where 450,000 people were detained. How many killed themselves? I could never get figures for the system as a whole, but I know that nationwide, across the entire breadth of the Soviet Union, people were ending their lives whether they were incarcerated or free. And this was because there really was no freedom. Everyone who lived in the Soviet Union was in jail. The first year that Leonid Brezhnev was in power (1965) 39,550 committed suicide in the Soviet Union, not including the suicides in psychiatric wards, concentration camps, and prisons. By the end of Brezhnev's rein, the figure would rise to 81,417.

Prison was especially tough on priests. If two or three priests came together to chat, the guards would immediately break up the conversation and the priests often would get 15 days in isolation.

What could I do but pray, and pray secretly. If you were caught in prayer, they would throw you into solitary confinement, or beat you senseless. They tried to persecute me at every step. And for the priests, it was every bit as bad. They had to "pretend" to say Mass, imagining themselves holding the Eucharist and handing out Communion. It was the only way to keep one's connection with sanity. If two or more priests congregated, this was immediately reported to prison authorities and the commandant—without so much as a brief investigation—would place the priests in punishment cells.

Yet these brave clergymen continued to preach. And they copied Scripture by hand to distribute among potential converts or to those who were already of the faith. They were constantly working with the young people. In prison most of the people were lost. Besides the religious and political detainees were men who were accused of incest and other distasteful crimes. We tried to minister to such people. We can't claim to have converted many of these to God, but the fact that we did not reject this category of people evoked a general attitude of sympathy toward us. The mafia criminals were superstitious. And some helped us not because of faith, but because they were afraid that if they laid hands on us or did something otherwise distressful to a person who believed, God would not help them steal. The ones who suffered most were those who were there because of nationalism.

Remember Olena, that medical student who I had met in Kiev before I was first imprisoned? She would communicate with me when she could. Meanwhile, I was always a student of the camp structure itself, on the lookout for ways of escape. In the case of Donbas, it was divided into blocks that were separated from each other by high walls. These walls were iron grates which enclosed barracks and playground. There were towers in every corner, manned by armed guards.

It didn't look like an escape would be very easy but how I yearned to try. The place was just so miserable. There were criminal homosexuals—always waiting for someone to rape—everywhere you looked. Young prisoners would come and the personnel of the camps would do everything to demoralize these people. They handed them over to the scum *(petushatnyk)*, who would rape them and permanently taint their mentalities. I think some people would rather die than be homosexually raped.

In one of the uprisings, 49 homosexuals were killed and 240 others burned to death. The 240 were cast into a barrack, the doors were nailed shut, gasoline was spread, and they were burned alive. The army surrounded the camp with tanks and entered with billyclubs, beating everyone. Along with about fifty other faithful, I climbed into an attic to avoid the utter mayhem. The authorities realized where we were and called us down with a bullhorn. They referred to us as the "prayer people." We were terrified. But instead of torture—this time, at any rate—we were sent to different camps in the Ukraine.

I was taken with Dmytro to PJA-128-59 in the Pishchanka area. It was January of 1965 and getting to be time for another escape. The captain in charge of the defense of the camp was named Vlasenko and the one in charge of the operative division was Lieutenant Dimarov. I noticed right away that the camp wasn't that well built.

I was a 22-year-old man who had never been intimate with a woman and the KGB decided to get to me through a female. They set up this woman who worked there as an engineer, Zhanna, and she pretended to be falling in love with me. She was married with a three-year-old son and soon our relationship became closer than anyone would have wanted—not sexually, but mentally. She explained the KGB set-up and I taught her about Christianity. She even took a trip to the Carpathians to be baptized.

Zhanna's husband was an officer there and didn't much like the closeness his wife felt for me. But neither did he detest me. In fact, he had helped me smuggle out letters to the Carpathians. When Zhanna returned from her baptism, she brought a cross and pictures of me and my family. Her husband found the pictures and confronted me. At the time, my prison job was to make tractor seats—a comfortable job in an otherwise uncomfortable camp. I had my own office and could do pretty much whatever I liked. She often came there. There was never anything intimate between us because I had totally different ideas about what marriage is supposed to be. Still, I was falling in love with her. We were both awestruck. Her husband came and showed me the pictures. "Josyp," he said, "I love my wife. You have to leave this place."

He was going to help me escape! Because he was a secret operative of the MVD (formerly the NKVD, or ministry for internal affairs), he knew what the KGB was up to and told me I wouldn't be able to escape alone while the KGB was so closely watching me. I began preparing to escape. I realized this was the only way out. I wanted my freedom, and I didn't want to do anything to harm his marriage. We are friends to this day. Unknown to me at the time, she had been instructed by the KGB to actually go so far as to marry me. The government would then greatly reward her with a well-established position. My mother was working behind the scenes, trying to get me away from religion and at the same time cutting a deal with authorities for my early release.

As far as I was concerned I still had nine long years in front of me. Had I known of the incredible events yet awaiting me, I would have been that much more intent on fleeing the camps and prisons. In my future were plans to permanently maim and murder me. But all I knew at the time was that I had an opportunity before me, and I formulated a plan in which five of us were going to escape.

Chapter 7

FUGITIVE

It was a tunnel escape. They made brooms at the camp and we burrowed from a deep pit beneath a huge power saw. The tunnel went under the barricades to a plantation of sorghum. My good friend Dmytro was among the escapees. They did not notice we were gone until later, at roll call.

We knew the KGB would search all roads throughout that part of the southern Ukraine, so I decided to head for the neighboring republic of Moldavia. It was summer—August 2—and we swam across the Dnister River, crossing near Kamyanka. I had a friend in a monastery and that's where we hid. There were three of us left. The other two had fled in a different direction. One of them had a stepfather who was chief of the MVD in L'viv. A few days later, Dmytro left for the rail lines. For some reason I followed him, and when I caught up with Dmytro I observed him at a train station. He had succeeded in getting across a first set of tracks and was soon on the platform. The MVD was there with dogs and I watched to my surprise as a captain approached Dmytro and embraced him. I was just terrified. I couldn't understand what was happening. They entered an office and Dmytro came out with some packages. He headed back toward the monastery.

I ran to the monastery and hid in the hay. I didn't say anything to Alexander, the third escapee. He was the son of a very well-known nationalist. Anyway, Dmytro comes, tells us he has some food—claiming it was stolen—as well as some money. I pretended I was happy with him. But what I did was take the money and some passports Dmytro had also been given, and snuck about a kilometer away from the monastery back to the Dnister River. I figured the MVD now knew our plan, which was to head for the Carpathians, and so instead I aimed south, for the Black Sea and the ancient city of Odessa.

I figured I would spend a month or two there before heading back to the Carpathians. I took a large log, lowered it into the river, and floated down with the current, first to Tyraspil and then by land east to Odessa.

At the camp in Donbas I had met a major racketeer who lived in Odessa and I had no choice but to look him up. This turned into an incredible and comical scene. The racketeer was politically connected and was certainly not short of cash. In the end I helped convert this racketeer to Catholicism (he has now forsaken his past and sends me religious poetry), but at the time he was still in the thick of things. His "job" was director of regional fruit distribution but really it was the Soviet version of the mafia.

I went to him and he decided to hide me at his *dacha* 120 kilometers away. It's where the comedy comes in. The place was lavish: sauna, heated pool. And once a month he had friends over for card games. Who showed up while I was there but generals, KGB officials, procurators and ministers of state, including a high-ranking official from Kiev named Ljashko. There I was, in the midst of Soviet bigwigs whose very men were searching for me!

The government and mafia were quite entangled with each other. The mafia provided women who were known to the public as cinema actresses but who in reality were callgirls. They gambled, drank, and had a merry old time together. Because the mafia was my host, no one could touch me. They let it pass for the time being. But had they been able to isolate me away from the *dacha* there would have been trouble. One major general in the KGB said that while no one would seize me at the *dacha* (the rule was that if the mafia introduced you, you were temporarily untouchable), if he got his hands on me a hundred meters from the *dacha*, he would bring me to prison and reap the reward. He said he would get two more stars and the rank of lieutenant colonel.

I stayed a week at the *dacha* and the racketeer forged false documents and so my name became Kovach Ivan Fedorovich. At times I disguised myself in a red wig, or used other aliases. My mugshot was on display through much of the Soviet Union, so it was a nervous time. I managed to evade the KGB and spent much of my time in Luhans'Ske at the far eastern side of the Ukraine, near the border with the republic of Russia. Armed with the false documentation, I enrolled at an agricultural institute. I had been given the stature of "leading Communist youth," or *Komsomal,* which is the entry stage into the Party. By day I was a *Komsomal,* while at night I was Josyp Terelya, Catholic activist, wanted for escape.

Eventually I had to flee into the mining country, where I was employed as a poultry worker, and then, in March of 1966, after seven months on the run, my freedom came to an abrupt and predictable end. I was spotted and arrested by the KGB in Luhans'Ske. They took me to Vynnytsya, a high-security prison where they had a cell ready for me. They were planning to kill me.

It was a very bad prison. There were five people in my room—hard-core criminals. I believe two of them were named Yurkyn and Tichomirov. We sat together a week in this room, and I became a bit suspicious. Every two days one of them was going to the doctor. What they were really doing was meeting with the director of operations and informing on me.

I was nearly too weak to think about it. I was cold and ill-fed. My energy was sapped. And while I was all but starved, these fellows would come back from the "doctor" burping as if they had just received a big meal.

On May 7, 1966, I went on trial. I was given seven years of severe-regime concentration camp. I had other time that also had to be served. My mother came for the trial and they behaved very politely with me. I was very surprised when they gave me good portions at lunch and dinner, even chocolates. Like always, I took advantage of the situation and ate everything they offered.

The Soviets had more in mind, however, than just a sentence of severe regime. At night they took me back to the cell with the same delinquents. Yurkyn and Tichomirov were naked to the belt. I saw that they were drunk, which meant the administration had smuggled them alcohol in payment for their undercover activities. But I pretended I didn't suspect a thing. One came up and asked if I wanted a drink. I said no. "You don't want to drink with us?" he said indignantly.

"I'm a believer," I answered. "I never smoke or drink and so don't talk to me this way." I turned around and lay on the lower bunk. I was very tired and when I'm over-tired I can't fall asleep. But finally I drifted into a deep slumber, only to wake up suddenly and in searing pain.

I was bleeding all over. There was pain throughout my body. Blood was flooding from my arms and legs. Some of it was spurting two or three meters. My cell mates had slit the veins on the back of my legs and had also cut my forearms near the elbow—down to the muscle, nerves and tendons—with big garden knives and crooked shivs.

I tried to fight with one hand against the five men. My blood was everywhere. The guards outside heard this pandemonium and broke in. Apparently they didn't know that the KGB had authorized these men to kill me.

With all the shouting and screaming, the other prisoners were jarred from sleep. When they realized what had happened they began shouting, "Murderers! Murderers!" The procurator came and took me to surgery. I'm grateful to the doctor who conducted the surgery. He did an expert job at sewing me up. But he also had bad news for me. He said I would not be able to use my hands any longer, nor my legs.

I was a cripple, a quadriplegic. He said I would be wheeled around the rest of my life. At the age of 22, I was a helpless man.

I would hear none of it. I was determined to use my hands. For many months I did an exercise that consisted of squeezing my hands and doing pushbacks against the wall, often for nine hours a day, until I got my strength and coordination back. I don't have the power I used to have, and there is still numbness, but the Lord granted that I'm alive and can walk. The fact that I stand before you indicates God's intervention. I regained the use of my limbs.

The whole prison was in anger over this. At that time there were numerous faithful, some in single cells, others doubled up, but in all more than five hundred believers, by my estimate. The commandant was General Kashirin, a truly awful person. He liked to come into a cell and terrorize the inmates. He'd put a glove on his right hand and hit you in the pit of the stomach. If somebody didn't fall immediately, he would mete out solitary confinement and then come to solitary and wait for you to beg—fall on your knees, kiss his boots, and say, "Our God is Commandant Kashirin. I consider myself guilty. I've sinned against the Soviet system."

When the inmate rose, he would unload another punch to the stomach.

"You're lucky you're now under the protection of the KGB," Kashirin informed me. "Otherwise you would never get out of here alive."

My attack had provoked enough of an uproar that the KGB had turned from maiming me to covering up their activities. The official version was that they weren't involved in the attack. Meanwhile, those who had stabbed me met with an unkind fate. Two of the young assailants were killed by inmates who considered me to be a "holy man." They had been murdered at a detention center in Kiev.

I hadn't yet developed a mystical sense but I prayed and preached incessantly. Gradually I could walk on crutches and, like I said, I regained use of my hands. My parents were appalled when they heard what had happened to me and had begun maneuvering behind the scenes. My mother purchased herbs for me and bought the helpful surgeon jewelry worth 15,000 rubles. My parents spent more than 100,000 rubles on me. Why was the KGB suddenly my protection—at least for the time being? Because my father went right to a general named Fedorchuk, who was in charge of the Ukrainian KGB, and raised the issue. It was one time it helped to have Communists in the family.

I was told I wouldn't be at the prison much longer but would be taken to yet another concentration camp. When I was leaving, the doctor said, "Continue exercising. We can't figure out how you can walk but it appears the will

of man is working." The will of man and the will of the
Holy Spirit. It was just the beginning of some truly awesome signs from Heaven. You will appreciate what I mean
shortly. I was also given certain inspirations. For instance,
while I was in the hospital I was relatively free to move
about and had access to paper. I began pilfering it and came
up with the idea for a rudimentary printing press. I decided
to print a little prayer card for the inmates—the *Our Father*
and *Hail Mary*. I stole a plate of glass and took it back to
my cell. I had a new cell mate, a member of the sect called
Jehovah's Witness. He tore off the back of a boot and we
burned it, making ash. If I was going to have a printing
press I'd need ink, right? I took butter and sugar, mixed
it all together, and made a pigment with it. I added some
glycerin, stenciled the prayers on the glass in reverse, and
there it was, a copying device.

By July of 1966 I was in the concentration camp PJA-128-39
at Hubnyk. It wasn't far, maybe nine kilometers, from my
friend Olena, the medical student. They kept special
prisoners there, especially escapees. I was already known
as something of a jailhouse Houdini.

The man in charge of regime was a fellow named Yarmosh, a sadist who not only tortured prisoners but also liked
to stab the bare breasts of his own wife with lit cigarettes.
He'd sit on a chair that was set up like a throne, spin around
on it like a madman, and make us plead for mercy. One
of the captains had been at the prison from which I escaped
in 1965, and he had quite a greeting for me. He raised his
arms and said, "Terelya! Now you're in my hands. You'll
never get out of here!"

His threat notwithstanding, within a month I was planning a new escape. There were many things working on
my mind. First of all, that printing at the previous prison?
They had found the plate. Besides the prayers, we had also
published appeals to the free world and had them smuggled out through the nurses. I could get at least three years
for that. The KGB from Kiev and Uzhhorod came to see
me about it. That was one reason for wanting to escape.
Then there was the medical student, Olena. After the matter with Zhanna, I had started thinking of Olena not just
as a pen-pal but as a potential wife. I wanted to see her.

The authorities said I could have visits from her if I provided
the information they were seeking. I didn't tell them a thing
and they threatened me with ten more years.

Fortunately my parents were always standing up for me;
anyone else would have been executed during the many
years I spent in prison. But I was in prison just the same.
I mulled over possible escapes. From what I could see, there
were three types of escape that could be attempted from
that camp and I carefully reviewed each possibility. At the
same time I was reviewing escape options, I was also busy
organizing a religious group that began surreptitiously printing appeals and religious messages again. We published
letters, posters, and leaflets, smuggling them out by hiding
them in large sacks that were made at the prison for a chocolate factory. On one of the leaflets I wrote an apocalyptic
appeal stating that the power of Satan would soon collapse.
This will seem ironic to you later. At any rate these bags
went from city to city, so our messages were soon appearing in Kiev and other places.

A KGB officer recognized my handwriting on the leaflets
and a general of the secret police came to see me. Trouble
again. I entered the camp offices and he began cursing and
blaspheming. "What are you doing?" he said. "Your mother
was just here. She asked for me to intervene. Your father
said you would behave. We can't cover this up because
Moscow knows of this. They think there's a large religious
underground, and here it's you with a couple of geezers."

"Go ahead and try me," I answered. There was no use
denying anything. My publications had been mentioned on
Radio Liberty along with my name. Sometimes I defiantly
signed my printed appeals, "Josyp Terelya, true Catholic."
Radio Liberty is a branch of Radio Free Europe and is based
in Munich, Germany.

In my two stays at Hubnyk I often found myself in isolation. It was miserable. It was like living in a box. There
was nothing to eat, nothing to read. It was cold and all
you could do was pray. But prayer is all you need. Let me
tell you, through prayer I was able to witness to many
inmates and even prison officials, including one director
of internal security who belonged to the MVD. The question often arises: How do we pray and listen for God? How

do we serve Him and obey Him? Remember the words of Christ when He spoke to the Samaritan woman. God is spirit and those who adore and bow down before Him must adore Him in spirit and truth.

What does this mean to bow down to the Lord? Before God? Through prayer we become one with God. When a man who believes seeks always to keep God in his heart, he becomes one with the Almighty. We must get down on our knees. Let me tell you that by doing this, and converting people, even the hardest guards, prison left me with some of my most joyous moments. I know this is hard to believe. But that's what prayer, self-denial, and faith can do. Prison was a purging and evangelical experience for me—soon to evolve, as I said, into an experience of outright mysticism.

Anyway, as for the isolation cell: I was there once and while I was out getting water five men began beating me, including a guard named Mychajlo Svyenko. Afterward I began praying for him. I asked Divine Mercy to enlighten this man, that His grace might come upon him.

Hearing my invocations, the guard angrily opened the wicket and cried out, "Quiet, Terelya, or I'll kill you."

I continued to pray for him aloud. In an hour he again opened that small window and said, "Terelya, I'm an atheist, a Communist. You can pray a hundred years and it can't help me. And if you continue to pray we'll come and beat you again."

I continued to pray aloud and he couldn't stand this. He opened the wicket yet again. This time he brought a stool to sit on. He said, "Look, Terelya, I beat you up. I treat you harshly. Why are you praying for me? There's no God."

I replied, "You say God doesn't exist but five hours ago you were beating me to death. You wouldn't give me a glass of water. And now you're talking rationally and calmly with me."

He turned all red, closed the cell window, and slammed the door. I continued to pray aloud for him and his family. He opened the window once more. This time he had an entirely different demeanor. He was there with a chunk of bread and a pot of hot water. He took his warm jacket off. "Look," he said, "you go back, sleep, and cover yourself with this jacket. An hour before wakeup I'll come back for the jacket.''

During my stay I conducted many discussions when this man was on duty watching me. Eventually he left the MVD and became a Ukrainian Catholic activist. Six years after his conversion—in 1972—this former guard was arrested and received his first sentence.

My stay at Hubnyk involved both conversions and another escape. As I remember, the breakout came on a Tuesday in the autumn of 1966.

They had these metal drums of diesel fuel in the yard, and when they were empty, the barrels would be trucked out and refilled. I managed to hacksaw one in half and devise clamps inside so that someone could get in the bottom half, lower the top half over, clamp it shut, and have it look like a whole barrel with the lid still fully intact. I got inside and sure enough a truck picked it up and I listened with great anxiety as we made our way beyond the camp barricades.

The dogs couldn't smell me because of the oily odor but after a while there was a different problem: I got claustrophobic. I needed to get out but I couldn't undo the clamps. I was afraid we would arrive at our destination and that before I could get out they would put a hose inside and fill it with diesel fuel. I said a prayer and then the thought occurred to me: Bang the lid with your head. I began banging my head against the top—so forcefully that blood was soon streaming down my face.

But it worked. I finally broke the lid, discarded the drum, and hid in a wooded area.

Chapter 8

WOLVES OF
THE WORLD

I wasn't free long before I was caught. They brought me back to camp and beat me severely. Starting in November I was in solitary for two full months. I got little more than cold water and strained gruel. Not even a shred of the third-rate meat.

The guards pummeled me with their fists and boots, or they would wake me by throwing freezing water on me. Yarmosh, a sadist, was director of discipline. I didn't think I'd survive. My job was to make road curbs from stone excavated in a nearby quarry. I was required to make two of these a day—a very exhausting task—and when I was finally finished Yarmosh would come with a sledge hammer and smash them so I would have to make two more. All of this labor was done on a daily diet of a mere 300 grams.

These are the types of techniques that are used throughout the Soviet gulag to break you down mentally. Many camps and prisons also have what we called the "bitch" rooms where homosexuals were kept. These perverts worked for the KGB and MVD and would rape prisoners who were thrown in with them.

I had a cross and an icon of Our Lady. Both were the source of enormous irritation to the authorities. But they didn't outright take them from me. They wanted me to hand them in voluntarily. It was a psychological ploy. They were trying to get me to come to the decision on my own. A decision to relinquish such sacred relics would have been a step towards shaking me from Christianity.

Naturally I refused and Yarmosh said I was violating prison regime. I was given those lengthy stays in solitary. Still, I refused to hand over my holy objects. In an effort to change my mind, they started putting me out in the cold with only a shirt to shield me against the elements. It was a very chilly autumn, with plenty of rain and sleet. One day I was brought out to work, lined up, and they opened my dossier. "Do you believe in this God?"

I remained silent because no matter what I said I would be beaten.

A captain named Volenko snarled that perhaps I didn't know how to speak. "Maybe you don't want to talk to Communists." He grinned sardonically. They brought out my icon and told me to hold it. "We'll see how God helps you," he said, leaving me to shiver in the cold breeze.

They left me there and the next day the same thing happened. Every morning all the senior officials would come out to see if I would take the cross off. They said they would keep me there until I got rid of it. Then they doused me with water one snowy day. Everything froze on me. This happened time and again. I stood there for eight hours at a stretch. They also deprived me of the regular rations, straining my soup through gauze to remove vegetables.

Miraculously, I was soon transferred out of there, held over for a few days in Vynnytsya (where I had been before), and then moved on January 5 to the prison in Odessa, where I spent two months. It was now 1967. Happy New Year.

On February 24 or 25, 1967, I was taken to Camp PJA-128-6 in the provincial town of Kirovohrad. The commandant was Colonel Cheprasov and the political adjutant was Loktjev. They greeted me nicely—that is to say, I wasn't immediately beaten—but the KGB had special directives and were looking for an opportunity to get even with me.

It is difficult to remember all of the horrors of captivity. During my years of incarceration I saw instances where religious believers were forced to drink their own urine, or to eat their own feces. I'm also told there were instances where the feces were shaped like a eucharistic host. Who but Satan could inspire such acts of blasphemy? One had to ignore the repulsive environment and persevere on the Christian path. Wherever I was, I continued to publish leaflets and evangelize at every opportunity. You can never give up. You can never compromise with the world. You can never give in to the devil.

I would like to divert a moment into the issue of ecumenism. During this time period, in Kirovohrad or the transfer prisons, I often had communication with other believers. For a while my cell mate was a leader in the sect known as Seventh Day Adventists. His name was Kozarjov. He was a Romanian citizen. How did I feel about such denominations? Firstly, I defended all the faithful—Protestants, Jews, Orthodox, Muslims. But I tended to avoid anyone who called himself a Christian and yet was critical of Scriptures. I didn't want to associate with those who denied the redemptive power of the blood of Jesus Christ. If I couldn't convince them I would avoid them—defend them, maybe, but avoid them.

I must ask any Protestants reading this to excuse me, but it is my conviction that *we* are the Church built on the foundation instituted by Jesus. The Protestant faith was initiated by Luther on October 31, 1517. It was a tumultuous time that shattered Christian unity. I believe the Mother of God is calling us to ecumenism, but my definition of ecumenism is a person who has truly received Christ and is baptized in the rites of the Catholic Church. I know this sounds radical these days, and perhaps even intolerant. But I don't believe in neutral churches. I am not against Protestants. I have always helped them. I have always given witness for them. They produce good, active Christians. But we Catholics must follow a truly authentic ecumenism, and our apostolate is to defend the Mother of God against the attacks of certain misguided denominations and work among the unbelievers. Disbelief in Christ, or the downgrading of His mother, is the work of demonic forces. So are all the divisions that have occurred since the 11th century, when the Greek Orthodox tragically separated from the Vatican in the "Great Schism."

We were always trying to convert people in prison. Even if you only convert one soul, the fruit is bountiful and sweet.

Conversion is a purifying process and an affirmation of one's own being. We converted many of the prisoners, and through prayer we were constantly purifying ourselves. We have so many obstacles to living a Godly life. Look at me. One moment I am calm, the next angry and impatient. The Mother of God herself, when she appeared to me later, in a prison cell and then at Hrushiv, corrected me for my impatience. We can never know when we'll fall into sin. A Christian brings the greatest good when he does good deeds. Not just prayer, but also deeds. You must proclaim your faith. You must expose and correct evil. If a man prays but takes no action when he sees another man in trouble, or when he notices evil, he is committing the sin of silence and inaction. A man who remains quiet is a greater sinner than the one actually sinning.

No wonder Jesus told us to go among the wolves of the world. We must go among the disbelievers and the indifferent. The indifferent ones are the most dangerous. You can transform a criminal—he'll repent—but an evil servant, the bureaucratic or intellectual type who knowingly spurns God, is much more difficult to convert. Yet we must. We must lift spiritual blindness. We cannot ignore evil. We're living in very awful times, the peak of the devil's activities. We must tear down the artificial and heretical distinctions between "secular" and "religious." The first heresy rose from this subtle distinction. The Church began to be subordinated to the state. The emperor Constantine became head of the Greek Orthodox Church, replacing the patriarch.

That's how religious atheism and secular humanism is born. It is only where you have the sacrament of priesthood that you find the Eucharistic Christ. The Catholic Church has the sacrament of the priesthood. The Russian Orthodox Church does not. Our duty is to teach the masses that they should be uncompromising with the world and Satan. One prison psychiatrist exclaimed: "You religious people are developing a unique spiritual masochism. You find satisfaction in that you're beaten. Nobody acts this way! You're separating yourselves from the masses." Perhaps we were separating ourselves from the world, but we were uniting ourselves with the crucified Christ and answering His call to arms. This was at the root of my uncompromising audacity. We must be unyielding, and we must prepare for the terrible times that are ahead.

At Kirovohrad they tried to give me a job at the camp and at the same time keep me under constant surveillance. Camp Number Six was responsible for manufacturing agricultural machinery that was sent to Africa and other countries. There was a school at the camp to train machinists. I was a janitor at the school. I had a little glass cubicle on the second level and we would clean machines, refill oil, and make emulsions. There was also a company that made drafting paper and I got the idea to make a printing press out of the drafting machine. I organized a group to set about the clandestine and risky task. I refused to compromise with the Communist system, no matter how many more years they kept heaping upon my sentence. There were three officers in the MVD and an officer's wife who cooperated with us. We had a rotary machine and stainless steel cylinder to run off the plates and could make 110 impressions from each waxen mastersheet.

Eventually we had more than 10,000 Christian flyers. It was quite a logistical challenge to smuggle them out of the camp. Some of our publications were hidden in the farm equipment and found their way into distant countries. What a stir that later raised! But we had many more to distribute and in the middle of July in 1967, I came up with another plan. We would shoot the leaflets into the wind. A national motorcycle contest was to be held nearby, which povided a large audience. The event was scheduled for July 18 to 21.

The second night of the carnival, we snuck the flyers to the base of the factory smokestack, which was very tall and had huge ventilation fans to propel out emissions. We began feeding our flyers into the updraft and the fans blew them out the stack, sending them over an area of twenty to thirty kilometers. The KGB started one of their inevitable investigations but they couldn't figure it out. At first they decided it had to be a plane or helicopter. They were looking all over the area when in reality the leaflets had come from their own prison.

Well, it's hard to get away with such a large-scale escapade. They sent in espionage and counterespionage investigators. They compiled a list of prisoners who in the past had anything to do with such shenanigans. One major named

Yakemovich decided that the tone of the writing was mine.
On August 14, 1967 they surrounded the factory office where
I worked and arrested me.

There wasn't going to be much leniency. They took my
escapes into consideration, along with my proclivity for publishing, and gave me a new eight-year sentence. I was in
trouble for any number of actions, including the Hubnyk
escape and another attempt to flee Kirovohrad. They told
me I wouldn't be kept in Ukrainian camps any longer. I
was going to be shipped up north, which meant I was ready
to experience the truly worst of Soviet prisons.

In all, I was sentenced eight times in Soviet prisons, and
in some cases all I needed to do was sign a document
denouncing my activities and agreeing to join the Russian
Orthodox Church in order to obtain early freedom. I refused
every time. In the case of the flyers, they demanded to know
where the hidden "printing press" was. If I told them, they
promised me a hospital diet, which meant milk, butter, some
meat and fruit. I told them it was in a Carpathian cave.
They went looking for it and of course never found it. I
knew they would beat me when they discovered I was leading them on a wild-goose chase but it gave me time to rest
before the new round of punishment.

When they returned I was placed in solitary confinement
for a month, without food or water some days. The other
problem was the cell's temperature. It was designed in such
a way that it was either shivering cold or unbearably hot.
They wanted to break me psychologically. I could tolerate
a little cold but not the heat. When it was cold I paced
to keep warm, and when it got very hot I would lie on the
floor and breathe through a crack at the bottom of the door.
I developed rather severe hemorrhoids as a result.

But was I "broken?" No. And I was certainly no less defiant. I collected scraps of bread and sculpted them into figures
of Marx, Lenin, and Engels. Then I unraveled a string from
my jacket and fashioned a noose out of it. Using the log
that served as my stool I played out a mock trial to vent
my frustration and pass the time. I "hung" Marx and Engels.
I also sculpted little animal figures to serve as the court-
room audience. They ran into the cell and stopped me from
hanging Lenin.

They took me to the republican psychiatric department at Kharkhiv Medical Institute. A Professor Zilberstein asked me if it was true that I thought animals were people and people were animals. I responded that the animals were closer to being human beings than Marx and Lenin had been.

"Were you hanging Communists?" he demanded.

"No," I replied. "I was hanging Satan."

In September, I had what was the beginning of a series of extraordinary dream experiences. At the time I was under investigation for the additional sentencing. I was also in frequent debate with two Jehovah's Witnesses and the fellow who was a Seventh Day Adventist. The days were long and boring with no peace. Ironically, it was after a discussion about the immortality of the soul—which the two Jehovah's Witnesses didn't believe in—that I had a dream precisely related to the issue of the soul's final place of refuge. We went to bed and in the dream I saw an immense field, sown with flowers I had never seen—mostly white ones. In the midst of this field was a small church and by it a house. Before the house was a well.

I flew over the fields and cities and came before this church and house. I heard the sounds of a choir singing in the church. The singing was more harmonious than any I had ever heard. My grandfather Ivan and grandmother Anna Sofia came out of the building. Behind them was my youngest brother, Sergius, who had died in 1951. I hardly knew him. Sergius was in white clothes embroidered in blue. He walked to the well and got water for my grandparents. "Sergius," I said to him. "Give me some of that to drink. I haven't had a drink in a long time."

"This water is not for you because you are not with us," he answered. "I'll give a drink to Aunt Olena."

My aunt was coming down the field all in white, her hair very bright, and in her hand were three candles—green, white, and yellow. It seemed strange to me, because everyone else was deceased, but as far as I knew, Aunt Olena was still alive. She entered the church and again I heard beautiful singing. It was a choir of angels praising the Mother of God.

I wanted to stay. It was beautiful there, while on earth, I faced a new trial. But in the dream my aunt spoke to me.

It was as if she were reading my thoughts, and that frightened me. "You still have work to do on earth," she said. "Not everything has been fulfilled that you are to do, Josyp. Pray to the Mother of God and God will help you."

We went behind the church and from there I could see the end of a large field. The thought came to me that this was God's meadow. My grandmother turned to me and said, "Look. See that woman in red?"

I looked and saw a woman gazing toward us. My soul was filled with an indomitable fear. My heart was squeezed with sorrow and grief. I looked at her and froze. My aunt said, "Pray for this woman but do not touch her body."

I looked and this woman began to take off her clothes. Her body was black and covered with horrible scabs. I was still too far away to see her face. A white bird descended from the skies and in its beak was a drop of water.

I felt a great thirst and wanted to take that drop. My grandfather stopped me and said, "You haven't prayed for that sinner." Still, I went to the bird. It moved away and headed to the woman.

The field disappeared and I saw I was standing in mud. And the woman—drunk and dirty—began shouting at me. When I got closer I saw that the woman represented Russia. I don't know how I knew that. She began to shout that I must not pray for her. She spoke as if she were possessed of an evil spirit.

Her mouth was foaming and her eyes were burning with a satanic glow. I was totally unnerved. I didn't know how to react. Then the white bird flew to me and gave me a drop of water and I experienced a lightening in my spirit. I crawled out of the mud and prepared to fly home because I knew I had to return there by morning.

Then I saw my aunt lying in a coffin and by her I saw the same candles she was holding at the church. At this moment the woman in red caught up with me, her face just hideous, her eyes burning with hatred for Christ. She swore she would eradicate faith in God. I was paralyzed with fear but found strength enough to kneel down and pray. The woman bent over and cried, "I don't want it. Don't do that!" I continued to pray and she turned her back to me and began to run away. On her back I saw many people praying secretly. I also saw that she was very tired and bound by chains.

A voice said to me, "Pray to Our Lady of Fatima and this woman will be saved." I trembled and awoke from the dream. I was covered with perspiration and my hands were trembling. Exactly one month later, October 27, my 24th birthday, I received a telegram about the death of Aunt Olena.

As you will see, that dream was only the start of a new mystical dimension in me. And how hard it was to return from the heavenly church. How hard it was to be in the real world and the reality of spending my youth in prison.

I was tried in November by a regional tribunal and immediately after began my journey north to a series of camps in the Mordovia region. Mordovia is south of Gorky and the big-time, as far as political camps. On the way I stayed at a number of transfer prisons, including one at Kharkiv, where I spent two weeks in a death cell because there was no separate place for political prisoners.

The next transfer point was in Potma and as soon as we got there all the camp directors came to look us over. We were detained there until they readied our permanent camp destinations. There was one separate unit at Mordovia, PJA-385-5, that was only for foreign prisoners and I was able to mix with them at the central hospital.

On January 18, 1968, a car came and the guard on duty called into my cell with the standard order that meant I was ready to go. "Prepare your belongings. Be ready in two minutes." I was somewhat confused because I was with others who were being tried for the same crime. The guards were obviously separating us. We began to say goodbye. The authorities dashed into the room and took nine of us away. With me was Father Yaroslav Lesiv, who had been sentenced for activities with the Ukrainian National Front. We were brought to Camp PJA-385-11, in the village of Javas.

It was a cold, damp region surrounded by swampland. I spent much of 1968 and 1969 at Number 11, but in 1969 I was also at PJA-385-3 in Barashevo and PJA-385-19 in Umor. We were stripped naked and they began searching us. They took away every shred of civilian clothing. They kept a special eye on me because of my reputation for escape. There were ten political camps in Mordovia and they were placing me in a unit with high-risk prisoners, such as foreign spies. The major approached and said, "Now, Terelya, if you escape once more, we will put you in front of the firing squad. We will play no more games. What you experienced in the Ukraine were just flowers. Here you will be collecting the berries."

When I entered there were five hundred prisoners waiting there. They were looking for news from the arriving prisoners. We were led to a camp store where we were handed mattresses, prison garb, and soap. There was a decree that I couldn't have any visitors. It was another form of punishment. In the gulag you would go months or years without family visitations, and depending on the camp, an equally long time without newspapers or letters. A cousin of mine was there, sentenced to 25 years of labor, but they transferred him a few days later so I would have no emotional support. I was assigned hard labor in the lumbering depot. It was frigid and wet. My job was to shove logs with a steel rod toward a sawmill. At one point I jumped into the water and began yelling that the Russians were trying to kill me; I jumped to get attention. I was screaming and hollering—and they pulled me out. The wind was so intense everything froze on me. They brought me in and had to cut off my clothes.

I began to play games myself. When I was taken to the staff office, I pretended that I didn't understand Russian and only spoke a Carpathian dialect. A week later, a KGB officer came from Kiev. The authorities already had a whole dossier on me. The officer was Major Chernjak. "You don't understand Russian, huh?" he demanded. "You're the son of the former delegate for the struggle against bourgeois nationalism, and you say you can't speak the language? A month of solitary. This I'm giving you myself, and after a month the authorities will give you whatever *they* feel is appropriate."

The solitary cell was made of concrete and had a small window at the top with a stump in the center of the room to sit on. The cell was maybe three feet wide and six or seven feet long—a closet. There was a chain hanging from the wall, and when they beat you, they strapped you to the chain like in the old medieval dungeons, hanging you by your arms with your toes barely touching the floor. Sometimes they made prisoners dangle like that for 24 straight hours.

The floor was coated with sawdust, and with nothing to read and no one to talk to, I paced back and forth to keep occupied and warm. It was chilly sitting there and I didn't have many calories to burn. I was fed two cups of hot water a day, 400 grams of bread, 63 grams of fish, fifty grams of beans, and some salt. By regulation, the punishment cells were supposed to be 16 degrees centigrade (or 29 degrees Fahrenheit, which isn't very warm as it is), but the temperature was often even lower.

It was the coldest at night and because of the chill, I couldn't sleep. Usually we wore an undershirt and the prison jacket, but in solitary you were allowed only one shirt. The guards shut off what little heat there was when they went off duty. I had to massage myself constantly to keep the frostiness off me, and when they gave me my daily 400 grams of bread and the hot water I would consume all the bread and most of the water, gaining a little heat from this. I would stick my fingers in the water and, for warmth, rub some of it into my skin. Then I would fall to the cement floor for an hour or so of intense sleep—making up for the sleep I lost at night when I paced to warm myself. I prayed constantly, and most other prisoners thought I was nuts because I was always in meditation. There are very few believing people in political camps, and while we shared the same revulsion for the Soviet system, most of the political dissidents were agnostic or disbelievers whose cause was entirely pragmatic—not spiritual. The nationalists, on the other hand, were believing people.

I came out of solitary on March 3 but it wasn't to be my last trip there. In fact, I ended up there so much I started to think of the cell as my private *dacha*. Once I was given ten days for not buttoning my collar properly.

Gruesome as it can be, it was in solitary at Mordovia around December of 1968 or January of 1969—I'm not quite sure of the month—that I had a very unusual experience. I had been beaten and I was trying to recuperate in a corner of the room. I would doze until it became too cold, then would pace to warm myself. It was during one little snooze that I had a nearly indescribable vision. In this daydream,

I was no longer on earth. I was on another planet—or rather, in some other dimension. There was no living environment, no trees, brush, or wildlife, just stones and a very powerful light, truly incredible. I was walking along this rather sterile terrain when I saw a white mountain reflecting in the light and what I can only describe as a cosmic mansion. The buildings weren't like our buildings; it was as if they were crystalline; you could see through them. They were like buildings on another planet. I entered the mansion, looked to the right, and saw an elevated structure that was something like a step pyramid; that is, there were layers leading up to a white throne. On the lower layers were many people in white and blue garments, and just before the top were 12 wisemen with long white beards. I got the sense that these were Christ's apostles.

On the white throne was Christ the King. He was fair-haired and perhaps thirty years old, and he too wore white garments but with purple embroidery along his mantle and decorations of gold. I felt comfortable and approached. It was like these cosmic people were patriarchs discussing the trials designated for my life and how I was proceeding with those challenges. When I looked I could see all the particulars—the color of their eyes, the wrinkles, the austere but very kind faces. I became very warm and possessed a great sense of comfort. Unfortunately, it was at this moment that I woke up to the realization that I was still in Mordovia.

I had no doubt Jesus was watching over me, but it wasn't my time to join Him yet.

Returning to the cell one day, I found another man inside. He was very strange. He was standing on his head and breathing through one nostril. I didn't know what he was up to. I greeted him but he didn't say a thing for half an hour.

I sat in a corner, watching him skeptically. Then he got off his head, sat up, extended his hand, and said his name was Kavalauskas and he was a Lithuanian nationalist. He had made a beautiful cross out of bread and had embroidered it with bits of straw. We became fast friends. He was a strong Catholic and we would meditate and pray together. He made rosaries with little balls of bread and for the cross he used matches dropped by a guard who smoked.

We were caught praying by a man named Schwed, the

non-commissioned officer in charge of solitary. He had crept up on us and began hollering. "You sons of bitches! You're praying to the gods! It's ridiculous. What does God do for you? Here you pray and are punished and I do not pray and am not punished."

It was the beginning of a remarkable rapport. Despite his initial hostility, the guard began listening to talk of Christ, and in the end, Schwed spilled his guts to me. He had been working there 35 years, and his life was as empty as a canyon. He told me that after attending school he was brought to Mordovia to work in the camps, and soon he had advanced to the execution squad.

Mordovia was famous as the place where condemned men were brought before firing squads. There were massive executions, and Schwed had taken part in a great number of them. Women didn't like to marry executioners, and his romantic life had consisted only of Black Sea prostitutes.

It was Schwed who told me about one of the greatest travesties my ears have ever had to sustain. Some day I will write an entire account of it. It happened around 1945. The Soviets had arrested 2,300 nuns and religious novices from the Baltics and Ukraine, transporting them to this area. There was a closed monastery nearby that had been barricaded with barbed wire and turned into another camp. It was about forty kilometers from our camp. And there, said Schwed, the nuns and religious were executed. He recalled that the executioners were led into the camp, primed with 400 grams of alcohol, and instructed to enter the barracks. They were told they could do whatever they wanted, as long as they killed the nuns once they were through with them. It was at night, and the intoxicated executioners began raping the sisters and stabbing them with bayonets. Some of the nuns fled up an old tower and threw themselves to the ground. Others lay humbly on the earth waiting for the killers to do their thing. "We murdered all of them," Schwed told me, "and then we dug a massive grave. A few days later we seeded the grave with birch trees."

It was eerie, gazing toward the little forest that hid a massive grave. It was also eerie knowing that at any moment we too could be killed—but in a more surreptitious way. One always had to be careful because they were known to slip a draught of poison in medication or food, and they were always trying to compromise those of us who were religious. At one point they brought three of us—mo, Yaroslaw Lesiv, and Wolodymyr Kulchitsky, who was a member of the underground—to a women's camp about 1.5 kilometers away. There they enticed us with a mini-skirted woman who wanted to shave us (we refused her services) and other females who scrubbed the floor in front of our cell with their bare bottoms pointing in our direction. No doubt if a man touched such a woman she would cry rape. And the man would receive another 15 years. It was all a set-up.

They told me if I cooperated with the authorities I could have any woman I wanted. They wanted to turn us into informers. "You're a young man," said one official. "You don't know what a woman is like. We'll give you one day to think it over." They used the same temptation on the others.

When they tried to send a woman into our room—ostensibly to clean it—I refused to let her in and instead took the pail and threw the water through the grill, soaking a captain. That bold act saved me from his provocations.

But it also earned me another two months in solitary.

Soon I fell ill with a bad cold. I was spitting large quantities of blood and the tension was eating away at my stomach. I was taken to the prison hospital. There I made friends with an American spy named Blomberg, who had been arrested in Latvia. He was initially sentenced for execution but this had been commuted to 25 years. I think his arrest had come in 1954, and I always thought it was strange that the USA was not doing more for him. I guess that's the breaks in espionage.

We were together three weeks and in this time we became so close that we began discussing ways to escape. It would be easier from the hospital.

Shortly we were joined by another spy, Ostrik, a Byelorussian who had worked with British espionage. He had studied history at Oxford and had also been a student in Belgium. We three would secretly meet in the morgue, talking there among the cadavers, where the KGB didn't have listening devices. The plan was to dig from the morgue to freedom.

We enlisted the help of other inmates and were able to start tunneling despite the KGB's precautions against another one of my escapes. We tunneled under the prison tower into a woods but had to abandon this escape when it was discovered. We were taken to the unit in Umor, which was about 25 kilometers away.

Immediately we began organizing an even larger tunnel escape. This time we set it up so that a hundred inmates could find their way to freedom. It was done very carefully and for reasons of security each person involved knew only the names of five others. We began digging a 45-meter-long hole that went three to five meters below the surface. Why so low? There was a tall spiked fence that was planted about three meters into the ground. It was part of a huge barricade that included a wooden fence, barbed wire, buffer zones, and more barbed wire. There were also electronic sensors that were meant to detect any digging in the vicinity. But the sensors were for detecting metal shovels and so we used spades made out of tempered wood. There was an abandoned prison building with an empty space underneath, then the hospital and camp road.

It was easy because it was just yellow sand. We'd fill up bags with the earth and sneak it to the abandoned prison building basement. To camouflage the hole at night, we fashioned a wooden cover with a hinge in the center and covered it with a piece of sod.

Alas, the guards suspected that something was up and in the end we discovered that a KGB informant had infiltrated our group.

I was tried and on September 25, 1969, sentenced to three more years—this time not in a camp, but in the infamous and detestable prison in Vladimir.

While they hadn't outright killed me—thanks to God and my family connections—the Soviets had tired of playing political games.

They were finally going to do away with me. They were going to rid themselves of me once and for all. They were going to hole me up in the highest-security prison under conditions that would break my health.

There was no question that death was waiting for me at Vladimir, but so was the Virgin Mary.

Chapter 9

THE VIRGIN
OF CELL 21

All I can do is report to you what I saw, heard, and felt. I tell the accounts that will follow with some reluctance, because I have no ambition to be labeled as a "visionary" or a "mystic." I am also reluctant because spiritual experiences are highly personal. But I have been urged to share them with those interested in supernatural phenomena, especially in the wake of Hrushiv and Medjugorje, and I believe they indicate that the Holy Spirit was watching over us and actively at work, despite the century that had been given to the devil.

Those who are not familiar with spiritual phenomena, or are directly opposed to it, will decide that the happenings I relate are proof that I am not rational. This was the attitude the Soviets took. Those who believe in the supernatural, but have not yet experienced God's profound and "coincidental" techniques, will hopefully see that the events which later erupted like a glorious volcano in Hrushiv were not isolated happenings but rather the culmination of long-fought metaphysical warfare. It was one in a hidden chain of events.

Some people say I am a mystic. Some people think of me as holy. Doubtless there are those who will think of me as deluded. I claim only to be a Catholic activist with human faults and frailties.

114

Nor do I think an apparition is crucial in and of itself. What is important is the *effect* of Our Lady's apparitions. The issue is this: Long before my experiences at Hrushiv I received visitations from the Virgin Mary and other celestial entities. They took the form of two apparitions and a series of visions and dreams. I am convinced that if and when there is better communication between the Soviet Union and outsiders, you will discover many other such remarkable accounts that had occurred behind the Iron Curtain during the darkest days of communistic materialism. I know of others who had supernatural experiences, and I have already mentioned that the Ukraine has a long history of Marian apparitions.

Add February 12, 1970, and then exactly two years later, February 12, 1972, in Special Corpus 2 at Vladimir Prison, to the list of her appearances.

Vladimir is a complex of multiple-storied buildings as drab as anything out of Dickens. It is set on a hill about 165 kilometers (or a hundred miles) northeast of Moscow. There are four prison buildings within the walls. There is also a military school, a building for officers, an exit gate, and most relevantly, a cemetery. Many famous prisoners have been detained there, and many have died anonymous deaths. Vladimir has held such people as the American spy Gary Powers, whose former cell I soon found myself languishing in.

Vladimir is also known as a place that is cold and cramped. In some cases, 20 to 30 people stood in a ten-by-ten-foot cell. But while there may not have been much sunlight, there was no dearth of artificial light. Vladimir is notorious for the lightbulb treatment. Bright lights were kept on day and night, driving prisoners to lunacy.

I can attest to the ill effects of constant light. After a month I began to lose my sight. It's a sort of "chicken disease." When a light is on constantly, it gets to the point where the prisoner cannot see once dusk arrives. I've been asked many times what the worst punishment was, and I have to say it's enduring the electrical lights 24 hours a day. The feeling was like someone pounding iron nails into my head and sprinking salt in my eyes.

The people who prayed and believed in God could endure it, but it wasn't easy for anyone. While in the camps, except

for periods of isolation, we could communicate with many
people and walk or work in the yards. At Vladimir you were
confined to the cell and I encountered long stretches of
extreme isolation. While there were times I had cell mates,
there were also times when, in order to communicate with
another human, I had to sneak notes or tap on a wall using
an alphabetical code.

When you sit for a long period of time with the same
people, conversation becomes difficult and prayer makes
everything easier. Each night I prostrated myself 120 times
before God. One had to be careful, however, lest such devout
demonstrations result in solitary confinement. In the prisons people liked to be with me. At one point there were
nine of us political prisoners together. Our cell was fairly
happy, but still, incarceration was something I couldn't take
for too long. I had to leave there, and knowing my character, the other prisoners begged me not to do anything that
might cause all of us to be punished. I devised methods
of escape and while I myself did not end up using them,
one plan was employed by some other inmates in a famous
escape during 1970.

I wasn't feeling well. My eight years of incarceration were
taking a physical toll. The body of the youthful boxer had
been reduced to about 120 pounds of skin and bones. My
weight at times dipped even lower. We looked like the survivors of Auschwitz. And I was ill from all the beatings,
dietary inadequacies, and cold temperatures at the camps.
I had encountered any number of physical tortures; at one
point the bones in my hand had been smashed and a thin
needle passed through the area near my wrist. I had been
kicked, clubbed, slapped, and punched continuously since
1962, especially after escapades like the smokestack flyers
or following escapes. My whole body ached, and I was
developing severe rheumatism. My kidneys and liver were
not in good shape, and my spine was out of whack. Back
at Uzhhorod, they had made me lay on my stomach and
then had bent up my knees to the point where three ver-
tebrae were thrown out of line. When the bones healed they
fused crookedly.

The beatings I could endure—I had a system for ignoring
pain—but the tortures were more difficult. Once I was placed

on a stool in front of a 1,000-watt lamp. It was excruciating. Even those who were physically strong couldn't take more than a few minutes before the lamp. Or the Soviets would club you with tubes full of salt or sand and you would be unconscious for nearly two hours.

I continued to see human agony at Vladimir. There were constant, echoing shrieks down the corridors, and relentless oppression. Prisoners on their daily exercise walks found only asphalt and concrete to commune with; they were not allowed to look sideways or up. "Stare at your boots! Don't step an inch sideways. Hurry or you'll be shot!" You saw just about no one but your cell mate and the omnipresent guards. They peered down from the 15-foot walls—menacingly.

The only "food" in great abundance was boiled water. Two or three cups a day. The guards were everywhere, checking everything, and while by regulation we were allowed to mail certain items (every inmate had the right to send mail to superior authorities), and while Vladimir had a passable library, which broke the monotony when one had access to the books, for the most part we were deprived of any external contact, and communication between prisoners was at the barest minimum. Prisoners at Vladimir were famous for communicating through the toilets. They would pump the water out of the toilet with a rag or other device, put their heads in the bowl, and whisper through the pipes to the next cell, passing on messages. This is what we were reduced to, talking into the toilets and being careful the guard didn't see. Later, I used other means of communication, including a stick that sent a note to the next cell like casting a fishing rod.

At first I was in Building or Corpus Four. I not only had an extended sentence to serve but was also punished with six months of a reduced diet. My weight would eventually go down to between 100 and 110 pounds. I was a breathing, bulgy-eyed skeleton. Originally there were the nine of us on strict regime, and for a month I put up with it like the others before deciding to take advantage of the regulation that allowed letters to prison or governmental authorities.

I wrote a note to Leonid Brezhnev himself. Brezhnev, a bull of a man who looked like a boss in the mafia, had become First Secretary of the Communist Party when Khrushchev retired in 1964. My father had told me about the food in Nazi camps, and it was better than what the Communists were giving us, I noted in my letter. I also noted that the guard dogs were better fed than we were. I wasn't being sarcastic. It was an actual fact. I had read a magazine called *Science and Life* and in the December 1969 issue there had been an article on how much the young, growing watchdogs were given to eat: 500 grams of white bread, 380 grams of cereal, 180 grams of sugar, two eggs, half a liter of milk, and three kilos of meat. What was I being fed? About 400 grams of bread, 250 grams of gruel, not a gram of meat, no sugar, no oil, 15 grams of salt, 50 grams of salted cereal, and 63 grams of fish.

It would have been better to be a dog.

I wrote this all to Brezhnev and told him they should put a metal collar around my neck and that I would then bark so I could be fed like a watchdog.

Despite the tenacious prison surveillance, I managed to have my declaration smuggled to the West. It got into the hands of a broadcasting unit—I believe it was Radio Free Europe or BBC. That infuriated the authorities. After about a week, a commission came and took me out of the cell. The Russian procurator minced no words. "You are taking part in anti-Soviet agitation and propaganda and we will put you to trial for this. Why did you write this declaration? Here you are calling out among all the world."

All of Vladimir knew of the letter and I was sort of a renegade. The authorities grilled me for a period of over two weeks. They were feeding me a bit better after a prison doctor examined me and saw how emaciated I was. I had been down to 100 pounds and they were going to get me up to 120. My skin was peeling like a snake shedding its hide and while my eyes would have devoured any kind of real food my stomach wouldn't accept it. I began to swell. It was very difficult to exert control over myself. I was in the prison hospital and they were going to feed me until I burst.

A short while later they took me out, dressed me in a civilian suit, put me in a car, and we headed from Vladimir for a mansion that looked like a clinic or hospital. People were walking around in white clothes. It was a provincial psychiatric clinic that was connected to the Serbsky Institute of Forensic Psychiatry in Moscow. Major Vynogradov had come from the provincial office of the KGB because they wanted to make a criminal incident of the last letter and were gathering documents for another trial against me. The system is that when you're accused of a political crime, you're taken for psychiatric examination. A group of soldiers and KGB agents escorted me to the third floor and a doctor came up to me. All told there were 12 doctors gathered at the clinic.

"Why have you brought him here?" the chief psychiatrist asked the KGB.

"He says he's a dog," a colonel replied.

The doctor asked me if this was true. I said, "No, *they* are the dogs, I am the human." The doctor didn't take it very seriously, and neither did he think there was much wrong with me. But the KGB persisted. They mentioned the commentary I had written to Brezhnev, and the psychiatrist demanded to see it. The KGB was surprised by the request and sent an officer for the letter, telling him no one else was to see it. But the doctor passed it around and the other doctors laughed.

The KGB was nervous. It was a situation that was in the public eye. The chief doctor reprimanded them and said his clinic could not perform an examination because they saw nothing psychologically amiss. My physical condition was a different matter. A woman approached, and told me to take off my coat. I stripped to the waist, and they quietly gasped at my condition. All you could see were ribs and ulcerating wounds. My legs were so gangrenous they closed their eyes. The doctors asked why I was so beaten up and the KGB lied that I had been hurt at transfer prisons. "That's not true," I blurted out. "I was beaten at Vladimir."

The doctor announced the prognosis. I was a mentally fit person. What I had written, he chuckled, was an example of healthy Ukrainian humor.

No one at the prison could have been very amused by my Ukrainian humor, least of all the commandant, Zavjalkin; his auxiliary, Colonel Zolotov; and another assistant, Captain Fedotov. They were going to get back at me one way or another. The procurator from Moscow, Yuri Nosov, wanted me to write a letter denying my previous declaration and saying someone else wrote lies about prison conditions under my name. They wanted the denial to appear in the publication *Izvestia*. They also wanted me to issue a denial on radio and television. Naturally I refused. It was turning into a dark comedy.

I mention this story because it helped get me thrown into the building known as Special (pronounced *spetz*) Corpus 2, the TON *(Tyurma Osobogo Naznadeniya)*. This corpus was one of the most isolated places in the Soviet prison system. It is like a jail within a prison, a redbrick building surrounded by its own walls. You were not allowed to so much as see who else was in the corpus and the names of those of us in there was a closely held secret. The special block was directly answerable to Moscow. There were at least 34 prisoners in the cellblock, including a Libyan spy. As usual, I had my ways of finding things out.

I was in Cell 21, and let me tell you, it was dismal even by the standards of Vladimir. When they wanted to punish you they had a way of forcing in cold air, and it was the middle of the notorious Russian winter—February 1970. There was salt on the wall that caused calcification and held the dampness, which eventually turned to a layer of frost and ice. There was an iron bed in the cell, with metal straps and a thin mattress stuffed with seaweed. There was also a small table on which to set clothes, a place to hang my towel, and a small compartment for a cup, a bowl, and a spoon. The towel I was given was changed every ten days and while the prisoners in the other sections of Vladimir were allowed to shower every week and a half, in solitary you were not allowed to thoroughly wash. I'd sit for two months without a bath. There was a quilt but it was so cold you had to wear your padded winter jacket all night. The window, which was the size of a wall picture, had iron bars and beyond the bars was a thin metal mesh. There were also wooden shutters so you couldn't see outside or get so much as a morsel from the sun.

Often I would awake in the middle of the night and pray. Such was the case on February 12, 1970, but during my prostrations I felt an unsusual warmth flow through my body.

It's difficult to recall the precise details after 20 years, and I tend to confuse certain details of this apparition with the one that occurred two years later, but the best I can recollect is that it was definitely after ten o'clock at night. Without a clock, and dozing in and out of sleep, one loses a sense of time. People had been asleep for quite a while, and so it may have been early morning. It was certainly long before dawn. The main lights were turned off but there was a faint light over the cell door. When I lay back down a brilliance of another sort suddenly filled the cell.

It was a most unusual light, similar to what I would see two years later in the same prison, and then 15 years after that at Hrushiv. I had never seen a light like that. It was silver, but it wasn't silver. It was like moonlight, but it wasn't like moonlight. The closest thing I can relate it to is the aureole around the moon on an exceptionally moonlit night. The field of light enclosed me and, like Hrushiv, it seemed to be a *living*, breathing illumination next to my bunk.

In this light the Blessed Mother appeared. It was a brief appearance, much briefer than the apparitions that would come later, and it lasted just a few minutes. But those moments meant the world to me. There was no doubt whatsoever that she was there. It was unlike any kind of dream, and while at first I wondered if I was hallucinating, the strength of presence, and the power of that light, were beyond psychological experience.

So was the sensation of fearlessness and peace. From this moment on, I lost just about any feelings of trepidation. I felt impossibly secure, despite where I was and what I faced in the immediate future. She looked at me with eyes so penetrating that you could feel the power of her gaze. Her eyes were dark blue, and while she was not what a fashion photographer would call beautiful, she was beyond beauty as we know it. The word "pleasant" keeps springing to mind. I was overcome by her pleasantness. A very pleasant young woman. She wore a veil that was pale blue, almost azure. I caught glimpse neither of her hair or feet. She wore what seemed like summer clothing despite the coolness of my cold, dank cell.

In such a situation the mind reaches, gropes, and nearly stalls. It was difficult to take in all the visual information presented in such otherworldly splendor. You cannot get enough of it. She was like a huge jewel in the shimmering light— majestic beyond words, as real as the walls and the hermetic door. My mind was so directed that I accepted her without question. Softly but firmly she spoke to me.

She addressed my personal needs, and my personality. She told me I had to overcome my impetuous, impatient emotions, and that I had to learn forgiveness. She instructed me to forgive everyone, even the Communists who had so brutalized me and my country. This was very important, she said: total forgiveness. She said all the Ukrainian people had to do the same. She said if we did not forgive, repent, and receive Jesus Christ, there would be monumental trouble involving the Ukraine. She instructed me to pray to the Angel of the Ukraine. In her right hand was a Rosary.

Her presence continued to work in a strange way on me. I was witness to a messenger of Christ. I lost all distrust. My faith was bolstered to an unfathomable degree. She told me that I had completed four of five paths in my life. I understood this immediately, but it is impossible to convey. *"You've traversed these four,"* she said; *"the fifth road is just beginning.*

"On one hand you have great faith but on the other hand you are not forgiving of your enemies, the Muscovites," she said. *"Until you overcome yourself and are able to forgive you will not find strength in yourself and your faith will be weak. You must learn to forgive those who persecute you the most. I will always be with you. But you're not ready. You doubt. You question. You must go through all of this. You must change your life and learn to forgive the Russians and learn to understand yourself so you won't be like Cain. There are difficult years before you, of trial and humiliation, but from today on you'll never have fear. I shall be with you. I have shed many tears. Many people are denying the future life. They are denying my Son. Around us is a very intense intolerance. Russia continues to remain in darkness and error and to spread hatred for Christ the King. Until people sincerely repent and accept the love of my Son, there will not be peace because peace comes only where there is justice. Pray for your enemies. Forgive them and before you there will be a very bright road."*

She said to look to the right. I moved my head towards the window and saw a mist unfurling. I saw four paths or roads.

"Look to the right."

I saw fire. I saw fire and tanks and I knew there would be war between Russia and some other country.

"From this day on I will always be with you," the Virgin repeated. *"No harm shall come to you."*

I understood this in the context of Scripture, when Jesus talks about every hair on our heads being counted, every part of our lives watched from above.

Our Lady vanished but the light remained for about ten minutes.

Gradually the illumination also disappeared, receding into a ball and then a point of light that blinked out, leaving me once more in the darkness of prison.

Chapter 10

ANGEL OF FLESH
AND BLOOD

Pg 130 - Wallenberg

In those precious moments of communion with Our Lady, all my sufferings, every pain at the hands of my oppressors, all the monotonous and anxious hours, were totally and inexpressibly banished. After eight years of harsh imprisonment, my faith had been totally vindicated and my life was irrevocably changed. I was filled with a strength that knew few bounds. I was determined to move forward with total confidence, and to publicly give Christian witness to everyone.

There was something within me—deep inside—that was not only affirmed but palpably strengthened. Though I was the same emaciated prisoner in Corpus 2, a new and brighter light had entered the recesses of my wretched being. Such is the power of the Mother of God. From that day forward I vowed not to worry about what I would say, not to laboriously plan how I would respond during interrogations, but to let the Holy Spirit do the talking and thinking.

"I will always be with you."

While I didn't have another apparition for two more years, intriguing dreams like the ones I'd had at Mordovia and Kirovohrad increased in frequency. They were dreams swathed in bright lights. I saw Mary, I saw Jesus, I saw many things that were not of this world—were certainly not of Vladimir Prison. Everything was brilliant but nothing like what can be found in nature. They seemed so far

124

from earth. Many of the dreams were associated with events of my life, and later, when I had the means to do so, I began to keep a diary. The dreams were often little prophecies. I'll give you one example. It was a bit beyond where we are now, in 1972. We're sitting in another part of Vladimir around lunchtime, I lean against the bed and lapse into sleep. I don't know if it was ten minutes or ten seconds. A vision appears before me, the door of the cell is opened, the guards enter into the room but they're all dressed in black. They begin searching the cell. The guard on duty, Stjunin, is dressed in black.

I told this vision to my cell mates. I told them Stjunin would be coming. He was the one who was so good at discovering our hiding places. I said he'd be dressed in black. My cell mates replied, "What are you talking about, black? The uniforms are not black."

We finished eating, did the dishes, and it happened as I foresaw: the guards came in, attired in black, and the mouths of my cell mates dropped wide open. It turns out that the prison workers had gotten the new smocks that day. My cell mates asked me to tell them the dream again. And they began writing down all my mental imagery—daydreams, evening dreams, and night dreams. Within five years we had several notepads full.

The KGB didn't pick on me because they were very happy I was so preoccupied with this newfound mysticism. They thought it was yoga. Very often I'd have a vision when I closed my eyes and I would see an image or vista that would materialize in the coming days. I am able to recall some dreams because I also mentioned them, when I got the chance, in letters to Olena. Often I dreamed of the Mother of God and it was because I had grown to feel so close to her that later, at Hrushiv, I felt hurt when she didn't immediately appear to me. Sometimes she would talk, but not frequently. Before some unpleasant incident was to occur to me or to someone with whom I was a friend, I would see the vision of a church and the Virgin would appear in monastic garb. To me that was the sign of an upcoming trial, sentencing, or pogrom. If something pleasant was about to occur, on the other hand, I would "see" the Mother of God in a brilliant sun.

The same year as the apparition, I had another strange experience. In a dream or vision—it's hard to tell if I was really asleep, it was so real—I saw myself in black monastic garb with a white cincture or rope around me. It was a beautiful, sunny day and the trees were in bloom. One was already bearing fruit—beautiful apples. But I felt if I picked an apple I wouldn't be able to fly.

In my dreams I nearly always flew, like a free spirit. I saw mountains and it was as if I was in the 12th century, when Tartar Mongols passed through the valleys. There was a monastery nearby and I had to warn the monks. The Mongols saw me and began to shoot arrows. I was flying. I flew over the briars and thistles, my garb tattered from the coarse vegetation brushing by. I got to the monastery, which was surrounded by a spiked wooden fence, and called up to the monks. But it was too late. The Mongols came with flaming arrows and soon the monastery was engulfed by fire. I was the only one who got away.

Later I had a smilar dream. It was another beautiful day and I saw a forest path and had a feeling I had been down that road before. The Mother of God appeared and smiled. We came to a fence and it was like the walls of the ancient monastery. But this time it was in the present—not the 12th century.

Much later, in 1984, I shared the dreams with a Basilian monk, Father Meletius Malynych. I described the hills, the path through the woods, the remaining wall. He was quite astounded. He took me by the hand and said, "Kneel down. We'll pray." His eyes were moist with tears. Then he took an album of old pictures, including one of the monastery site, and said, "Josyp, I've known you from grade one. You're an adult man now. I'm showing you this book for the first time." Until the Mongol invasions there had been an old wooden monastery precisely as I saw in the vision. This monastery, he explained, had been destroyed by fire.

"The fact that the Mother of God brought you to the walls of this monastery and you saw it before it was destroyed is a sign that the Church will rise again—resurrect as a phoenix from the ashes," he said. "You have been chosen for this role and your obligation is to carry this burden to the end regardless of how heavy it is."

I can't explain what this was all about but the monk also explained that it is very difficult to understand dreams and better not to analyze them too often. The more I was tortured or emotionally wrought, the more I would have these visions. I became fascinated by them. I began to classify them according to even days and odd days. Then I would subcategorize evening, day, and night dreams. Intellectually, we can't grasp it all but I concluded from my own experiences that dreams are not simply something that happens by chance but that instead the person—the subconscious—is working spiritually. I also decided that if someone has a goal in life, the dreams are oriented *towards* that goal. If someone is weak emotionally, the dreams are meaningless.

There were also nightmares that caused me to wake up perspiring and fatigued. There were moments when I felt the evil of our times. These were not symbols but real, live situations, and everything I saw *really* took place. News of my ability spread through the prison and when the prisoners woke up they would call out demanding that I analyze their dreams.

Let me give you another example of my nightly ventures. I'll leave it for you to decide if this was a meaningless dream or a mystical experience. It was toward the end of November in 1970, and it concerned a Ukrainian woman named Alla Horska, the daughter of a KGB general. Both Olena and I knew her, and we knew that although Alla had been raised on philosophers like Schopenhauer, she had come to the conclusion—from reading these pessimistic philosophers—that God did indeed exist.

Perhaps it was the barrenness of those atheistic philosophies that convinced Alla that they were off base. Whatever the case, Alla, an artist herself, was married to a painter named Zarytsky and became very involved in Ukrainian affairs. This nationalism, and her belief in God, caused violent arguments with her father. Had she been of some lesser family, she would have been immediately eliminated. But because she was the daughter of a high-ranking military Communist, there was an attempt, at first, to cover up her unorthodox thinking and behavior. Even though they persecuted the children of Party members, they hesitated to kill them because of the family.

The dream about Alla started with me raising myself out of the prison bed. My cell was filled with an intense light. I didn't know where the light was coming from and there was a sense of fear. I knew I had to journey to somewhere far away but I had to hurry so I would be back in prison before the morning wake-up siren.

I floated to the rafters of the cell and looked at myself lying down there in bed. Through the wall I could see the security guard. It was as if I had x-ray vision. The intense field of light that had entered my cell carried me through the bars and I began to fly swiftly across the republic of Russia, heading south to the Ukraine.

Below me I saw cities flickering and at train stations the nameplates of various localities. Everything was on fast-forward. I approached and started to pass over the Ukraine. I circled around Kiev and then flew to a small town I've never been to, Vasilkovo. I had the sense, in this dream, that something was going to happen there. The dream lasted so long I had time to actually mull over the happenings, and that was why there was so much trepidation. I was flying as if I had wings.

I looked down, saw two cars, and began following them. There was the road and orchards and vegetable gardens. It was typically hilly terrain. I lowered myself but was careful not to touch the earth itself, because somehow I knew that if I made contact with the ground, it would greatly slow me. Instead I hovered several inches above the grass.

Somebody came out of one car, and then I saw that there were three people. They went to a house, knocked at the window pane, and the second car came with three more people. They went around the house and barged into the door. Alla was standing there, her eyes wide at the strangers. I followed them. They were unable to see me.

I stood behind one of these men, breathing carefully. I was cautious not to stand on the ground so I wouldn't be like a mortal being. They took Alla into a room down the corridor and there was an agitated conversation. One of the men had unnaturally thick eyebrows.

I looked into the room and watched in horror as they raped and beat Alla. After an agonizing while they brought her out. They had put a coat around her and as if with contempt, her bra had been strapped on the outside of it. The fellow with the thick eyebrows brandished a hammer. He approached Alla and she gasped as he smashed her head so hard that blood and pieces of brain splattered across the wall.

I felt a tremor through me. I rose and flew away. I realized it was time for the prison wake-up bell and when the siren sounded, I jerked up from that startling and lucid nightmare.

Upon release from prison six years later, I was at a party and began speaking of my dream. The people were shocked. I learned that, two weeks after this dream, Alla had indeed been killed in the brutal fashion I had envisioned. I heard about it from a woman named Nadia Svitlychna, who had gone to this town with a dissident poet named Yevhen Sverstivik and saw the scene of the crime. Alla's body had indeed been left in the cellar where she had been thrown with the coat and bra, her head bashed in. The walls had been washed but a criminal investigation ascertained that they had been covered with blood. Nadia had also found a pair of false eyebrows in the garbage. The investigative team had not gone through the garbage but Nadia had. She never spoke to anyone of this and as Nadia put it, my dream was so accurate that if she had not been sure I was in prison at the time of the crime, she would have thought I had been there during the actual incident.

I had many similar dreams. Sometimes, when I had heavenly visions, I would "awaken" surrounded by a beautiful fragrance unlike anything we know, and once a guard came into my cell because he smelled the scent and, knowing I hadn't received a bath in months, began searching for what he was certain had to be perfume. I don't know whether they are dreams, visions, or out-of-body experiences, but I feel I am physically at the events and scenes.

In reality, of course, I was still at Vladimir and terribly alone: all I had were my dreams and a little mouse that was so accustomed to me that it ate from my hand and slept on my hat. I found myself detained in Corpus 2 on more than one occasion. I knew the American spy pilot Gary Powers had been there because he had scratched his name with a needle on one of the walls. He had also been in Cell 25. They were always moving prisoners around up there. As I've emphasized, the first and second floors and some of the rooms on the third floor were used for detaining prisoners whose names weren't mentioned. Yet, little by little I learned who was there. One of the prisoners was a man who had witnessed an infamous slaughter of Polish officers in 1941, when he was a 12-year-old boy. The Soviets hate witnesses. That was his "crime": he knew the Soviets had murdered thousands of Poles and blamed it on the Nazis. In cell 33 was the Arab military attache I mentioned previously, and I would also learn of a man named Nick Budulak-Sharygin, who was associated with British espionage.

The most intriguing of all the prisoners, however, was an old emaciated Swede named Raoul Wallenberg. I need to give you some history here. They are facts I came to learn only later, when I spoke to other prisoners, or facts I learned after my release. Wallenberg was a truly remarkable and historical man. He was known as the "righteous Gentile" and the "hero of the Holocaust." Few words could adequately describe him. He was an extraordinary soul. He was like an angel of flesh and blood.

Born in 1912 to a wealthy Lutheran family in Sweden, Wallenberg worked at his nation's embassy in Budapest. His mission was to save Hungarian Jews. Many people believe that Wallenberg rescued more Jews from the Nazis than any other single person. By hiding them, or issuing them protective Swedish passports, it is said that Wallenberg probably saved between 30,000 to 100,000 men, women and children from German death camps in the mid-1940s. He was a selfless man who worked day and night getting Swedish documents to Jewish women walking in death marches.

When a Jew was taken from the claws of death—returned to a family that had given that person up as dead—there was one word on the family's disbelieving and eternally grateful lips: *Wallenberg.*

It is beyond my ability here to fully describe Wallenberg's selfless and courageous accomplishments.

Towards the end of the war, Wallenberg had contacted

the Russians, who were then on the outskirts of Budapest, and asked for food and other supplies for the Jews he was protecting. On January 17, 1945, he and his driver, Vilmos Langfelder, left Budapest for a meeting with the Russian commander, Marshal Malinovsky. It was the last anyone saw Wallenberg as a free man. He was taken into the custody of the NKVD and vanished in the Soviet gulag.

Why would the Russians bother Wallenberg? Why would the Soviets, who had just barely escaped Nazism themselves, attack an enemy of the Third Reich? Remember what I said about Nazism and Communism bickering between each other, but both belonging to the empire of Satan. Once more it was paranoia and irrationality. Stalin was so demented he even arrested dedicated Communists if they had been foreign born. He imagined all kinds of plots and counterplots. In the case of Wallenberg, the Soviets probably assumed he was some kind of spy.

When Sweden inquired about Wallenberg's whereabouts, Russia lied that Wallenberg had been killed by the Nazis or Hungarian fascists. By 1957, with pressure still building for a disclosure of his fate, the Soviets switched their tactics and produced a phony document stating that Wallenberg had died ten years before at Lubyanka Prison in Moscow. The Soviets were now caught in a web of their own lies. Wallenberg's internment was an international embarrassment, and there was no greater secret in the prison system than Wallenberg's location. Why the Soviets didn't kill him and be done with it is anyone's guess. You try to figure out the psychosis of evil.

But the fact is that Wallenberg wasn't dead. There were sporadic sightings of him in prisons such as Lubyanka, Vladimir, and Vadivovo Camp in Siberia. Most of these sighting, I learned later, had been in the 1950s and 1960s, and anyone who so much as mentioned seeing him was subject to immediate death. There was no topic more taboo in the gulag than Raoul Wallenberg. At least one officer who had helped interrogate Wallenberg was executed; former cell mates were placed in solitary for long periods of time; and when Dr. Aleksandr Myashnikov—who was Khrushchev's personal doctor—let it slip at an international medical conference that he had seen Wallenberg in a mental hospital, this esteemed physician suddenly suffered a fatal "heart attack."

In 1970 I knew nothing about all that. I knew only that I was in the surreal netherworld of captivity. In April I was transferred from cell 21 to cell 30 on the same floor. In the cell was a Russian nationalist and monarchist named Igor Ogurtzov. He was from an old Russian family, and he was a believer, a moderate Orthodox. We got along well. Across the corridor, in cell 25, was a mysterious prisoner who was later moved to cell 33. I caught sight of him during a nightly trip to the bathroom, where we emptied our *parashas,* the buckets we used as latrines.

It was about the middle of April, two months after Our Lady's appearance. The toilet was next to cell 36 in Corpus 2. There was an exit nearby and also a security desk, telephone, and guard on the floor. The guard usually led prisoners to the toilet starting with cell 18, but at times they would change the sequence. On this day the mysterious prisoner was second to last for the routine visit to the bathroom.

My cell was last. The guards were normally careful that prisoners from one cell did not catch sight of prisoners from another cell, opening our door only when the previous cell was out of the toilet. But on this particular day the security guard was rushing things and his timing was off. He opened our cell before the previous cell was back from the toilet.

The door to the toilet was open when I got into the corridor and a man came out, bald at the pate, hair on the side that was two fingers deep, wearing a windbreaker— which was unusual, in that such apparel is certainly not standard prison garb. The jacket was dark brown, patched but clean, and he was alone. Obviously he did not have a cell mate.

I decided to make contact with the peculiar prisoner out of simple curiosity. This was possible because the guard that night was a man known as "The Fool." We called him that because he was flatulent and often passed gas loudly and with comical histrionics in the corridor. He was an unusual guard in that he had a sense of humor about himself. He was also easy to bribe for little things—which is how I kept up a certain contact with the outside world—

and I felt freer in his presence than I normally would have. I walked by the mysterious prisoner, who was thin and in his late fifties, and at first I said nothing but as I was going into the toilet and he was returning into cell 25 I asked in Ukrainian, "Where are you from?"

The guard called for me to be quiet. But I repeated the question, this time in Russian. The man remained silent. Then I called out to him in Hungarian. The aging prisoner trembled and his *parasha* splashed some of its contents— fresh water and a chlorine tablet—onto the floor.

"The Fool" pushed this prisoner back into his cell and I had to mop up the water he had spilled, since it was my fault the prisoner had trembled. The guard was very afraid because this was a secret prisoner and I had seen him. The KGB was watching so we all had to be careful. Over the next few *parasha* changes, I began asking, "Who is that prisoner?" The guard answered that it was a fascist who had killed many people. The guard himself didn't know who the prisoner was.

Some days later, I was able to obtain a long nail through surreptitious means and with it I drilled a few holes so I had a better view of the corridor and the "recreation" area behind the cells. The walls were concrete slabs and a hole near the door afforded a lateral view. I began watching the movements of the fair-skinned prisoner in cell 25. One day I saw the old man being led out of his cell with his belongings. They were moving him to cell 33. The door clanged shut. "The Fool" was on guard that night, and I asked him if I could have a table I knew was in the cell which had just been vacated. "The Fool" liked me. He enjoyed listening to my experiences and philosophies. I asked him to do me a harmless favor and bring me the table from cell 25. He did, and on April 25, 1970, the last Saturday before the holiday of Mayday, when everything had to be spruced up, I began cleaning the table and when I turned it around I saw that someone had managed to write on the back side of it. There was a large circle and the words, "Miranda Martina." Below that, in indelible purple ink, were the words, "Shweden Raoul Wallenberg" and some more writing with a date at the bottom. The writing was probably in Swedish. I didn't understand it.

This is how we came to know that the mystery prisoner was a foreigner by the name of Raoul Wallenberg. It was the first time we'd heard of him. I decided to find out more about him and established contact by leaving him a tiny note on toilet paper. We immediately set up a system whereby we exchanged additional messages. While the guards were supposed to inspect every crevice of the toilet after each cell was finished using it, they did such checks haphazardly and missed many transactions. In the bathroom there was a peg in the wall for hanging up jackets and hats. We left each other messages by pulling out the peg and inserting a note, then reinserting the peg.

I identified myself to him and Wallenberg wrote in Russian that he was a diplomat arrested in 1945. He told me that he was arrested with his chauffeur. He wanted to know if anyone knew what had happened to his driver, Vilmos Langfelder. That's all he seemed to want: knowledge of what had happened to his friend.

The notes with Wallenberg were just, who are you, where are you from. I had copied the addresses from the table and sewed them into my coat. Miranda Martina was a friend of Wallenberg's and I took down her address. When I was released I personally conveyed all this information to Wallenberg's family and the American embassy, which did little about it.

For all we know, Wallenberg is still alive.

Chapter 11

THE RETURN
OF MARY

So that was my encounter with a different kind of heavenly messenger. Mainly, however, my contact was with the messengers of Hell.

Guards, KGB, sadistic doctors and nurses. In 1971, I was transferred to a large corpus with ten men in one cell. It's one of the places where I had my many dream experiences. Why didn't the Soviets oppose such mysticism? They didn't understand where it was coming from. They probably thought I was involved with yoga, which was fine with them. The Soviets not only allowed but even encouraged the prisoners to involve themselves with yoga, freely dispensing books on the subject, just like they would probably dispense books on the New Age and occult.

There were five political cells on the fourth floor of the corpus, and fifty people would be taken for exercise at one time. The political inmates talked about refusing to do the required prison work, but I argued that we should continue to labor so we had the capability of spreading religious leaflets. We were packaging items and sending notes in the packages, as I had done before. By now I was a well-known prisoner both in the gulag and on the outside. My escapes, protests, communiques, and letters had made many people aware of my defiance. I was occasionally an item on the radio. When I conned the administration into letting me

work at packaging, the Soviets broadcast this as proof that
I was now cooperating and rehabilitating myself!

The first dispatch of leaflets went out—five hundred of
them. How was such a task accomplished? Our job was making little bags for sugar and we would hide our notes in
there. Alas, one of these bags found its way to the political
commissar. His wife opened the sugar, finding the note.

He was frightened because he could lose his job over such
a matter. They came directly to my cell, but really, the
authorities didn't know what to do with me. I would pull
off one stunt or another and they would change all the prison
guards. When the commissar found other of our leaflets he
asked if any of them had been dispensed abroad. I admitted
that they had. That made them extremely paranoid. They
certainly didn't want anything from the gulag finding its
way to the West, where my name was also starting to be
noticed.

Other camps were also making these packages and so they
had to confiscate thousands of them and burn everything.
They didn't torture me because of the trouble I had already
caused with my notes to Moscow. But the Soviets were so
intent on halting the spread of anything about Christ, that
in Latvia around this time, they put radioactive traces on
paper used by Baptists so that, by helicopter sensors, they
could track the shipment to a rural house where the Baptists were printing New Testaments.

My own little printings drove the Soviets crazy, but I also
whipped them into a frenzy by going on a talking strike.
That is, I hardly said a word for a full year. May 21, 1970,
to May 21, 1971, I communicated mainly by notes.

Why was I not using my vocal chords? It was both a protest and a sign of mourning. There had been a severe flood
in the Ukraine and the Soviets had done very little to help
the victims. Hundreds were killed, and when such calamities occur, the Soviet Union is supposed to declare three
days of national mourning. But not in this case. So, I decided
I would make up for it by a year of my own mourning.
I was also mourning over an earthquake in the Caucasians.

They came from Kiev to question me over a pending case
but I refused to speak. Instead, I wrote a declaration of protest. They tried everything to break my silence—chocolate,

apples—and when they couldn't destroy my resolve they threw me back into solitary.

I was accustomed to solitary, even the cold cells of Corpus 2, but I didn't know what was ahead of me. There were rumors that they had come up with a severe new form of solitary, but I thought it was just a ploy to scare us. It wasn't. The Vladimir administration had done it again. They had engineered a truly hellish torture. In the bowels of the prison, deep in the dungeon, there were holes in the cement floor, and from those holes, which must have been connected to a sewer, came the coldest, foulest air I had ever encountered, turning the high, narrow punishment cell into a fetid Siberia.

You could *see* the frigidity coming out of the holes. In no time, I experienced spasmodic pain. What to do? I began to run in place, keeping my blood flowing, but it was almost impossible to breathe the foul air. I took off my jacket and covered two of the holes, took off my pants to cover the third, and removed my undershirt to stuff into the fourth aperture. In that way, I was able to last quite a while, much to the confusion of the guards, who didn't see what I had done. Usually, a prisoner could last there only two hours before screaming horrendously, but I seemed to be doing fine and when I heard them coming, I would hurriedly put my clothes back on so they didn't know what I was doing. The Lord gave me strength to resist in such circumstances, but it was very trying. The walls were damp and slimy and I coughed up a black phlegm.

I was also subjected to the "hole" treatment as sort of a late Christmas gift in December of 1971. My mother had visited me and what she did was basically try to brainwash me into keeping my beliefs to myself. She suggested that I forsake my nationalistic inclinations and settle into life as an Orthodox priest. "Leave your nationalism, write a declaration, and you'll be home in a week," she said. "We've even found a girl for you. You will live in Uzhhorod. Think of it."

I don't know why, but after her visit I was given twenty days of solitary. It was probably to accelerate my decision. The solitary was cold but sufferable, because the cell was near the guard's table and he kept turning up the heat for himself. However, after 15 days of that idyllic existence I was moved to room 9. In an hour I felt the extreme cold coming out of three holes the size of a fist. The skin on my face became taut and I was barely able to move my lips. Then they temporarily raised the temperature.

I was filled with an intense anger and I cried out like a man gone mad. I don't remember what I shouted, because I was filled with an intense hatred and anger. I couldn't believe it myself. I couldn't believe my emotions. When a guard came in to ask if I wanted anything—expecting to hear me beg to be taken to another cell—I stubbornly replied that I needed nothing from him. Soon it was so cold I was nearly powerless to move.

Around suppertime I was given a cup of hot water. I heard a friend of mine arguing with the supervising guard and I called out for more water so my friend would hear my voice and know I was in the adjacent cellblock. "Guard, give me water."

The guard ran up to the window and hissed. "Why are you shouting? Do you want another 15 days of solitary?"

I asked for another cup of hot water. He answered, "No way." The guard was a young Ukrainian. The inmates didn't like him one bit. He was always shouting at us. "I'll show you. You're undermining the strength of Russia!" The other inmates laughed and called him a skinhead.

Sort of a wild shouting frenzy erupted among the prisoners. It was nearly like a riot and soon a group of guards dashed into the solitary section and began putting inmates into strait-jackets. The cries were so loud it nearly made you crazy. I was paralyzed with fear and forgot to pray. But I didn't get beaten. Commandant Zavjalkin came into my cell. Still I was left alone. But the cold began biting at my skin again.

A wild anger filled me again and prevented me from concentrating. How easy it is to make a man into a beast! I heard some sounds as if something was going on in a nearby cell, including the voice of the prison doctor. Soon the guards came into my room with a wooden cot and placed it over the holes spouting the frigid air. Shortly after, they brought in an inmate who was badly beaten and put him on that cot. He was groaning and asking for water. They left me a cup of hot water and the guard on duty said, "You, painter, look after him. If anything happens bang on the door."

The two of us remained alone. I took a sip of the hot water, which was a scandal in that the water was his. I was happy they had covered the holes with the cot and I began to pray. But my prayers were stiff and I still couldn't concentrate. I dozed as best I could but soon noticed that my new cell mate was not making the slightest sound. I feared he was dead. Slowly I got up and went to him. He was cold as ice. I began beating at the door. The guard came and asked what I needed. I told him that my neighbor wasn't moving.

The door opened and the commandant dashed in, along with the doctor, who felt for the man's pulse and opened his eyelids. "He's ready," was all he said, and they carried the corpse away.

The next day they took me out of the solitary block and I was assigned to cell 12 in the first block. I emptied water from a toilet and spoke to my friend through the pipes. They caught us and that night I was back in solitary for another ten days.

There were so many ways they tried to break us. There and elsewhere they would deny us water, they would place me in a cell so tiny that when I sat on a stool my knees were crammed against the wall, they would isolate you for thirty days at a time, in circumstances that caused severe claustrophobia. At other times I was surrounded by spiritless prisoners who were destined for execution. My prayers and my parents were all that had kept me alive. I should have been executed five times by now. But the Virgin was watching over me, and my parents, despite their embarrassment, were spending a small fortune behind the scenes to keep me from death.

I appreciated their efforts but my entire existence was meant to be a protest. I refused to give into the Communist system. I managed to maintain contacts with the underground Church, and there was great power simply in my willingness to suffer prison. It gave my messages to the Church forceful meaning and encouragement.

I didn't have the opportunity of systematic study in prison, but I devoured any books that were available, studying physics, chemistry, or anything at all. And then there were my own "books." Once more, God gave me the opportunity to print my literature, even in prison. At Vladimir, I published several pamphlets using the glass-plate method— making ink from burnt shoe rubber and mixing it with sugar and bread paste. One of the publications was *The Triumph of Satan* by Zinowij Krasiwskyj. We made four copies of this. There were even illustrations. There was also a collection of my own poems, called *Hirkoty* (which means "poison"). The authorities couldn't figure out how such underground literature had found its way into Vladimir.

They began investigating the whole prison. At the time, I was also publishing a composition entitled, *Letters of the Mother of God to the Ukrainian People.* The KGB knew it was me but couldn't prove it.

Some of those who helped smuggle out my letters were guards who grew sympathetic to our cause or underwent a conversion. The power of God prevails in the most harsh, most extreme circumstances. It's a funny thing about guards and prisoners: they often develop a mutual psychological dependence and empathy by virtue of familiarity, and because, really, both are in captivity. There is an assimilation of character. Other guards, unfortunately, develop antipathy for the prisoners and practice sadism.

Such was life at Vladimir, while on the outside, down in the Ukraine, the Eastern Rite Catholic Church had been officially stamped out of existence. The Communists were now focusing upon the Evangelicals and Baptists. Lutheran preachers such as S. Ostapovych were in exile in Siberia, and although denominations such as the Seventh Day Adventists were officially recognized by the state, they too were subjected to Soviet torment. Jehovah's Witnesses were also severely persecuted. Secret Jewish religious groups were also persecuted, and so were the Jews who tried to leave the country.

On February 11, 1972, an investigation began over my Articles, poetry, and other publishing ventures. My arrest was in conjunction with articles 70 and 72; they were read to me by Major Yevsejiv, a KGB agent, and the procurator.

At first I was in cell 20 on the third floor of the fourth block, but then, on February 12, after the official arrest, they transferred me back to cell 21 in Corpus 2, the same cell where the Virgin had appeared in 1970. This time that ice-box of a cell promised to be the end of me. The Soviets were going to kill me but leave no overt evidence. If you freeze someone to death no one can prove the prisoner was intentionally killed. In this way, they avoid the legal work involved in formal executions as well as the political repercussions in the outside world.

Cell 21 had been turned into a veritable freezer. It was the middle of winter and they were forcing in frigid air. The walls were coated with ice so thick that you could make it ring by tapping an object against it. They stripped me of my winter clothes, leaving me there in a light shirt. In half an hour I felt my jaws freeze shut. I couldn't move them. And the very roots of my hair hurt.

My mind was working, I was aware that I was freezing, and I gathered my strength. I climbed the grate on the cell door to warm my head against the ceiling light bulb.

The guard on duty looked through the peephole, saw this, and switched off the light. I sat on my bed and began to freeze. There was an old quilt you could see through and I wrapped myself in it, garnering what little comfort it could afford me. Too weak, I finally lay down, praying and awaiting my fate. Within another ten minutes my lips wouldn't move, and my eyelids felt like they too were freezing shut. My head was splitting, my eyes, my temples, my jaws. I could still think but I couldn't move my limbs. I was freezing to death.

It was then that I became aware of an intense flash in the room, a very powerful light, and heard what sounded like someone walking in the cell. My eyes were clamped. I couldn't tell who it was. I can't explain what happened— lying there with my eyes shut, in a state approaching paralysis—but somehow I became aware that the room was illuminated. And the cell was starting to feel warmer. Against my eyelids I felt the palm of a woman's hand and smelled the soft pure fragrance of milk.

When the hand lifted I was able to open my eyes. There before me was the young Virgin I had seen in the same cell exactly two years before. *"You called to me,"* she said, *"and I have come."*

Chapter 12

RUSSIA
IN FLAMES

Because I had been nearly unconscious, I wondered if I was hallucinating. I knew that when people are close to freezing they often see and hear imaginary things. But the sight was too extraordinary. She was right there next to me. This time Our Blessed Mother wore a heavy plaited dark blue dress and a kerchief with fringes, like the Carpathian mountain women. Instead of the breezy summer apparel, she had on an old-fashioned church veil.

Otherwise, her looks were like in 1970, the same young, overwhelmingly pleasant face.

It wasn't like the dreams and visions. It was an apparition. I saw her with my physical eyes and I heard her dulcet voice with my eardrums.

"You don't believe it's me," she said in that soft, beautiful voice. *"But it is me. You have called me in your daily prayers and I have come to you."*

I'm doing my best to remember the exact words. I may be off in sequence but I will give you the essence of the apparition. Let me repeat that there are times I confuse certain details of this apparition with the previous one. Two decades have passed since they occurred. I do remember that I remained very calm. The cell continued to warm. She was surrounded by the same huge aura of light, and again it enveloped me. My body started to feel like I was in front

142

of a stove. My whole body was hot—my face was hot, my palms were hot too. I had the feeling of talking with her just as I am sitting here now, speaking with my translator and co-author. Just like I would speak to you. The only difference is that I felt a tremendous uplifting. I was excited. It was similar to little butterflies in the stomach. I can still feel the same sensations, I can still see every detail of her in my mind's eye, down to her eyelashes.

"You will not leave prison soon," she informed me. *"You are only halfway through the process, but do not worry because I am always with you. There are many years of prison and suffering before you. That road I told you about is beginning. Do not be troubled. You will not be released home. You will not be released at this time."*

I was still in disbelief. My mind couldn't accept it. The Virgin Mary was there in the fullness of being. She was neither a hologram nor a vaporous ghost. I extended my hand and actually touched her. She felt normal, a solid body there. I wasn't hallucinating. In her right hand was the Rosary again. She smiled and said, *"Why are you disbelieving? It is me."*

For the next two hours I gawked, prayed, and listened as the Mother of God consoled and instructed me. She said that while I was only halfway through the time I was to spend in prison, and that certain situations would be painful and precarious, no harm would befall me. She began to predict events that would occur in my personal life, events that I have since seen happen right to the minor details. She said I would be released in April of 1976 (she didn't give an exact date), but it was obvious I would be persecuted, rearrested after the release, and imprisoned again.

She also made predictions for all of mankind. She drew me into prophetic visions. The wall melted and instead of the freeze-cell, I saw tremendous, real-life images materialize before my eyes. While such visions in 1970 had been cloaked in a mist, this time they were as clear and real as anything that can greet your eyes. It was not as if they were on television, these sights I was led to see, but instead they were full-scale and occurring before me.

"Now, look," was the way she put it, reaching with her left arm.

I saw a map. I saw a map and parts of it were burning. Russia! There were fires erupting all over Russia. Surrounding countries were also involved. There were flames in various parts of the world. It was what could happen if mankind does not come back to her Son. I saw entire landscapes. I saw a river I recognized, the Amur. I don't know how I knew it was that river. I saw many islands there. I saw tanks on the Soviet side—but not the Soviet type—and a city in flames. Siberia was on fire to the Ural Mountains. I saw Moscow, and the people there had faces that were twisted and deformed. Moscow was sinking, and throughout the city were strange creatures running down the streets. Their faces were those of rats and their tails were long and fat with scaly skin and hairs sticking out like spikes. They were as big as a dog and whoever the creatures spat at would fall to the ground, as if by venom. There was a tremendous fear that filled Moscow, and the city was falling into the earth. I saw hills, forests, cities, walls. The whole countryside was aflame. And all these explosions were taking place. . .

Prophecies are difficult to interpret, and they are not always set in concrete. Was it civil war, or solely war with a foreign power? All I understood was that this was war and saw one country against whom this war was waged— China! The tanks were Chinese. This war is inevitable and I got the sense it might come before the year 2000. If it does, the war will be a warning to all of God's people. The Virgin wasn't speaking, but I knew what some of this meant. It was so clearly impressed upon me that I could paint it. And though most of it was smoke and fire, it ended with a sunny day.

"The Ukrainians should also repent," said the Virgin. *"You're an unfortunate people because you love each other so little. You've dedicated your better forces to ungodly goals. God punishes a nation as he punished Cain for the slaughter of Abel."*
Then I saw myself among my people, Zarvanystya village, and I saw myself among peoples from other nations. I was being persecuted. I saw a king with a scepter in his hand. He was wearing a crown and sitting on a throne. The

king was dressed in white with purple sewn on his robe. I thought: this is a fairytale image. A mirage. But when I was thinking this, I heard the Virgin's voice again, continuing her messages:

"You have to follow that road that has been set for you. There shall be many builders but many are without my Son and without His love. There will be many who use His name to aggrandize themselves. But do not fear. They are not the builders. The builders are those who are humble before my Son. Without love and without faith, people can attain their own desires, but not that which has been foretold by the Lord Jesus Christ, my Son. I shall always be with you. Pray and work for the conversion of Russia to Christ the King. Do not lose faith. The world is cold and spiritless, as it was before the Flood." And the woman continued to speak about that which would happen.

She was asking us to repent and purify ourselves. She was asking us to develop questioning consciences. She was asking us to repent of our fratricides. These are all fundamental tasks, and the alternative to accomplishing them is clearly an undesirable future.

After a long while, in another very powerful flash, the Mother of God disappeared. There was still the beguiling smell of farm milk. It remained even after she was gone. When I was released years later, I related this apparitional experience to a doctor and asked why he thought the Virgin would exude such an aroma. The doctor told me to go back to my childhood and think of the dearest memories associated with my grandmother. I did, and I recalled an Easter Sunday when I was in grade two—a very happy day, a beautiful and joyful Easter. I had come home and my grandmother was laying out the table for Easter breakfast. She had caressed me on the head and her hand smelled of milk because she had just milked the cow. The doctor, who was a close friend of mine, explained that even if I hadn't realized it back then, my grandmother's caress had actually been my first caress from God.

The doctor continued questioning me and asked what I smelled when I saw the flames during the apparition. It wasn't the smell of burning, as I recall, but like moldy sod or decaying mushrooms. The doctor said it sounded like the smell he encounters cutting cadavers during autopsies. It was the smell of death.

After the Blessed Virgin disappeared on February 12, 1972, I took off my shirt and started walking around the cell. That's how warm it was. I was sweating. I heard the boot heels of guards clamoring up and down the halls. Apparently they had caught glimpse of the flash of light and thought there might be a fire. A siren was wailing.

They began to open the little peephole in the door and people were looking in at me. After half an hour the KGB and hierarchy of the prison came into my cell, along with the doctor. They couldn't believe I was alive. They couldn't believe I could be standing there without a shirt. They had come rushing in wearing very warm coats and fur hats. You could see their breath. They were touching my hands, looking me over. The administrator arrived, his face flushed with raw hatred. They asked what I had set fire to. "There's no smoke," I pointed out. "What do you want of me?"

"What were you doing?" they demanded. "Walking around? Praying?"

"The Mother of God was here with me and nothing has happened to me," I replied.

During the initial inspection, and in subsequent days, the KGB, prison administration, and medical experts, including psychiatrists from the Serbsky Institute of Forensic Psychiatry in Moscow, struggled to understand what had happened. A doctor commented that I must be out of my mind. The superior authorities, General Zavjalkin and Colonel Zotow, didn't even try to conceal the fact that I had been put in the freeze-cell to die. They were beside themselves. They couldn't comprehend how I could be walking and how my skin could have warmed. They formed a commission that included psychologists and physicists.

They shuttled me from the offices at Vladimir into Moscow, where, during 1972, I would spend time at the Serbsky Institute and in prisons such as Lubyanka, Butyrka, and most of all the main KGB center of detention, Lefortovo. These prisons are as infamous in the USSR as Attica and The Tombs are in America. Especially renowned is Lubyanka. It has been said that the very name causes the average Russian citizen to tremble. During the Stalin years, it was not only the center of torture but also—if one survived—the gateway to Siberia. It is located in the same complex as that of KGB headquarters at Dzerzhinsky Square—a couple blocks from the Kremlin. And hundreds of men, famous in Soviet history, including several discredited chiefs of security, met their fates at Lubyanka, herded into its execution chambers.

Yet, I nearly enjoyed my visits to Lubyanka, which was sort of an interrogation and investigation center. For one thing there was better food at Lubyanka than at the other prisons, and anyway, I had become almost inured to the atrocities. So severe were some of the tortures in the camps that back in 1966 one young man had tried to end it all by swallowing a light bulb. What could we do but pray the *Our Father*, while the evangelists sang psalms?

So Lubyanka was nothing special, and I was only sent there for interrogation. My visits lasted just several hours at a time and at the most a few days. Besides the improved food, it was a nice drive getting there. They would talk to me for fifteen or twenty minutes, then I would be given lunch. I spent somewhat more time at Lefortovo, where I arrived in June of 1972. It was the standard hellhole, the same murky walls and gloomy asphalt floors and prisoners whose eyes were cast into an inhuman gaze.

The authorities were formulating their new case against me and everything foretold in the apparition was to transpire. They sent me from one doctor to another. There was an intense persecution. I was often totally isolated and even the guards were prohibited from talking with me. Major Vynnogradov had begun the judicial inquiry and they made it clear that after all that had passed, they couldn't release me. I asked them, "Why aren't you setting me free when my sentence is finished?" "Oh," they said, "you haven't been behaving well in prison and we're opening another prison sentence against you." I heard Vynnogradov say, "If we let him go free it will be known to all the fanatics. The Catholics will raise him up. They'll make a saint of him."

One of the "experts" who was involved in my case, Yelena Butova, a well-known prison doctor who was equally well-known as a lesbian sadist, had immediately proclaimed that what had happened was self-imposed. "Terelya was taking

part in yoga and he has brought himself to such a state,"
she had said, trying to explain the inexplicable warmth in
the freeze-cell the night of the apparition.

Yoga! They were grasping for straws. I told them the
Mother of God had come to me and that the Mother of God
had saved me. The prison doctors continued to insist that
I had been in some kind of yogic trance. They demanded
that I tell them the technique of meditation and psy-
chodynamics that I had used.

"The Mother of God came to me, and there will be a war,"
I insisted to my various examiners. "Before the year 2000,
Russia will be at war. There will be an awful fiery war for
12 years. Many will die."

They asked me who the war would be against.

I told them of my impression that it might be China. "But
even before that," I added, "there will be *major* changes
within your own nation."

They noted these things tangentially, scoffing and disbelieving. How can an atheist accept an otherworldly visitation? The mere thought of it enrages scientists and those
many others—both in the East and West—whose entire system of thought is narrow and materialistic, restricted to the
physical senses. It especially enrages those whose thoughts
and actions—whose patterns of intellectual evil—were
formed under the mistaken idea that there is no eternal
punishment. An atheistic scientist is no different from a
dyed-in-the-wool Communist. In fact, the thrust to replace
religion with science was the single greatest thrust of
totalitarianism. The microscope became the Bible, the cosmonauts became saints, and the institutes of mathematics
and psychology were the new cathedrals. Priests and bishops
were replaced by physicists. The confessional booth was
replaced by the office of a godless psychiatrist.

These doctors and psychologists insisted that I was making fun of them. No, I assured them without any fear, I
was not. The Virgin Mary saved me and warmed the
freeze-cell.

There was a young psychiatrist by the name of Stella, and
she was the only one who believed me. Today she is a devout
Catholic. But the others were not nearly as open-minded.
And beneath everything else, they were just plain scared.

I prayed and believed what had been told to me by the Virgin, despite events that *seemed* to contradict her. Where Our Blessed Mother said I would be released in April of 1976, the authorities were tacking 15 years to my sentence, which, added to the time I already owed, meant I wouldn't be released until 1999. I remained silent and did not talk with my captors. The interrogations sometimes went on for six hours a day. At Lefortovo I did not utter one word—not "good day," not "goodbye," nothing. I would go back to my cell, fall on my knees, and pray. They would write their questions for me and I wouldn't say a thing. Major General Bokov of the KGB said I was psychiatrically abnormal and that there was no use trying to talk to me. The criminal investigation was led by Captain Pleshkov, who was also of the KGB. They wanted to take me out of the political arena and get rid of me.

I spent a lot of time at the psychiatric institute, which was known for its fake diagnoses and drug "therapies." I was moved there on July 5. The chief psychiatrist on my case was KGB General Daniil Lunts. He directed a special diagnostic section that declared people of sound mind but opposing political and religious views to be paranoid schizophrenics. Lunts said, "Fine, Terelya, we know you are a fanatic believer, but we want to know what system you used to overcome the freezing temperatures. Own up to what system of yoga you used to prevent your freezing."

"I am telling you what I have seen," I continued to insist. "I am not going to lie to accommodate you."

Thus commenced my continual examinations at the Serbsky Institute. Besides Lunts, I remember some other examiners named Margareta Taltze, Adalbert Fokin, and the academician Snizhnevsky. "Tell us, why are you so stubborn?" Taltze wanted to know. "Deny that you have seen the Mother of God and you will go home. We have to conduct experiments to determine what we are to do with you. You must cooperate."

The doctors said they were interested in me as a case study. On one occasion, I recall Margareta asking how a young man like me, raised in good Soviet schools, could believe in God and more than that, how I could be so silly as to believe in the Immaculate Conception. "Did you not study biology in school?'' she asked.

"Yes."

"Do you know how cells are formed? Do you know what a sperm and egg are? Do you deny that a child is conceived in the womb of its mother?"

"No, I am not denying that," I responded. "This is how people are born. But God was not born in this fashion. He is not an ordinary man."

At times, under the persistent questioning, I grew angry. "You're awful, you're ugly," I shouted at Margareta. "Let the KGB take me away. You're a satanist."

"Let's continue talking on religious issues," Dr. Lunts said on another occasion. "Why do you believe in God?"

"I don't want anything to do with Babylonians," I replied, refusing to answer him.

He said, "We see you're an intelligent man and we want to prove this. Do you really believe a woman can be made pregnant without a man?"

"This is a dogma of our faith. I don't want to talk on this theme because this offends my religious convictions."

"You believe this?"

"I am totally convinced," I said. "I myself can inseminate a woman from a distance."

It was a ploy on my part, the claim about insemination. Not only was I defending my faith, but also striving towards a diagnosis of schizophrenia. I *wanted* to be declared insane. And so I gave them reason to think I was crazy. I had decided that it would be better in a psychiatric hospital than back in a camp or prison. While places like the Serbsky Institute also had the reputation for torture—they placed inmates in wet straitjackets that shrank as they dried and nearly squeezed stubborn "patients" to death—there was the likelihood that my life would be over if I was returned to prison. I was being sentenced under Articles 70 and 72 of the codex. Article 70 charged me with anti-Soviet agitation and propaganda, but more serious was Article 72, which involved organizing subversive organizations. The punishment for that charge was execution.

I led myself correctly in interrogation, but from time to time I would utter statements to make them suspect I wasn't normal. I screamed at the doctors. I pretended to suffer from a persecution mania. I criticized Margareta's looks. I brazenly stole their pens and claimed they were mine. Playing on their obsession with my belief in the Immaculate Conception, I continued to pretend to also believe that I myself could inseminate someone at a distance. I claimed to be the son of a 1,000-year-old prince and the most intelligent man in the Soviet Union.

At one point I was brought before a huge forum of doctors from around the Soviet bloc and asked to repeat my claim of being able to impregnate women at a distance. Lunts introduced this demonstration. It was to catch me in a lie. I continued the charade. "I will demonstrate this," I said at the convention, up there on the stage. "I will inseminate women here. All those who are virgins please stand up." I knew there wasn't a virgin in the audience. Those doctors do not live very morally. They burst into laughter and applause.

While the Serbsky doctors suspected that I was feigning insanity, the idea of insemination-at-a-distance they found to be such a bizarre idea that I must be out of my mind. It was only God's grace and the promise of the Mother of God that she was looking after me that enabled me to go successfully through this period and avoid execution.

Even at Serbsky I managed to get messages to the outside world, and in some ways life there and at the subsequent mental wards was one of relative leisure. The food was certainly an improvement. It was in January of 1973 that I was transported to Sechovka, a psychiatric concentration camp in the Smolensk region. I wasn't in the best of physical condition—my liver and stomach acted up—and I suffered beatings from the male nurses, who once tied me to my bed for two months. I also suffered seeing all the violence, the homicides committed by mafia types who had bought their way into this prison. But I was able to receive parcels from my girlfriend Olena, who I hadn't seen in eleven years.

There were about three hundred political prisoners in the tenth block of this psychiatric camp, including Muslims, a Lithuanian Catholic, an evangelical Christian sentenced in 1941, and a Ukrainian Catholic. There was also a secretary of a local Communist party sent there for his belief in God. Other detainees were indeed mentally unstable, poor souls who suffered actual psychological maladies. Besides the murders, there were homosexual rapes, infusions with pharmaceuticals, and little tortures whereby political prisoners were forced to swallow live frogs.

There were so many injustices I couldn't conceivably log them all. In the Soviet system, it is not uncommon for a man who murdered a pregnant wife to be released after just one year, while a political detainee was sent for five years of "therapy."

Meanwhile, outside the dingy two-story buildings and rows of barbed wire, every last vestige of the official church was being stomped out like little campfires. In 1974 a clandestine convent was discovered in L'viv, and Uniate Bishop Vasyl Velychkovsky, after completing a prison sentence, had been allowed to leave the USSR and died in Canada, his health ruined by his imprisonment. Other priests such as Ivan Kryvy had been apprehended for reprinting 3,500 copies of a Ukrainian prayer book. As the historian Valentyn Moroz put it, the anti-Catholic campaign was tantamount to an attack on the very spiritual structure of the nation.

But once again, the Divine Father was sending warnings to those destroying His Church. In the village Sokilnyky, a suburb of L'viv, was a high school language teacher named Maria Panchenko, who propagated atheism fanatically. She was a real Communist. She was so vigorous in her atheism that even the official Party organ criticized her as going overboard in anti-religious activities. During one of her classes at the end of June in 1973, she said something to the effect, "If there is a God, have him punish me! Our god is our Party, our Lenin. If you don't listen to us, we can punish you, but where's your God?"

After that class she was supposed to take a bus back to L'viv, where she lived. But she decided to walk and as she made her way home—the same day she made the challenge to God—a large transport truck came along and hit her. She was thrown into a pole, seriously injuring her back. After that she was in a wheelchair. And anyone who went to visit her heard this teacher admit that God punished her for her atheism.

My punishment was meted out by omnipresent KGB. They were infuriated that I had managed to get myself committed and vowed that I wouldn't be there for long. They wanted me back in the regular prisons.

My sentence was life and I should still be there. But God granted that my parents intervened. Along with certain well-placed friends (including the cousin of my father, who was first secretary of the Carpathian Communist Party), they concocted a fictitious legal proceeding whereby I was deemed cured of my "schizophrenia." It was another little miracle. The judge was a man who knew my father because they had spent time together in a Nazi prison. They drew up a decree of release, and caught off guard, the KGB didn't have time enough to refute it.

As the Mother of God foretold, I was released in April of 1976.

Olena, Josyp, and Daughter Marianna—1981

Chapter 13

THE
CROSS

The precise day of my release was April 7. I wasn't about to lay back and bask in my liberty. I immediately set about organizing Church activists and celebration of the underground liturgy.

During my freedom, which would last a full year, I also married Olena. We had now been corresponding, off and on, for 15 years. And she was to suffer punishment—including internal exile—for her persistence in maintaining contact with me. Olena was by now taking the higher medical courses, a very brave woman of 34. I was 33. She lived in Vynnytsya, and we were married in that region toward the end of May.

The marriage was very romantic. We went into the Carpathian Mountains, where a catacomb bishop was preparing for our encounter at midnight. They arranged for a honeymoon room in one of the villages and the owner of the inn didn't know who was going to occupy it. Like everything else, our marriage had to be conducted in secrecy.

News of my release was all over the radio and the KGB was steaming. My release, of course, was not really legal. It was all a clever political maneuver through the hospital, circumventing the regular prison system. As I said, it was my father's group that orchestrated it—at a neutral court in Mukachiv. They printed a false decree to which the local judge placed his stamp. The stated reason for my release was that my mental "health" had improved and I had supposedly abandoned my fanatical religious convictions.

By this time there were some interesting changes taking place with my father. He had occasionally betrayed a hidden streak of nationalism, but now he was also showing signs of converting back to the faith of his parents. He had experienced some sort of inner crisis and now had kicked his smoking and drinking habits. He was also quietly helping Catholic families. He maintained communication with an underground priest (who posed as a dean in the Orthodox Church) and hired Catholics after they finished their prison sentences. He also was secretly lending financial support to a parish or pulling strings to keep young men out of the camps.

My mother wasn't thrilled about my marriage to Olena, and she certainly wanted me to tone down my overt Christianity. The idea was for me to maintain my freedom by renouncing Catholicism and joining the officially sanctioned Russian Orthodox Church. It was really a game, but it was also all the Communists wanted: for me to publicly recant Catholicism and stay away from the nationalistic element.

This would have been a blow to the underground and would have led to other recantations. There were many times I could have gotten out of jail by simply signing a document of renunciation. After my release, I had been shooed out of the Carpathians and ordered by the government to live and work in the less nationalisitic and less Catholic Eastern Ukraine. But I worked for the Church wherever I was. One of our greatest leaders, Bishop Fedoryk, had taken ill, and I had a lot of work to do. It was work of an administrative nature. I was responsible for the underground treasury, raising funds to support persecuted nuns and priests. At the same time, I organized summer camps for the "Church of the woods." I had to plan many of the clandestine meetings, teach catechism to the children, and present a short course on the history of the Ukrainian Church.

There are large virgin forests in the Ukraine and it's there we often met for religious youth camps. We pretended that the kids trooping into those woods were Soviet scouts. In the forest we had tents, a mobile altar, and an icon of "Our

Lady of Perpetual Help.'' There was also a candelabra and
rosaries.

The children would be rustled awake at 6 a.m., wash up
and come for prayer. There was a dress parade and assign-
ment of chores. The youths were divided into groups according to age, and each group received a particular type of
instruction. Such meetings were taking place in different
parts of Carpathia. To give them a sense of reality, the students were often visited by activists like Vasyl Kobryn or
me. It was exciting for the youngsters, meeting a mysterious activist, and I suppose it was like my experience as
a youngster with nationalistic guerrillas.

I am sometimes accused of having trained religious
fanatics. Let me hasten to say that they were *not* fanatics,
they were very strong Catholics. We taught love, not hatred;
forgiveness, not revenge. The children would have a morning snack of a bun and jam and go into the woods, where
a nun often conducted prayer.

During lunch one of the older boys would read Scripture
or recite another prayer. Some people ask what sense this
made—reading while they were eating. Well, it had important meaning. The children experienced an authentic Christian relationship and were given a taste of monastic flavor.

After lunch there was a rest and then: running, swimming, and more prayer. In the evening they would listen
to stories about luminaries such as Saints Alphonse and John
Bosco. There were also intense discussions at which they
shared their deepest thoughts, and the children developed
a comradery just as I had in Catholic Action. We continued
the tradition of the "Last Supper," breaking bread and eating fruit, cabbage leaves with mushrooms, and cooked beans.
"Lord merciful God, send your guardian angels upon the
ways of all those present," was one favorite petition. Evening prayer lasted an hour and then it was time to sleep.
The youngsters were proud and happy.

During our gatherings we would agree on which Roman
Church we should go to for Mass. For nine years the KGB
couldn't understand how we were able to communicate
throughout the region. They did everything to figure it out
and only met with success when they sent a KGB officer
from L'viv to infiltrate us. The Roman Catholics were still

tolerated in some areas—though just barely—and during the Mass people would come from all the regions and slip each other notes. As during my teenage years, there were clandestine Eastern Rite Confessions in the choir lofts.

The Roman Catholic priests risked their lives for us; there were only 11 of them left in all of Carpathia. Most of their surviving churches were used by us Eastern Rite Catholics.

Besides places to worship, we also needed to start up more in the way of publication. It was difficult to get access to printing machines because they were all registered by number. We had young groups from Catholic Action and the Apostolate of Prayer who, after school, would copy the text of prayers, psalms, and sections of the liturgy by hand. One such publication, a book of Gospels, was presented to the Holy Father and is now in the Vatican museum. Although he had no idea how many of us there were, the Pope knew of our Church because certain of our documents were presented to the international press, or in Basilian reports to Rome.

Led by Bishop Fedoryk, we continued to organize the underground and translate Catholic literature. We had three hundred lay missionaries and we broke them into groups of five or ten. Their mission: to infiltrate the high schools and elementary schools, reversing atheistic propaganda. Many people didn't even know the sign of the cross let alone how to pray, and at first, the only religious books we could get our hands on were three volumes of a catechism that had been in my father's library.

There was a whole group of people working to photocopy these books on sort of an underground assembly line. They would never acknowledge who did what, because prison awaited all of them. My own dedication could not have been stronger. The apparitions of the Virgin had instilled me with a closer association with the Holy Spirit. Although always a believer, I was 28 when I first had experienced the reality and truth of God—in 1970.

It's true that every person has his own way to God, and when I ask someone if he believes in God, I want to know about their experience with the *living* God. This business of going to church and knowing about God isn't faith in God. We have to *experience* God, feel His grace, and this experience does not come to everyone at the same time and in the same way. There are good Christians who live their whole lives without experiencing the living God. How do we make God come alive? One must remember to continually build up the momentum of faith, remembering and meditating upon little prayers that were answered, then recalling somewhat larger heavenly favors, and finally knowing with full confidence that—if it's God's will—even the largest prayers will be answered. A little doubt can poison an otherwise profound prayer.

After the night services I would address ecclesiastical issues and talk about the problems with Russian Orthodoxy —how it was controlled by the Communists. The Soviets were everywhere. One of our faithful was the mother of a brutal militiaman who liked to smash crosses and other religious articles. He was consorting with an immoral woman and his mother prayed for him endlessly. At the time I was under constant surveillance and the KGB had learned that the militiaman's mother was meeting with our group. That meant trouble. In fact it was nearly the death of me. One of our meeting places was accessible only by a path that went along the side of a cliff, and it was so steep the tops of the pines were below us. Well, one evening this woman failed to show up for services and late that night, as I was returning along the precarious cliff, under a starlit sky, several men rushed me from behind and pushed me so violently that I began to somersault downward.

By all odds I should have taken a 30-foot fall and landed on sharp rocks, but as I started to fall my jacket was caught on a thorn bush. I bumped up and down and landed easily.

There wasn't so much as a scratch on me.

When I looked to the top, however, I broke into a cold sweat. It was ghastly realizing how close I had come to an early end. I became weak and my legs began to tremble. I started to pray, and I cried like a child. But then I went right to the militiaman's house to confront him, and you should have seen his face. It wasn't fear. It was wild terror. It was like he was seeing a ghost. "Is your mother home?" I asked calmly but sharply.

"Yes, she's home."

It was morning by now. I said, "Tell your mother we're

gathering at such and such a place tonight.'' I turned away and left. But he got the message. He was possessed of the fear of God. And he was certainly concerned that I would tell his mother about the attempt on my life.

I never did tell the woman. The only one I told was Olena after we were married. I won't mention this man's name. He is now a colonel, and he has quietly converted to the faith. Every first Friday he goes to confession and he has returned to his first wife.

If I could convert prison guards, I could certainly convert members of the militia. God gives each one of us an established role and it all depends on how each of us has worked. There's no doubt Satan always stays with a person while he is on earth. But we must push on. Man is in a constant state of warfare.

My countrymen have been fighting Satan for more than seventy years, and from my own experience, I've come to the conclusion that a person who's never had interior conflict, or doesn't want to know his own shortcomings, will never be able to build God's perfect kingdom. It's very easy to tell someone to do this or to do that, but hard to do it ourselves. The easiest thing to do is to fall into sin. Basically this struggle is a struggle for man's soul. Our worst sin is when we are silent, when we understand that through inaction we are sinning and yet remain silent. I cannot emphasize enough that a person who remains silent creates a greater sin than he who is doing the actual sinning. Jesus has come to us in order that we too convert sinners, and now we're all witnesses of the purification. In the Soviet Union more than fifty million have died since 1915, while in America, there is a holocaust in the form of crime and abortion. There is nothing that demands our raised voice more than the issue of murdering the unborn.

When I say we can not remain silent, I am also referring to seemingly little things like blessing ourselves, passing a church. Catholics everywhere must give an example to the nonbelievers, and one way to do that is to make public demonstrations of our reverence for Christ the King. How many people in Western countries make the sign of the cross in public? Let me answer for you: very few. Yet, in the Soviet Union, where people are killed for their beliefs, the older folks publicly tipped their hats and made the sign of the cross when they passed a church, hoping to make an impression on atheists.

In the Soviet Union, Satan worked through suffering and want; in the West he works through wealth and well-being. Both countries share the plague of abortion. Let me leave the subject with this fact: A doctor who performs abortions is no better—and perhaps worse—than the commandant of a concentration camp.

In the Ukraine, speaking out against sin took the form of carrying a finger rosary on a bus, or making the sign of the cross on a crowded street. It was hard on the Catholics who worked on the collective farms. They might be making 22 rubles in spendable currency a month and yet be slapped with a 50-ruble fine. But the answer was not to stop. We concluded that the active element could no longer remain silent. We stepped up public displays of our reverence, and the atmosphere became electrified. The Communists intensified their surveillances (through the regional committees of the Party) and the activists were increasingly fined or threatened with the prospect of psychiatric hospitals.

To expose oneself to 12 years of forced labor or a mental ward is a lot to ask. Somebody had to stand up and give an example of boldness. I thought or at least hoped that I wouldn't be arrested immediately because I was well-known by now and had just been released. So I decided to step forward. I wrote a letter to KGB Chairman Yuri Andropov, openly declaring that I was a Catholic and that our Church existed in the catacombs—despite KGB claims that we had been completely liquidated.

The KGB were surprised at this. They were also very angry. I was arrested and brought to the provincial office in Kiev at Rose Luxemborg 16, room seven. A Major Hupak was there and all the incriminating documentation was on the table. "Is this all yours?" he asked.

I waited to see what they had to say, and what they said was that they were returning the letter to me.

It was addressed to Andropov and that's who I wanted to get it. "How is it that it ended up in your office?" I demanded. "I'm going to write another open declaration that the KGB from the Ukraine is not allowing letters from the Ukraine to go through to Moscow authorities."

They warned me not to start playing games. They said I was under official surveillance according to a decree signed by the procurator of the Ukraine. They also said they had permission to interrogate me. They wanted me to sign a paper documenting our conversation, but I refused because it inferred that the Catholic Church no longer existed and was instead part of the Russian Orthodox Church. It amounted to a declaration that I was joining the Orthodox.

"I'm not signing."

"Then you're not leaving this place."

But after five or six hours they let me go, with the warning that I better not write any more such letters.

I paid them no heed and began writing open letters to Western countries. I proclaimed that our Church existed but was forced into the underground. It was then that the KGB began investigating my court release in an effort to nullify it. But in some ways, it was too late. My name had reached the United States and other countries.

I spent much of my time organizing parishes in Olena's region, Vynnytsya. I was protected at times by a Russian officer who was a member of the underground—we had our people everywhere—but the authorities began to demand I leave this province and go somewhere else. The KGB made it clear that it might be easier for them to kill me than put me back in prison. And one official said that if I had anything to do with the Jews, he would really come after me.

Another thing that probably bothered them was an escapade of mine with the Russian Orthodox Church. The Church had made overtures to me and I decided to infiltrate it. How was I going to do this? By becoming an Orthodox priest! At first my application was denied by Bishop Agafongel of Vynnytsya, but soon he changed his mind and decided to accept me. On September 21, 1976, I went to meet with the Orthodox bishop. He said he had decided to ordain me as a priest and send me for further studies in Leningrad. I found out later my father was behind all of this. They knew it was hopeless to turn me into a Soviet, but they still had hopes that my religious fervor could be channeled in an acceptable direction. My father had even gone to visit the First Secretary of the Ukrainian Communist Party. They figured they would make me a bishop.

The Orthodox bishop told me I should officially establish myself as a psalmist at St. George's in Vynnytsya, which is what I did. The superior or rector of this church was Father Nicholai, who was also an army major. He was provoking me to see if I was sincere.

But back for a moment to September 21. It's another incident that points out the currents and cross currents of Communism. After my discussion with the bishop, a young man had approached me. "Are you Terelya?" It was dark and nearby was a large limousine.

"Yes," I answered. "Terelya is my name."

We got in the car. They were sent to see what went on at the meeting. I thought they were taking me to a parliament building. They said they wanted to talk to me and that I should leave Vynnytsya and go to my home province.

I said I couldn't, that I had been chased out of there, too, that I was being chased out of all the provinces. These men in the limousine, I learned later, were KGB agents. Obviously, what I was doing didn't sit well and they had been instructed to cool off my religious fervor.

One of the more insistent ones said, "Look, don't imagine all these things about Jesus Christ. It's all just imaginary things." He said if I didn't stop, they would fix me.

I told them I would continue to go to church no matter what they said. I felt that they might be testing me to see if I was a truly committed Christian. I still didn't know who they were.

They continued to drive. We were heading away from Vynnytsya, to an abandoned cemetery. There were many abandoned graveyards in the Vynnytsya area. They took me out of the car and as they did one of them hit me, knocking me to the ground. They began beating me.

When I regained consciousness they were tying me to a cross! The cord cut into my flesh painfully. They put a scarf around my mouth and told me to think everything over.

I hung on that cross from September 21 to the 23rd— three days in the cemetery. Most of the time I was in a state of semi-consciousness. Fortunately it wasn't all that cold out but still, it was no fun hanging up there. I didn't suffer physically so much as mentally. It was quiet—there was no wind because the cross was surrounded by trees—and every time I heard a strange noise my heart would begin beating a mile a minute. Whether it was a squirrel scampering or a crow flying, it nearly gave me a heart attack.

When the men returned they untied me and roughed me up some more. They put me in their car and warned that if I told anyone, I would end up in a psychiatric hospital.

Perhaps they had gotten wind of my infiltration of the Orthodox Church, or were trying to do my father a "favor" by tempering my religious ardor. At any rate, these operatives obviously had taken their instructions to an extreme and let their imaginations get away from them. I don't believe anyone had ordered my torture and I know the higher authorities didn't want their names associated with the incident.

If it seems odd that I would try to infiltrate the Russian Orthodox Church, recall what I said about the Communists controlling that church's hierarchy. I am not basing such a statement on mere rumor but on facts. As the American journalist John Barron has reported, the Archbishop of the Russian Orthodox Church for all of Africa was a heavy-drinking KGB agent named Anatoli Kaznovetsky who kept vodka near his crosier and miter. He was but one of the Church leaders who are really agents of the KGB.

My problem with the Russian Orthodox Church went beyond its pro-Soviet hierarchy. While the Eastern Rite Catholics attend services that, to the untrained eye, may seem more similar to the Orthodox Mass than the Roman Catholic liturgy, the Orthodox are separated from the Pope and their liturgy is different from the Catholic Mass in certain cloaked but fundamental ways.

My thoughts on the Catholic Church and the splinter denominations, such as Orthodoxy, are as follows. The hierarchy of the Russian Orthodox Church teaches that God is not One in three Persons, but two. It would appear on the outside that the Orthodox believe in the Trinity, just as we do, but when you look closer, the Son is not like the Father, and the Holy Spirit does not proceed from the Son but only from the Father.

Is the Son not equal to the Father?

The true and authentic Church teaches that Mary's holy soul was never in the state of original sin. Our most Holy God, preparing her to become His mother, preserved her from sin so that Satan could never say that the Mother of God was at any time in subjection to the Evil One.

The history of the world for 2000 years is tied closely with the name "Jesus Christ." The name of Jesus extends its influence into the history and lives of most nations. Never downplay the importance of Jesus, and never ignore the hope He gave. When Jesus established the Church, He said to Peter that he was the rock and the gates of Hell would not prevail over the Church founded on that rock.

What are the gates of Hell?

The enemies of the true Church, the demons and Satan.

Who are these?

Those who deliberately instigate satanic activity against the Church. Communists, masons, and atheists are prime examples.

Jesus warned about this struggle and told us not to be cast down in spirit. We Catholics must be sure that Hell does not overcome the Church, but at the same time, we should be very circumspect and defend our Church as good stewards of God's vineyard.

The events of the Ukraine unfolded before us as the progress of the anti-God battalions. The Communists have allied themselves with the religious atheists of the Russian Orthodox Church for the common fight against the Church of Christ. This plot against our Church is so extensive that we are surprised that they have not yet destroyed us. And again the words of Christ echo in our ears: *the gates of Hell shall not prevail.*

We must oppose this attack on the Christian faith. Every true Christian must understand that the Church of Christ is one and the same, even if the form might be different. In the Catholic Church there is no such thing as fashion or mode. The Church proclaims one immutable truth while the Soviet system spreads egotism, fosters beastly self-love, and nurtures hatred.

What is a Ukrainian Catholic? A faithful son of the land who didn't give Communists the opportunity to destroy the accomplishments and culture of our forefathers. We proclaim and profess the *true* ancient Ukrainian Orthodoxy. The mentality of the Catholic is very broad: from the causes of the Universe to the question of man's ultimate goals. The Ukrainian Catholic has always cultivated the sense of a person's dignity and freedom. In all things the Catholic abides by the rule of spiritual primacy over the material.

Our Church does not believe in compromising idealism but at the same time trains us in spiritual realism. And sometimes, being a militant is part of that realism.

This is what I proclaimed to my Communist tormentors, and this is the attitude I would not waver from. The harassment throughout 1976 and into 1977 was unending. The KGB was always calling me in for questioning, and on November 4, 1976, while I was working as a carpenter in the hospital where Olena was employed, the militia came to pick me up for no other reason than to keep me out of circulation during the national holiday on November 7—celebration of the Bolshevik "revolution." It's a time when dissidents and nationalists are known to act up, I suppose, and I was isolated for a month in a psychiatric hospital. You may wonder why the Soviets bother treading lightly at times, while totally ignoring their own rules at other junctures. I don't know. It has to do with the national psychosis I mentioned. You see, the USSR is worried about what outsiders might think, and in order to feel like a legitimate nation, the Soviets do abide by certain legalistic technicalities. For example, since I had been diagnosed as a "schizophrenic," they could not officially liquidate me; if they were to attempt this, they had to do it surreptitiously.

I was also kept alive by my contacts with the West—the letters and declarations I managed to have smuggled to diplomats and radio outlets in Europe. These messages proclaimed the existence of our Church and the conditions at various prisons where the persecuted were being held. The Soviets hated this more than anything—the civilized world learning of Communist atrocities. It was a sensitive time because the Helsinki Accords, and other human-rights agreements, had just been signed by the Eastern Bloc, Western Europe, and the United States (who Russia feared because it was so strong militarily).

Soon, Helsinki watchdog groups were springing up all over Communist countries. They were composed of dissidents and democrats who demanded, with Western support, that Communist governments live up to their pledges on human rights and freedom. I supported them but didn't actively join their ranks because I didn't feel they paid quite enough attention to the important differences between certain religious groups, and because the Helsinki Accords proclaimed the USSR's borders (including as they did the Baltic states and Ukraine) as inviolable when in fact the Soviet borders were contrived and illegal.

I also felt certain dissidents were a bit too quick to embrace a socialistic philosophy. They were compromising when they should have been standing firm. There is no way to compromise with evil.

I was a hot item, and I got hotter for the Soviets when, during my illegal detainment, people in Western Europe raised a hue and cry. Even Voice of America publicized the fact that I had been arrested again. The Soviets tried to discredit me by claiming, in one ridiculous article, that I had never sat a day in prison. Other articles said that my religious activities were just a cover for my nationalism.

In March of 1977, Olena and I left Vynnytsya where it was impossible to live because of the clamor raised against me in publications such as the *Zhovtnevi Zori*, or "October Stars." We were told to leave Vynnytsya or I would be arrested again. We returned to Svalyava, where my parents were.

The KGB worked feverishly to track down the judge and unravel the fictitious legal proceeding that had released me from the psychiatric prison. The judge, who was 73, was arrested and submitted to severe interrogations. He would pass out and they would bring him to by dousing the poor old man with water.

One Saturday, while we were coming from the public baths, Olena and I noticed that a car was following us. As we approached my house several other cars arrived. My father was at the entrance and was calling out. It was the last time I would see him there. He died the next year.

I was dragged into the car and Olena jumped in after me. Bold Olena! She sat on the knees of one of the officers and began shouting at the top of her voice.

They grabbed her roughly, leaving black-and-blue marks, but it's hard to stop Olena when she is intent on something. As we were approaching a bridge she pounced at the driver and we nearly went off the bridge. They stifled her by grabbing her neck.

At the time, she was pregnant with our first child— Marianna.

They brought us to the regional office of the militia, sat me down, and presented me with a document stating that I was again being sent to prison. The charge was very serious: "anti-Soviet agitation." The arrest was on April 28, 1977, and the decree for my previous release was nullified.

Chapter 14

MICHAEL AND
THE EAGLE

I was held at the provincial prison in Uzhhorod (where I had been held as a much younger man) before I was taken by convoy to a special prison in Dnipropetrovs'ke, which is at a bend in the Dnipro River.

I tasted a brief period of freedom when I managed to free myself from a hospital in between Uzhhorod and Dnipropetrovs'ke. I had gotten myself placed there by putting on an award-winning act, pretending I was not only physically ill but also a zombie—insane. I sucked blood from my gums, which were diseased from all the years of neglect, and would then cough loudly, letting the blood flow from my mouth like I had a serious disorder. I also acted as if I couldn't walk or talk.

The KGB wanted to take me back, but the doctors wouldn't let them. When I was led out for walks the guards put a straitjacket on me. But the security was so lax at the hospital that all it took was Olena to bring some cognac spiked with tranquilizers. This we gave to the hospital guards. The guards passed out and I was able to get a key to a grate and descend from a three-story window. This was May 16, 1977, the Feast of the Ascension. But they found me within a couple weeks and that's when I was shipped off to solitary at the special Dnipropetrovs'ke prison. I was to remain there for three years.

Most specialized "hospitals" didn't want to receive me because of my obstinacy, my evangelism, and my proclivity for escape. But finally they found a place for me. I was taken to Dnipropetrovs'ke on September 2, 1977, while the KGB manufactured a case against me. They stripped me naked, gave me the prison garb, and sent me to the criminal corpus. I ended up in the third block. The red and blue marks in my dossier indicated that I was both a propagandist and an escape artist.

From my previous interrogations I knew the KGB was going to try to connect me to the unsolved deaths a few years before of three KGB agents. I knew nothing about it, except the rumor that the agents got into a fiery auto accident after drinking to the point of intoxication. Their absurd attempt to pin this blame on me reached newspapers in lands as far away as Canada.

I am not going to recount the entire three years of my new captivity, but there are certain matters that should be discussed, including the fact that the captain, Nella Butkevich, was another sadist. She accused me of anything she could imagine, and throughout 1977 and 1978, I was submitted to all sorts of beatings, treatments, and psychological terror. During these three years I was kept in cell 21. They didn't allow my name to be mentioned to anyone, and I wasn't even on the list of inmates. The orderlies abused the sick at the instigation of the doctors, denying them water and making them wait long periods of time to go to the bathroom. One invalid, a teacher, was beaten to death.

"Do you seriously think that you'll ever get out of here?" Butkevich would ask me. "Do you want this handed to an international tribunal? We are the tribunal. The fact that you call yourself a Christian shows you have a sickness and we shall nurse you until such time as you reject all your hallucinations. You're a sick person."

I answered that there were many more Christians than she thought and that beyond the Soviet Union there were even national leaders—such as the President of the United States—who were Christians.

"The Soviets will arrive at the rotten West and cure everyone," Butkevich boasted. "Christianity is a symptom of schizophrenia."

Yet, in spite of her, there were elements of the prison that weren't all that horrible. I had a good bed, good pillows, a table and chair, a reasonable mattress. Compared to some places it was a penthouse. It wasn't really solitary but rather a single room. Through certain cooperative nurses and doctors, I was able to establish contacts with people on the outside, passing out information to such media organs as Voice of America and Radio Free Europe. The information pertained to the treatment of political prisoners. Olena came by and the KGB noted that every time she did, something seemed to make its way to a radio broadcaster. They began following her and interrogating me. They slapped my face and injected me with caffeine.

My father died on March 20, 1978, but I didn't find out about it until 1980. I was still in cell 21—isolated completely from the world—when Butkevich had called me to an office and locked the door. Quietly, she took out some documents. First she mentioned that they were going to be prescribing new medicines to "help" me, then she turned to the window, which was fogged up, and scribbled on it that my father had died. Strange, aren't they? Then she began shouting that I wasn't cooperating and that I had to cast away my religion.

I later learned that my father had experienced a full Christian rebirth. He went to Confession before he died, and while the Communists wanted a funeral with music and banners, he had expressed the desire to have a priest bury him. When the people learned of that—a leading Ukrainian Soviet wanting a priest!—they were galvanized. Many people attended my father's funeral and it is a cross—not the red star—that marks his grave.

I don't want to say much about it, but I always wondered if my father's death was a natural one. My mother claimed he died of liver disease, but I suspected he had been poisoned by the Communists.

That same year, on June 17, I had a most peculiar dream. It was a time of internal struggle at the Kremlin between factions led by Brezhnev and Andropov. There was also a third faction, composed of former Khrushchev loyalists. It was a dream and yet I wasn't really asleep. I saw Moscow and limousines arriving at a large building. Once more I was flying above it all. Out of one of these limos came two leading Communists, Fedor Kulakov, who was a member of the Central Committee, and Petro Shelest, a former secretary of the Ukrainian Communists. I was there watching but these men—political has-beens—couldn't see me. Shelest says to Kulakov, "We have to be very careful and not trust Andropov."

Kulakov says, "Josyp is flying over us. And he'll tell us if there is danger from Andropov."

And Shelest answers, "We shouldn't have dragged the son of Michael into this. He has to take revenge for his father."

I saw a black cloud looming toward us and I understood that if this black cloud caught me I would fall and wouldn't be able to fly. I saw Andropov's car approaching but I didn't see Andropov. Yet, I recognized some of the people who had been in the KGB and I knew they had allied themselves with him.

In my mind was the thought that they had betrayed my father. Just then, the black cloud burst around me and I fell to the ground. I landed near a wall, in a flower bed.

Through the flowers all I could see were boots and shoes passing by—civilian and military. Then I saw a man approach Kulakov and shoot him in the mouth. This dream was so intense that I was under its influence the rest of the day.

What did it mean? We will wait and see. I don't believe it was meaningless.

The drudgery of confinement wore on and for much of the time I was forbidden to write or paint. I always enjoyed sketching or working with oil paints, and it was difficult when they took my pencils and paper from me.

I also dabbled in poetry. I would like to share excerpts of one poem called "My Melodies":

> *I carry the cross of illusions, and I mark my time*
> *on this, the thorny path of expiation...*
> *My being, like a dog, continues to whine—*
> *but mutely—there's no sensation.*
> *I carry the cross of illusions like one condemned;*
> *obstinately pulling shadow to light—*
> *and from the sides: he's damned, he's damned!*
> *resounds with malice and with might.*

I didn't know it then, but by now the political atmosphere was starting to change around me. The Ukrainian Catholic Church and numerous Christian Churches in Europe had risen to my defense. So had Pope John Paul II, who obviously had heard of my plight. Amnesty International also knew of me, and I also had support from the Dutch, English, and French embassies. The attitude of prison officials began to improve as human rights became an international issue. Much to my surprise, it was announced that I would soon be released. I was anxious for freedom not only because I was needed by the Church, but also because our first daughter had been born. Marianna was already three.

It was after a review of my case in October of 1980 that I was moved back to Berehovo, the provincial psychiatric hospital with an improved regime. I was allowed to grow my hair and wear civilian clothes and Olena could visit every day. The doctors were relatively friendly and were asking me how I would behave in the free world. "Tell us, if you're released, what will you do during the day?"

I said I had a wife and child and would live and work for them.

They asked if this meant that I would become involved in further political activity.

I answered that a person who was as sick as I was would not have the energy for such activities.

They told me to remember one thing: "When you're free, you may say nothing good or bad about the special prison." They asked if I considered anything they had done to be torture, and I coyly replied that it was better where I was than where I had been.

They weren't quite ready to set me free, however, and before they did, I had another unusual experience. It happened on April 12, 1981. I'm going to quote here from a letter I wrote to Olena:

> "I've written you before that almost every night there is a strange light over my head that seems to be shining in from the window. I have remained silent about this because I don't want the psychiatrists to use it against me. You yourself know that one should not say anything in a psychiatric ward. But April 12, Mary, an older nurse, was on

duty (she's one of ours) and I spoke at length with
her and then went to sleep. There is also a worker
named Maria, and she witnessed the event. After
midnight a light began to shine. It was shining
with a silvery-blue gleam into the room. It's hard
to say where it came from because we could see
no source of light high in the sky. The silver blue
light began to spread throughout the room, fad-
ing and becoming brighter. Maria stood at the
entrance (there is no door to my room in the ward)
and asked, 'Are you sleeping?' I answered, 'No.'
She called out, 'Our Lord, do you hear us? Forgive us sinners.' She fell to her knees and began
to pray. I did the same at my bedside. The light
disappeared as suddenly as it had appeared.

I quickly fell asleep and in the morning I helped
Maria distribute medicine to the sick, saying nothing of this to anyone. At the end of her shift, Maria
said she would go to a priest and tell him what
we had seen. She was convinced this was God's
grace visiting me in the form of the Holy Spirit.
She asked that I not talk about it. It's hard to
describe the events because I don't have the words
to describe them. When I close my eyes, I see
everything in detail but how can I convey this in
poor human words? I don't know, but when I see
this light and it surrounds me, a sense of deep
grief overwhelms me and the tears well up in my
eyes. I'm very weak during prayer. I would
describe my state as being ill and at the same time
uplifted. I can't convey it in words..."

There were a number of times that I found myself illu-
mined by that strange light. It appeared over the course of
several months and when it did, I experienced a warmth
that was touching and deep. It also seemed to bring along
the fragrances of fresh milk and cut hay that seem to follow
me.

I was haunted not only by manifestations of the supernatural, but also by prison memories. I couldn't forget my
encounter with the Swedish diplomat, Raoul Wallenberg.
And ever since that exchange in 1970, I had endeavored

to find out what I could about him. A Lithuanian patriot, whom I met in 1973 at Sechovka, told me he too had seen Wallenberg, but many years before, at an Arctic camp called Norilsk. The patriot, whose name was Bogdonas, was also imprisoned with Wallenberg in 1953 at a special hospital in Kazan. He said the Soviets were "curing" Wallenberg of his megalomania—of his claims to be a diplomat. Beyond the borders of the USSR, people knew I had met Wallenberg and later I gave details of what I had seen to his family. I was obsessed with Wallenberg because while his chauffeur died in 1948, I believe the old diplomat may still be alive.

The Soviets were terribly nervous when they heard indications that I was talking about Wallenberg. Officials from Moscow arrived and posed the question, "Did you really see Wallenberg?"

I said, "No, I didn't see him, I don't know anything."

"Terelya, think about it. You can tell us the truth."

"I am telling the truth. I didn't see any Wallenberg."

"Who thought of the story that you saw him? You know that you have sat for this reason in these cells."

I continued to deny it. The Soviets were unbelievably paranoid about anyone sending reports of the diplomat. They executed people who saw him, or at least stuffed you for years in solitary. "I will from this day forth never speak of it again, because I have not seen anything," I insisted. "I have not seen Wallenberg."

They left it alone—for now—and after a week I was set free. My release date was June 23, 1981. They called me into the office, handed me an internal passport, and gave me a bus ticket to the Carpathian village of Dovhe.

Soon after my release there was a family gathering attended by certain Communist friends from Kiev and L'viv. By this time my mother had moved to Prague, but maintained a secondary residence in Kiev. I began to demand that the officials gathered at this social event tell me the circumstances of my father's death. I didn't get very far. They told me only that he had taken ill while returning from a trip to Moscow. They said he had been hospitalized.

During the same discussion, I learned that Kulakov, the man who I had "seen" shot, had died at the time of my vision. But no one said he had been shot. When I described the dream to these officials one of them stood up, rubbing his hands.

Did Kulakov die a natural death, or was he killed in the same way other aging, useless, or otherwise awkward leaders have been quietly slain? I can assure you that there are many Kremlin intrigues that have never been exposed. There were always rumors, for example, that Stalin had poisoned Lenin.

Nor has the West realized that even in Russia, masonic lodges wield great clout. I believe Kulakov was wary of the masons and this is why they killed him. While *Tass* declared that he had died of a heart attack, and a second version of his death claimed it was a suicide after an attempted coup, I believe that is all a smokescreen, that he was shot. And whatever the case, it was the beginning of Andropov's rise to power.

Yuri Andropov! A sinister man, a product of the KGB. There are many who believe that he was the mastermind behind the attempted assassination of Pope John Paul II in May of 1981. There was certainly a connection to Bulgaria.

I went home to my small family and right away there were problems. Olena's landlady, who had been intimidated by local officials, would no longer let us stay there. They were trying to force me out of the province. A friend of a nun took us in for the time being. Because we had living quarters and my wife had a job, they had to allow me to register in that region. I found work with a brigade of woodsmen. We ground pine needles to make medical products and livestock feed. It was a good job because I earned a decent sum (much more than Olena did as a doctor) and because I could arrange secret meetings in the woods.

Soon the KGB got wind of this, however, and decided the job wasn't so good for me.

Nonetheless, in 1981 I was once more a free man—or at least as free as one could be in the Soviet Union. In some circles I was becoming known at the "Gray Cardinal," a power behind the Catholic underground. I was certainly working hard to resurrect the beleaguered Church. And I decided to remain very bold. Besides organizing the underground we began establishing units that could disseminate Catholic literature and establish contacts with Western broadcasters. Our continued goal: to let the West know we existed but were on the verge of liquidation.

We also strove to convert as many people as possible. In Georgia, there were Orthodox who wanted to establish relations with Rome. The problem was that the Georgian priests were married. Many Lutheran priests would also have converted to Catholicism but they too were betrothed. Our attitude was that we had to reunite Christians, and my staunch belief was that our Church was the true Church. The authenticity of the Catholic Church was eloquently expressed by a provincial Basilian superior, Father Nicholas, who died on January 15, 1979. In his last testament, he stated that, ''I remain always faithful to Rome, for when the apostle of the Slavs, Methodius, converted and baptized Slavs, they went neither to Peking nor Constantinople to proclaim themselves but made their declaration to the lawful successor of St. Peter, namely, the Pope...''

My eerie dream life also continued to unfold. On July 9, 1981, I was in Dovhe when I had a vision of the entire world covered by fog. There was a gray-black smoke billowing from the earth and from this smoke I saw tongues of fire. Once more I was flying. I looked to the ground and in the midst of a large, burnt field was a cement block building without windows—a huge building.

In the dream I entered the building, climbed the stairs, and went into a large room. I felt like I was covered with red velvet. In the middle of the room were three coffins. There were also stools, and on them were three men: Brezhnev, Chernenko, and Andropov. Brezhnev was all yellow— almost dead. Chernenko was very pale and holding a book in his hand. Andropov was holding a bottle and giving Brezhnev a shot of whisky to drink. He drank this with satisfaction but I realized it wasn't really whisky but some mysterious fluid. I was flying near the ceiling and they couldn't see me. But Andropov seemed to sense something. ''There's someone here and he's praying because I feel a fire burning in me,'' he said.

At this moment some very frightful people entered the room—very frightful. They took Brezhnev by the arms and placed him in one of the coffins. I was hovering but worried that at any minute I would fall. Again Andropov said,

"There's somebody here. Catch him and give him a year of prison. Let him know not to spy on us." I fell into the hands of these men, who laughed hideously. Then I saw myself on trial. I also saw Olena with a child in her arms. She was in the chambers telling me a little girl had been born a month ago.

Well, we did have our second child, Kalyna, in 1983. During the rest of 1981 and throughout 1982 I maintained a pro-Catholic writing campaign. I issued essays, declarations, articles, and other documents that eventually found their way to the West. These essays would later be used by Soviet authorities to give me another prison sentence. In August of 1981, in the Estonian city of Tartu, I prepared what a Soviet prosecutor would describe as a libelous text in which I attacked medical institutes, the MVD, and the KGB. Later that year I also wrote an essay that was entitled, "Humility and Opposition." At the same time I put together another "scandalous" article that the government described as calling out to the Russian emigrés to fight against Soviet authorities. At the end of December I prepared the text of a letter to the president of the Central Committee of German Catholics, who was also the Minister of Culture in Germany. In it I described the subjugation of Ukrainians. The Soviets were especially upset with my denial of Communism as an "historical reality."

"He spreads false information about the status of the faithful in the USSR and contemptuously scorns the peace-loving policies of the USSR," they were eventually to charge. "He called the Western countries to an economic blockade of the USSR and called upon the anti-socialist Christian forces to organize against the USSR. This letter, through channels we haven't been able to determine, went beyond the frontiers to be used by centers of massive propaganda."

The Soviets were referring to the fact that my documents were later aired over Radio Liberty and a German station.

Perhaps most upsetting was my organization of what we called the Initiative Group for the Defense of the Rights of the Faithful and Church in Ukraine. It was sort of an offshoot of the Helsinki "watch" groups, but with a more specific orientation. It was founded on September 9, 1982, in L'viv and it sought to extend earlier efforts at legalizing the Eastern Rite Church. We were trying to bring Catholics out of the catacombs and included in the first meetings were such people as Stephania Petrash Sichko, who was with me in good times and bad, and Father Hryhoriy Budzinskyi.

The Initiative Group grew increasingly skilled at disseminating information and during the 1980s we printed many documents that were delivered throughout the Soviet Union. How did we do that? We would take ten copies of a document or newsletter to each of the provinces, where regional groups would then surreptitiously make many more copies of them. Some local organizations had their own photocopy laboratories.

The same month as we founded the Initiative Group, I prepared a letter to the Central Committee of the Ukrainian Party. In it I complained about the persecution of our faithful and denounced the Soviet Union—which the Soviets interpreted as a call to destroy their nation. The letter was written in the Lithuanian city of Panevizhes. I was evangelizing in the villages or converting people in republics like Georgia.

I was everywhere and that much harder to find.

Sundays our people had to use Orthodox churches and sometimes a priest was there, but other times the worshippers were on their own. The Soviet army set up loudspeakers to play jazz during services in one village, Keretski, during 1982, and the villagers organized a strike to protest that. The following Monday, nobody went to milk cows or feed the poultry. The women told the authorities that they wouldn't work if they couldn't pray.

Naturally, I got the blame for it. I was known as the "fanatic from Dovhe," and I soon found myself in prison again. I was arrested during 1982 and shuttled between the prison at Uzhhorod and L'viv concentration camp HSP-7-385-30. I wouldn't see freedom again for a year.

On May 19, 1983, I wrote to Olena about two recurring discomforts: harassment by the guards and disputes with non-Catholics. The guards had found a book of Gospels that were hidden in my pillow; and if it wasn't trouble with the guards it was trouble with sects such as Pentecostalists and Baptists. We were soon enmeshed in all kinds of theological debate. Sometimes dozens of inmates gathered to hear us argue back and forth. Certain of these people believed they knew everything by virtue of their memorization of Scriptures, and I argued that memorizing passages wasn't enough; one also had to understand them in proper context. The Protestants were especially bothered by the claim that our Pope is infallible. I answered that except for Jesus and Mary, everyone has been a sinner. Popes are not sinless. But when it comes to issues of faith, they are indeed infallible.

I also toiled with personal thoughts. I wondered if I had discovered the meaning of my life, and I wondered whether imprisonment was a good enough sacrifice to God. I had become convinced that without sincere sacrifice we can not attain anything. I don't remember exactly, but Pascal writes about this. It was something like, "I don't believe in histories in which the witnesses did not bring sacrifices of themselves . . ."

I finished the letter by telling Olena about another dream.

"The Prisoners went to bed late," I wrote in 1983. "I fell asleep before dawn and had a strange dream. I'm in freedom and a large number of people came on a pilgrimage. In the dream I see a strange light over a church. There was a wire fence surrounding the church. I fell to my knees before the cross and this light stood over me and the thought came to me that this light was the grace of God. I felt very good. I really felt that light as if it were alive and I smelled the fragrance of fresh hay and heard the voice of a woman. 'Have you seen the face of God? If you haven't seen it you shall see it . . .' I awoke full of confidence, and the whole day I felt good. I am not able to describe all of this now but I felt filled with a strange strength. There are things you cannot talk about when you are among skeptical faces. Glory be to Jesus. I am praying for you. Josyp."

L'viv proved to be the setting for dreams and visions more extraordinary than anything I had experienced since the apparitions a decade before. In October, I wrote Olena of another incident. I had been placed in solitary for 15 days. The officials had been questioning me about the death of my brother Borys, who shot himself in Polijana rather than be captured by the militia and MVD. (He had died on June 10, 1982, for the cause of nationalism.)

Anyway, I was languishing in solitary with two other men. One was a young drug addict and the other an old thief. My first days in solitary were always filled with conflicting thoughts that gnawed and ate away at me. Had I acted properly? Was it wise to resist all the time and keep getting sentenced to solitary?

Here I had 15 days again. But I was consoled by a lucid dream. I saw a great green forest, and it was difficult to scramble through the thickets. I saw a wooded glen brightly illuminated by the sun. I was all torn from the thorns and branches but I made my way to the center of the glen.

There I heard a beautiful choir. It was the angels singing. How do I know this? How does a child know his mother is his mother! I looked and saw a golden throne above me and on this was Christ the King. His nose was long and thin and he wore the expected beard. All around the throne there was singing. I knelt down and began to pray. Jesus stood up and from his side I saw a white cincture and on it the inscription, "King of kings, Lord of lords." But the end of His cincture was tainted with blood. I was very much afraid but the singing comforted me.

Blood was flowing like a river stopping just before my feet. I was terrified. The fear paralyzed my will. I heard the blood speaking to me. "The Lord Himself is with you, what are you afraid of? Do you know the Lord blossoms like the tree of life at this time of year?"

I awoke in a fit of perspiration. I was back in the cell; the dream was over. But right away I noticed it: Two fingers on my right hand were bloody. There was actual blood on me. I felt myself all over but I had no cut or infection.

It was my twelfth day of solitary. The whole day I was half asleep. I didn't want to eat. I gave my ration of bread to my companions. The old thief looked at me and said, "Josyp, you're strange today. When you come close to me I feel warmth."

That evening I was released, three days before I was supposed to be.

In December of 1983 I had another dream in which I saw myself called to an *Ovir* office, where passports are issued. A man in a gray suit turned to me and gave me documents for exit from the Soviet Union. He had a chain hanging from a velvet button. Remember this dream, because it comes into play later.

But the most dramatic vision was described in a letter to Olena on July 17, 1983. I was down in spirits. A prisoner who had recently converted to Catholicism had mysteriously died (the authorities implied it was suicide), and I found myself with another stint in solitary because religious articles had been found in my possession. They allowed me to take soap and my toothbrush. I don't know why but I wasn't placed in the usual cement cell. I was put in one with a wooden floor.

I was tired, struggling to fall asleep. I woke up to a sound at the door. It was the supervisor, who called out that I was sleeping at the wrong time and I would get another ten days of solitary.

I stood and began walking because my legs were freezing. It was damp and raw in the cell. After supper they gave me hot water and bread but the next day only cold water. I had buttons on my shirt and I was saying my Rosary on them.

I was very tired so once again I crouched in a corner. I don't know whether I fell asleep or was wake. I saw myself in Zarvanystya. It was night. I saw myself in the center of a meadow and all of a sudden an intense light illuminated the meadow and I recognized a familiar aroma spreading around me. The odor was like apple blossoms.

A large white eagle came and settled on the field and told me I should not fear. In the distance I saw an old man dressed in white. I remember only his face. And he said to me: "Why are you so troubled? Suffer and do not give in because you are under the protection of the Mother of God and after your release from prison there is a bright road spreading before you. The Church will rise."

I asked who he was and he said he was a servant of the Lord. "I know you and you know me," he said.

His voice continued in this dream or vision. "The Lord is now gathering the good men against the evil," he said. "The world would long ago have been destroyed but the soul of the world would not allow this."

I asked what he meant by the "soul of the world." He said the soul of the world is composed of the Christians. "As the soul preserves the life of the body, so do Christians preserve the life of the world," he added.

The old man went on to give me a long message, and I related it all to Olena. The man told me rebellion against God extended across the world and apostates were presenting themselves as prophets. "There are many false teachings and false churches," he said. "And the false churches are preparing for the degeneration of the peoples. There are many pious people who are confused and are falling into the darkness of false beliefs or faiths because people have lost the true faith. Even worse times are approaching than the time of Luther. There are many faithful and even members of the hierarchy who will fall into neo-paganism. You shall be in liberty soon and do not look around but take yourself to work. God needs fervent and constant sons. Prayer will help you to find a solution to difficult situations. In four years you shall meet the Pope and his Cardinals and they will listen to you. A year later great miracles will take place and the testimony of hundreds of thousands of Christians of the true faith will verify your words. The Pope will call you once more but bad priests and apostates will confuse and cause problems for the Holy See.

"You shall go through the ways of the world and give witness, and in the end God will punish the apostates because only through this punishment will God be able to bring man back to sound reason. And when the faith and love shall be reborn, Satan will begin a new persecution of the Christians. Times of persecution will begin, of priests and the faithful. The world will be divided into the messengers of God and messengers of anti-Christ. After the great revelations of the Virgin Mary, renewal of love of Christ will begin. You will see the rapid rise of devotion to the Immaculate Heart of Mary."

I asked him whether I would still be in prison, and this

ancient, celestial man answered, "Yes, but not for long because God has other plans for you."

I asked again, "Who are you? What is your name?"

His answer: "I'm a servant of God, the archangel Michael."

Tears streamed down my face. When I came to I didn't know if I had dreamed it or really seen it.

Meanwhile the guards smelled the aroma of apples and began searching the cells. But of course there were no apples to be found.

Chapter 15

GENTLEMEN
OF THE JURY

I wonder how many other prisoners, if they were alive to tell their stories, found consolation in events of a supernatural nature. It was obvious that during the high reign of the Red Dragon, God in His mercy was quietly intervening.

Inside and outside of the gulag, Christ, through His mother, was preparing a rescue and a message. The humanists will never accept this, and the secular intelligentsia will mock the very possibility of a supernatural mission. But that's what seemed to be taking shape and I leave it to the political scientists to explain why they could neither foresee nor rationalize the sweeping changes that were to come in Eastern Europe and the Soviet Union.

When I left the gulag it was like leaving one prison for a larger one. Everyone under Communist rule was an inmate. I was released from L'viv on December 26, 1983, and this time I would remain in "freedom" for a year and four months. I was traveling everywhere. We were organizing a large number of underground churches and making journeys through all the Ukraine, as well as to Georgia, Latvia, Byelorussia, and Lithuania.

While I was imprisoned, a group of Catholics, including Mychajlo Danylash, had already decided to start publishing the *Chronicles of the Catholic Church in Ukraine*. Naturally it was a clandestine publication, and its job was to record the devastation of churches, the abuses heaped upon believers, and the arrest of priests. The first issue was printed about two weeks after my release, on January 14, 1984. The publication was enshrouded with great solemnity. An underground bishop celebrated Mass. Soon the *Chronicles* was in the underground pipeline. Before I was rearrested we got 12 issues out.

Our *Chronicles* reached publications as far away as *The Christian Science Monitor* in America. As the *Monitor* reported on March 6, 1985: "A Soviet *samizdat* (underground) journal on religious dissent in the Western Ukraine that has recently reached the West could prove to be a source of considerable embarrassment to the Kremlin."

There was much to report upon. Persecutions were still in high gear. Between 1984 and 1985, 35 more churches in Western Ukraine alone were turned into museums, funeral parlors, or piles of rubble. The same was true elsewhere. In Smolensk, the Church of the Transfiguration was transformed into KGB archives.

I was too busy evangelizing and publishing to care about being arrested again. I converted the president of the Helsinki group of Georgia, and the Georgian Catholics began their own newsletter. We passed on an immense amount of information to the free world and the Ukrainian press began discussing this. Officials in Rome established a Ukrainian Catholic bulletin that reached the United States and Canada.

I also made an appeal to the general secretary of the United Nations, Javier Pérez de Cuéllar. Excerpts from my letter:

"Forty years have passed since the end of World War II and we see that we will not be returned to the past. People on our small planet are directing their efforts to peace and mutual understanding. But we see that desire is not enough. In the city of L'viv, in the Ukraine, there was a concentration camp during the time of war, near a cemetery. There the Hitlerites destroyed more than 100,000 people of different nationalities and among these, 920 Jews. After the war, the Soviet Russian armies occupied Ukrainian lands and on the spot of this concentration camp they built one of their

own twice as big as the one used during the war.
This camp continues to exist to the present day.
On May 29, 1984, the Ukrainian Catholic priest
Father Potocniak, a Basilian, 72 years old, was
killed. The number of the prison is VL-315-30.
"We members of the Initiative Group for the
Defense of the Faithful and Church in Ukraine
appeal to you personally, that on the territory of
this former Hitlerite camp, and now a Soviet concentration camp, that a monument be raised to
the victims of Russian-Stalinist and Hitlerite genocide. People of goodwill remember and do not forget that the Russians are conducting an
unproclaimed war against the Ukrainian nation.
They robbed us of our past to deprive us of our
future."

It was also signed by Vasyl Kobryn and Father Budzinskyi.

As usual, the KGB was everywhere I turned. I was living
in Dovhe and the agents had a small truck parked day and
night near my home. They picked on anyone who came
to see me. Although I wasn't beaten seriously, I was roughed
up and provoked on any number of occasions. My protection was my growing notoriety and the fact that diplomats
were inquiring about me.

The KGB tailed me everywhere, which ironically made
me feel safer when I had to travel at night on public transportation. But the agents were not exactly a hallmark of
bravery. Once, on the train to Carpathia, a bunch of hood-
lums wearing jackets and no shirts came aboard. They liked
to pick on old women or steal kerchiefs from local peasant
girls and jab cigarettes into their skin. I turned to one KGB
officer and told him to do something.

He was afraid because there were 15 of these punks and
they had chains around their hands. I got up and started
yelling in criminal slang.

This act of aggression startled and scared them. They
calmed down and we started talking. We didn't stop chat-
ting until Lavochne. They had heard of me, and I ended
up getting some of them to come to a place of pilgrimage.

The organization, Young Catholic Action, also worked

with punkers and converted at least three hundred of them. We taught our people to spread the Good News everywhere. I printed instructions on how Catholic activists should behave and urged them to carry books of religious instruction when they boarded buses or trains.

During the summer of 1984 I was traveling from L'viv to Carpathia on a bus packed with villagers, a few intellectuals, and a militia commandant from Muchakiv. I had a Bible and two L'viv university students who were with me had rosaries in their hands. One woman asked, "Is that a Bible you have in hand?" She asked if she could hold it in her hands. She said she had heard of it and simply wanted to touch it. I began to discuss Scripture.

Then I began debating with the commandant, who was in civilian clothes. "What trinity do the Communists have?" I asked rhetorically. "I will tell you: Marx, Lenin, and Engels." I said that the prophecies tell us Satan will try to ape what Christ's Church does, and that in the place of Christ will be anti-Christ. Satan is an idea that Lucifer gave to the world and an idea that is spread through people. I explained who anti-Christ was—those who bow down before the triad of Marx, Lenin, and Engels. At every Communist center there is a little room and, in a corner, a table draped with red cloth with a bust of Lenin. It's Satan imitating Christ's altar.

I began explaining who the anti-Christ is—a person who willfully and deliberately steps out against God. I think the founder of Communism in Russia, Vladimir Ilyich Lenin, was one anti-Christ referred to in the Bible.

Consider some facts: Lenin's mother was named Maria. That mimics Christ's own mother's name. Her full name was Maria Blank, and her mother's name was Anna. From the prophecies we know the anti-Christ was or is to be the illegitimate son of a Jewish woman, from birth different from anyone else. Maria Blank's father, Alexander, a doctor, was a converted Odessa Jew. Some think he may have been born in the Ukraine. Her mother was a German Lutheran. Maria married a Russified Kalmuck, Ilya Ulyanov. He was in his thirties then; Maria was given in marriage. Anna often went to the meetings of the brotherhood of Masons. The main themes of talk at such sessions were anti-religious in nature.

The prophecies say that the mother of the anti-Christ shall identify or tie in with people of ill-repute. It was in this masonic movement that Maria was filled with ideas of skepticism and cynicism. This is how she later educated her own children.

In 1170, St. Hildegard prophesied that an unclean woman would conceive an unclean son and the same deceitful serpent that deceived Adam would overcome this child so that there would be nothing good in him. The unclean woman is a woman with an immoral mind. The serpent is Marxism. The father of the anti-Christ was or is supposed to be a servant who shall leave a Muslim-like faith and accept Christianity. And, indeed, the biological father of Lenin was a convert Kalmuck who had been born in territories where—until priests came—there had been a shamanistic type of religion. The area was known as Astrakhan. It used to be Mongol territory, and in time these lands fell under the rule of the Ottoman Empire.

This is the characterization of the father of Lenin: sharp, active, vengeful, jealous, pallid, short, a high and bulging forehead, straight and unkempt hair, black gleaming eyes. Despite his countenance, some describe the father of Lenin as gentle and jovial. Although he became a teacher, his family ancestry included serfdom. What obliged Maria to marry a man she didn't love? Muslim people were subhuman, according to that day's thinking. She became the wife of a teacher and Kalmuck.

Maria was very calculating and self-controlled. She did only what she wanted. She was silent and sly with beautiful dark hair. She loved to read but did not like poetry. Her hobby was the occult. She didn't believe in God. She considered faith in God as the folly of her age. At times she would go to church because it was a custom. Let me repeat, the prophecies tell us the anti-Christ will mimic the person of God. Maria gave birth to her son on April 22, 1870, in Simbirsk. Her name was Mary, like the Virgin Mary, and her mother was Anna. The son's name was Vladimir—the one who rules the world.

What was Lenin like as a child? He was tempestuous. He was a chronic liar. He broke toys. He screamed at the top of his lungs. He tortured animals. He especially liked a song called "The Little Goat" about a helpless young goat eaten by wolves. Vladimir sang the last verse with a fierce look on his face, according to biographers. He bellowed triumphantly, "And there was nothing left for granny except the little hoofs and horns." He also sang the aria of Valentin from Gounod's *Faust*. He avoided contact with schoolmates and one director wrote to Kazan University that the young Lenin showed a chilling remoteness and an alarming lack of ordinary humanity. One evening his sister heard him muttering to himself and realized he was talking nonsense—delirious, like he was talking to another world, in an unknown language. The spell passed, and he grew to become the Soviet godhead, deceiving much of the world. In an *Izvestia* article Karl Radek, himself a Jew, declared that Lenin was a "Messiah who led the proletariat out of Egyptian bondage."

In many ways, Lenin was a false messiah and an anti-Christ.

Back to where I was: Two weeks after the bus debate I had another experience on public transportation. I was going to Svalyava and had bundles of literature with me. From Svalyava, I was to go on to Dovhe. Nine kilometers before Svalyava, in Poljana, a group of militia and KGB boarded the bus. My heart leapt because I had two suitcases with me. It wasn't just religious literature but also nationalist material, and for this you got 15 years.

I moved a distance from the suitcases and though I was taken to the procurator's, they couldn't prove the literature was mine. I caught them on a technicality: they had let the other passengers go instead of securing proper witnesses against me.

It was also during the summer of 1984 that I came up with a fairly radical idea: to form a group of army types to try and spring Raoul Wallenberg from Vladimir Prison.

I still knew where that poor old diplomat was. They kept him in the surgical divison, cell 53.

How to get him out? There were several ideas. Some of the proposals I rejected because they involved gunfire. That would simply not work. We might be able to get him out of that unit by using guns, but I knew that if someone fired, causing noise, we would never get him out of the prison itself. I began studying the possibility of slipping Wallenberg out secretly. I had already examined the prison from the outside—all the entrances and exits. I watched the place and took pictures of the gates. One day, we saw them take out a coffin. Near the prison was a cemetery. I began thinking about sneaking Wallenberg out in a coffin. There were two men who dug the graves and I walked by with a woman, pretending to be a passerby. I asked off-handedly how they buried the dead. I learned that they leveled the grave even with the ground and drove a big spike next to it, two or three meters tall, with a little number attached on a hook at the end. I learned that the little number remains there for three years in case of exhumation.

I returned home and had a conference with my group. I told them we could get Wallenberg only if we could supplant a criminal scheduled for burial and put Wallenberg into the coffin. Wallenberg was in the hospital, which made matters much easier. All we needed was some money, which was in very short supply. I went back to Vladimir, established contacts with a prison doctor I knew, and got additional information from her. She was a pathologist who did autopsies. Everything was planned—we were ready to initiate the jailbreak—but I was still woefully short of the necessary money. Suddenly, a series of new arrests erupted—arrests of our religious-initiatory group. I had to scurry back into the underground.

It was terrible, the other ways they persecuted us. For instance, if they found out you were a Catholic, they might find a way of taking your children to specialized schools for brainwashing and deprive you of your parental rights. Some of the Catholic children who refused to relinquish their religious articles were placed on bread-and-water diets. I went to visit one such "school," where the daughter of a friend was being trained. "Mr. Josyp, I'll run away from here with you," she said, pleading.

I said, "Look. I came here by foot. I have no car."

"You don't need a car," she insisted.

"Okay," I answered. "I'll wait for you."

The school (camp) was in an old monastery with a wall that reached to a plum orchard. I waited until the free time after lunch. The gates were locked and the supervisors were watching, so I had to be careful. I climbed one of the trees and was able to see over the wall. By this time the girl had organized a dozen or so other children, including two Baptists. "Mr. Josyp, we want to go with you too," they said. They pointed to a hole in the wall, an opening that had been used to throw garbage, but which the Russians had sealed with boards. The children removed the boards and often crawled out at night. Now they were crawling out for good. We took off by foot.

By this time the school administration had informed the militia that I had been there and we heard the military vehicles near a field of corn. We hid among the stalks and evaded them.

That was an adventure, but most of my work was organizing and administrating. My main tasks, of course, were with the initiatory group we had formed in 1982. We had an inner circle that maintained contacts with international organizations, and this had to be done in top secret because we could have been arrested for "spying." It was much more dangerous than just springing a couple kids from school.

During my stints of freedom, I also worked in Georgia, converting such nationalist leaders as Eduard and Tenghiz Gudava to Catholicism. In the 1920s there had been talks between Georgia and the Vatican and we tried to firm up those ties. Georgian Orthodoxy is closer to Rome than to Moscow.

I watched as resentment of Lenin continued to grow through the USSR. On November 7, 1984, there was the annual celebration of the "October Revolution" and in Borzhavsk and Keretsky, young boys came and smeared statues of Lenin with fecal matter or threw paint on them. In Svalyava, they painted a statue of Lenin red with eyes of phosphorous. And on Lenin's outstretched hand they hung a sign that said, "In 1985 we'll be living in Hell."

I was arrested again on February 8, 1985. You may think I was asking for it, but I believed the only way to beat back the Communists was to be uncompromising and relentless. They shuttled me between Uzhhorod and L'viv, secretly transporting me so I was unable to establish any outside contacts. They also removed a commandant who was suspected of aiding me.

During conversations with the KGB, I was told that should I repent and renounce my faith I would be released from trial. God gave me the thought to ask for a sheet of paper. On it I wrote a long declaration to the effect that I, son of Communists, now understood that the only really authentic Church was the Orthodox Church and that I was repenting.

They didn't know what I was writing. I left the paper on a table and went out for a walk. I knew they would read this. When I came back I had lunch and a whole bunch of officials arrived, including KGB agents and the second secretary of the Ukrainian Communist Party.

Because I was supposedly going to recant, they decided to have an open trial. It would be great public relations to have a leading Catholic activist openly renounce Catholicism. How their attitudes toward me changed! They gave me a good hospital meal three days before the proceedings and Olena was allowed to bring me a new shirt and a pressed suit.

They took me into the auditorium of the provincial court, where priests, nuns, and a mass of others were waiting. The top KGB echelon from Kiev and L'viv were also there because I was supposedly going to recant. The procurator came up and asked how I was going to behave. I said, "Well, I'll maintain a position and then come out with this statement of repentance."

It was just a ploy of mine to secure an open trial. By this time, I had torn the declaration to pieces and flushed it down the toilet, where it belonged. Then I wrote another declaration. When I stood up, I began a verbal attack on Moscow. You should have seen the officials in the room. They were squirming all over the place. The first day of trial was a total fiasco and the second day they brought a group of psychiatrists in by helicopter. I simply stated why I was a Catholic and what our convictions were.

They brought me back to prison and the hatred was tangible. They took me to the bath and had me change back into prison garb. I announced to them that from what the

Mother of God told me, in two years or so, despite their efforts, I would be free.

They laughed at me. They were talking about how I would never return.

The indictment was based upon Paragraph 62, Number One, of the Ukrainian SSR code. It was indictment 8200485. They were charging me, Josyp Terelya Mychailovych, with being "antagonistic to Soviet authorities with the goal of destabilizing Soviet authority and fomenting nationalistic sentiments."

Me, antagonistic?

What it amounted to was a diatribe against my activities from 1981 to 1985. They were putting everything into one neat package. They mentioned my essay, "Humility and Opposition," and a letter I had written with Father Anton Potochniak in August of 1982 to an international conference in Madrid. The text, which the Soviet prosecution described as "of libelous content against the government of the USSR with the intent of subversive action," beseeched other countries to press the USSR to legalize the Ukrainian Catholic Church and free people from the prisons.

What irritated the Soviet officials more than anything was that these articles and declarations found their way outside of the USSR. In charge after charge, the indictment brooded over the fact that my documents, "through unknown channels, went beyond frontiers to be used by centers of massive propaganda." The Madrid letter, for example, was broadcast over Radio Liberty.

These and other documents were cranked out on my little Olympia typewriter. The Soviets mentioned an essay entitled "Paschal Talk," which had been distributed among the residents of Dovhe, and a document I had sent to the Polish union leader (and now president), Lech Walesa. I noted to Walesa the persecution of religious in the Ukraine and the connection between Satan and Communism. This material was broadcast by Radio Canada on February 24, 1985. The prosecutor also noted that Vasyl Kobryn and I had prepared an open letter to Catholic Action in Switzerland.

As the Soviets heatedly described it, my correspondences proposed that a government in the Ukraine be formed without the involvement of Communists. Think of how reasonable that sounds today. One such commentary found its way to the *Ukrainian Word* in Paris and was broadcast by the Voice of America on March 14, 1985. Throughout the indictment they mentioned the *Chronicles* and were upset with my stand against the war in Afghanistan. They were incensed with a statement Kobryn, Budzinskyi, and I had sent on June 21, 1984 to the defense minister, Marshal Ustinov, concerning that horrible war and also political genocide in the Ukraine. Another letter, this time to the President of the Supreme Presidium (Chernenko), had given authorities an ultimatum for the liberation of 72 political prisoners.

Our correspondence to Chernenko is a story in and of itself. How did we get something to the President of the Supreme Presidium? It was through people who had access to the inner circle and were willing to risk their lives. Chernenko had come to visit a health spa in the Carpathians and an employee who changed bedding at the spa agreed to take our letter and slip it onto Chernenko's nightstand.

The KGB was beside itself with fury. The letter made it known that contrary to what the KGB might be telling him, Catholics still existed in the USSR, and it led to a meeting with several high-ranking officials who tried to mollify us by proposing that a Catholic Church be formed in the Chinese model—which meant without contacts with Rome.

"So through 1984 in the place of his occupation on a collective farm, in the presence of the director, Terelya continually adduced libelous actions against the USSR, against the payment system, and affirmed issues as if the Ukrainian people were subjugated and there was a so-called 'Russification' of the Ukraine," the prosecutor charged. "(He) continued his anti-Soviet activity during a conversation to which he was called at city hall where in the presence of the secretary at the mayor's office and inspector Starosta of the militia, he affirmed the low standard of life in the Soviet Union. Terelya called for struggle against social structures."

During the official investigation, I had told them that between 1989 and 1990, the kingdom of Satan would come tumbling down. At my sentencing they laughed at this statement and asked what 1991 would have in store for them. We'll have to wait and see.

Anyway, at that sentencing on August 20, 1985, the provincial court of Carpathia, under presiding Judge A. A. Stryzhak, in the name of the Ukrainian Socialist Republic, found me guilty of "systematic involvement with anti-Soviet propaganda with the purpose of destroying the Soviet authorities." I was given the maximum: seven years in concentration camps and five years of internal exile. The procurator indicated that they were ready to retire into chambers. The judge gave me a last word in self-defense.

I turned to the people and began to speak:

"He who lives in love, lives in God and God in Him. Today the judicial trial against me has been completed—not the first nor probably the last. This is the end of the twentieth century. The persecutions against the Christians, as in the first centuries, are not ending. Russian ethnocentrism has reached its apogee. The Ukraine is at the crossroads of its own self-contradictions. Christ, crucified by His colonizers, asks God: where shall I go, how shall we find the way; and the answer comes from within our hearts. Jesus is that road because only He is truth and light. All who go to the Father go through Jesus. There is no other way. They robbed Ukrainians of their history, their language, their religion. They oblige us to pray to strange gods. Whatever Ukrainian raises his voice in protest is immediately accused of treason and nationalism. The danger lies in this: that Russian ethnocentrism permeates our educational system and we see the trail of Russian ethnocentrism in the textbooks and the teachings in our universities, high schools, and colleges. These falsified textbooks will grant no mention of the three artificial famines in the Ukraine: 1921, 1932-33, and 1947. Even today's trial is conducted in Russian. The empire, whatever color we paint it, will always strive to uproot any foreign language that is used in these territories. The culture and the language of the conqueror is forced upon us. The normal course of a nation is disturbed. A Ukrainian,

robbed of his nationality and his religious faith,
does not understand his place in the history of
cultures and peoples. He has no desire to come
to understand his own reality. I am being judged
only because I dare to cry out, 'I am a Ukrainian.
I am a Christian.' "

Chapter 16

HELL
ON EARTH

They were sending me to camps in the Perm area, which many consider to be the worst in the Soviet system. If Vladimir and Hubnyk had their moments, what lay before me was Hell on earth. Certain of the detention centers in Perm, especially Kuchino Number 36-1, were not concentration camps but death centers.

Perm is located on the western side of the Ural Mountains. On the other side are the lowlands of Siberia. During winter the mercury drops well below zero. It was the kind of climate one did not seek for a *dacha*. Before I was shipped off, Olena managed to arrange a meeting with me. She brought along our children. Besides Marianna and Kalyna, there was now a boy we named Paul. He was just nine months old. It hurt to leave them.

I was transferred to Kharkov, where I was placed in solitary. I had never been in such a dark and damp cell, and it was so small I couldn't even stretch out my legs. With room only for me and the toilet bucket, it was like being kept in an outhouse. I spent two weeks there and then was moved to special prison ST-2-OD-6 in Kazan.

Kazan was a transfer point for Ukrainian dissidents. There I managed to make a Rosary out of bread and paint it nicely. Then it was on to Perm. For all I knew, I would never be returning.

To look at such camps is to see rows of solid fence topped with barbed wire. The barricades enclose peaked buildings that could be mistaken for army barracks. Perm was very dark, cold, and unpleasant in every way. Like Mordovia, there was a series of camps in the area. I spent time at Kuchino, Polovynka, and Vsesviatskaja. Initially, I was thrown into a cement room with twenty other people. The authorities came and forbade me to sleep in a dark corner. "Now you're in our hands," said one official. "No West will help you here."

I didn't know it, but on November 1, 1985, a petition signed by 151 U.S. congressmen was sent to the new Soviet General Secretary, Mikhail Gorbachev, asking for my release. The Soviet response, thus far, was to bury me that much deeper in its gulag. Two weeks later I was off to dreaded Kuchino. They took away my regular prison garb and gave me their own. The jacket was so thin you could nearly see through it—and I was supposed to go out in subzero weather with it. I was led down an alley and brought to a solitary building in the corner of the camp. It was for quarantine, they said, but I didn't like the looks of it at all. I began to rebel. The walls were coated with salt, dripping and malignant. I could see myself dying in that little isolated building. "Take me out of this room!" I shouted at the top of my lungs. "This is a punishment cell, not quarantine."

"We know how to deal with you," was the response. "We know who you are."

I attacked the security guard and brought two clawed fingers to his face, threatening to poke out his eyes. "I know you have taken me here to kill me, but while I still have strength I'll take a few of you with me," I screamed.

They called Major Dolmatov, who came and asked why I wasn't going into the room. He took me through the barracks to prove to me that all the other rooms were taken.

I refused to work in the yard and on the fourth day of my little strike they gave me only three hundred grams of bread, 63 grams of fish, and two hundred grams of vegetables. Everyone in the zone knew that "Terelya" was there. By this time they put me in the severe regime zone, Number 36-1. They said they would get back at me and that

I wouldn't get away with what I had in Mordovia. This wasn't Dnipropetrovs'Ke, either. They said I would never get white bread or be able to get news out to the free world. "I have a camp that even a mosquito can't pass through," boasted Major Vakulenko.

I responded with defiance. "I've been in prisons where even air can't pass through and I've gotten out."

Meanwhile the Soviet press was writing terrible stories about me and Borys, my deceased brother. They began denouncing me as a nationalist who hid under the cover of Christianity. What did I care? Only a fool believed what was in the Soviet newspapers.

I began writing a declaration that demanded transfer into the work zone so I could make money for my family. Colonel Khorkov arrived. He was in charge of MVD detachments in all the Perm region. They were all nervous. Somehow news of where I was had hit the free radio waves. Khorkov and his henchmen wanted to know how the information had gotten out. A gypsy name Captain Rak was sent to provoke me and I received 15 days of solitary. I began to shout, "The Russians are killing me!"

Rak and another guard jumped me and twisted my arm behind my back. They were trying to break it. I finally managed to kick the security guard and Rak began punching me. There were a number of guards converging on me. The commandant came with KGB. I was taken to solitary, the coldest cell, number three.

Yet still, I prayed. Yet still, I survived. Still I remained defiant. When a group of KGB officers arrived from Kiev and Moscow, we fell into a debate. It was over the meaning of Christianity. One KGB officer insisted that Jesus was talking about the poor in money—not the poor in morality and spirit—when he spoke of those who are hungry and thirsty. The Church distorted the teachings of Christ, he said. Christ was a leader of the proletariat. I retorted: "You have twisted the teachings further by trying to claim Jesus was the first to teach communism."

They threw challenges at me and I kept volleying answers back. "Why doesn't your Jesus help you? Here we throw you into solitary, we beat you, and Jesus doesn't help you."

It was the old, hackneyed refrain. I answered that when

I prayed, my mind was granted peace and I didn't experience their prison.

Next came the question of love. "Can a good and meek man be so without love? Look at me. I'm a good man by nature but I don't love you. Is this a sin? Christianity teaches a schizophrenic love—love for everybody. Psychiatrists prove this is impossible. I don't need the love of Jesus. I can love without Jesus. People like to eat well and dress well. How many people are there like you? People like you are masochists who find pleasure in being tortured."

"What can I say about you unbelievers?" I responded. "It's not to be wondered that Christ prophesied that those who do believe would be persecuted for His name's sake."

A colonel laughed. "What do you want, that the people should persecute us and then the people will believe, and then we will believe?"

I told him I was talking about Christians. He said, "We don't believe Christ existed or that God exists. That's for childish minds. Do you think we can ever find ourselves in a situation that will make us believe?"

I answered, "It's a matter of being worthy of Christ."

One of the KGB said, "According to your Christian doctrine, I, a KGB officer, am a sinner. What are you going to do about it? These twenty years you have spent in prison, what benefit is it? You can't answer it—why have you wasted all these years."

I answered: "Each soul makes an examination of conscience daily. The issue is not physical suffering. We seek to purify our consciences. And the greatest sufferings are moral sufferings. You officers should acknowledge your sins and do penance for your sins. You claim to be good, so do penance for your sins."

They commented that God was a "Jewish myth."

Eventually they became violently angry. It was all a provocation. They wanted to get me into a Jewish issue. My comment on the Jews was that a truly Christian Europe would not repress those of Jewish faith. They brought up the point that most of the world was gentile, not Christian. I acknowledged that yes, this was our weakness.

"Josyp, you say the Catholic Church is a militant Church. How can this be if it is loving and tolerant?"

I said, "Yes, it *is* tolerant, but in going among the wolves
of the world, our Church has become militant."

"We've come to the conclusion we have to punish you,"
I was informed. They took out a blue document, a decree
from the procurator. It was August 3, 1986. They read me
a sentence of two months of solitary.

I was not a well man and was in and out of the Perm
hospitals. The KGB had once boasted that if I ever got out,
I would spend the rest of my life paying for medications.
They were right. I was physically broken. I needed heart
medicine as it was, and I had high blood pressure and joint
problems. I suffered miserably from the cold and damp.
When I was able to read, I encountered massive headaches.
The climate in the northern Urals is not for the sick, and
I often had blood coming from my ears and throat.

All of this served to challenge my faith. I struggled to
remain firm but there were moments of doubt—when I complained about myself and my destiny. Prayer was my only
relief. Prayer gave me confidence and helped me remain
faithful to Jesus.

I am prone to angry outbursts and I realized this was a
sin. It's not given to everyone to patiently carry the cross.
Blessed are the meek! And how difficult it is to preserve
oneself from evil. I couldn't have sunken lower. My time
at Kuchino was nearly all in solitary, and my fellow inmates
were dropping like flies—a third of them between 1984 and
1986. Many of the deaths were intentional. The administration did just about nothing to heal the sick. They knew *perestroika* was about to arrive and they wanted to eliminate
everyone who might pose problems in a freer society.

During 1986 I was placed in the centralized hospital at
Polyvynka, where I had been many times before. At one
point I was to the far right of one wing and the Jewish refusenik, Anatoly Shcharansky, was to the far left. The rest of
the wing had been emptied. When Shcharansky was led
from the hospital I heard a guard say, "Shcharansky, with
your things." I knew they were taking him out and wondered what they would do with me.

There were persistent rumors that I too would be set free.
My cause had become familiar to such people as William
Casey, director of the CIA, as well as President Reagan, who

took my name with him for the summit with Gorbachev
in Iceland. Reagan always watched over the persecuted Jews
and Christians, and I had written letters to all kinds of foreign leaders: besides Reagan, Mitterrand, and even Chinese
Communist Party leader Deng Xiao Ping. Mitterrand was
the first to begin talking about me in 1986. Queen Beatrice
of Holland had also become involved.

The rumor was that Gorbachev, reacting to the demands
for my freedom, referred to me as a "common criminal."

Needless to say, I don't trust Gorbachev. I believe he is
a secret mason.

All the while, poor Olena hardly heard from me. In two
years, she received only six letters. The only way she knew
I was alive was because I was still mentioned on the radio
when there were broadcasts of anti-religious propaganda.
In April 1986, while in Hospital 35, I began to feel very
depressed. I felt as if there had been some kind of tragedy.
It went on for two weeks and I had trouble concentrating.
It was as if a black vacuum was swallowing me. Later, I
learned that my depression had preceded the nuclear disaster at Chernobyl. When we heard bits and pieces of the
news, it was very heart-wrenching. I painted my first picture of Chernobyl as an image of death—the world on fire.
Out of a skull emerged the Soviet snake.

A week later, I made another painting of an immense skull
with the atomic cloud and an open jaw with crosses in the
picture. Then I began painting a series focusing upon the
children of Chernobyl. All but one of my paintings were
confiscated.

The extent of damage near the nuclear reactor escaped
our initial comprehension. More than a thousand square
miles of farmland were contaminated, entire towns were
abandoned, and the loss of electricity was soon to cause
problems for an area that, in 1988, was the center for celebration of the millennium of Christianity. It was in the very
region of Chernobyl that the first Rus tribe, in 988, had converted to Christianity. Now, through greed and sloth, evil
forces had spread radioactivity there, poisoning the land
of the first Rus Christians and causing 37,000 children in
Byelorussia alone to develop pre-cancerous symptoms.

Behind bars, I was isolated from such news, including news of my own pending release. I knew something was in the wind, but no details. It turned into an excruciating waiting game. To occupy myself, I put up a picture of Lenin and prayed for his soul. The guards couldn't stand that and ordered me to take the picture down. "No," I said. "If I tear the picture of Lenin off, you'll give me another sentence. I want to see *you* tear the picture off so I can write a letter of complaint."

They gave me 15 days of solitary for disobedience. At the time, I was hooked to intravenous tubes and they took the tubes out, put me on a gurney, and it was off to punishment. Then I was moved to Camp 37, where the commandant was Major Zgogurin. His wife was a doctor who for some reason was friendly to me. She was intrigued by my history of escapes. But there wasn't much else in the way of cordiality. I was put into the camp hospital and forbidden to speak to anybody.

There I found myself next to a priest named Father Sigitas Tamkavichus who was editor of the underground *Catholic Chronicles* in Lithuania. There were close ties between us and the Lithuanians. They accepted many of our men into their seminaries. The KGB were very worried about this relationship and also the sisterly contact with Christians in Georgia, Armenia, Latvia, and Estonia. Their placing me with Father Sigitas was a ploy to eavesdrop on what we might discuss despite the rules.

We said nothing, although Father Sigitas did hear my confessions. I would pace back and forth in prayer and as we passed I would whisper my confession to him. He had a consecrated host in his vest pocket and even snuck me Communion. During my long stints in the camps there had been times when we had been able to celebrate Easter. Starting a few months before, we would begin stowing away sugar, garlic, and white bread, and we would collect butter from the hospitals and preserve it in salt. From these ingredients we would make things like cottage cheese, and at Mordovia we would even set up tables to celebrate. This goes to show you that there were some good guards working in the camps.

But then there were always the bad ones, and they were in evidence at Perm. "That bitch has heard your Confes-

sion," said an officer. "Terelya, tell us, what was your confession? Tell us or we'll put you on your feet for five years,
in such a way that you can never go to confession again."

A priest could have been charged under 138 of the criminal code for religious services. I flatly denied this allegation.

I established contact with an expatriated German nurse
from the Volga area and she snuck letters of mine out of
the Perm region. One was an open letter to be beamed on
Radio Free Europe. I kept it under my shirt and when this
woman came to put a mustard plaster on me, I slipped the
envelope into the sleeve of her dress. She took the letter
and mailed it from Siberia.

The letter discussed the fact that I was being given solitary again and it complained about the deprivation of religious articles. A contingent from Moscow arrived and began
talking to me. They took me into an office and informed
me that the issue of my freedom was at hand. I didn't know
it, but Shcharansky was out. I thought they had simply taken
him to another prison. "If you behave," they said, "you'll
soon be out too."

They didn't know when I would be released, but soon
I was taken to the hospital and given all kinds of food. I
knew immediately what was going on: they were trying to
fatten me so I would look healthy upon my release. I refused
to eat. They were setting white breat before me, and liters
of milk. Still I refused. They said they wouldn't release me
until I weighed 130 pounds. I was shuttled back and forth
between the hospital and solitary during 1986 and finally
I began to eat.

A new year arrived, 1987. It was to be the most dramatic
year of my life. Even though I still had many years to serve,
one night in February I was taken to the normal zone, and
then set free.

Chapter 17

WHERE ANGELS
PRAYED

Not in my fondest dreams could I have foreseen the super-natural sign that was about to manifest itself. Long vener-ated in the Ukraine, Mary had never forgotten us. She had been there all the while, waiting for her time. Now her time was coming. The century of Satan was drawing to a close. It was as if all that I'd experienced—the dreams, the visions, the visitations in my cell—was building to an unsuspected climax.

There was truly an invisible battle in progress and by the grace of God, I was positioned to give witness to it. Perhaps because our country was consecrated to her, Mary had long been a presence in the Ukraine. Throughout the nation are places of pilgrimage and magnificent icons showing the Vir-gin holding her precious Son. Many of these icons have been proclaimed as miraculous. They have smiled, frowned, and shed actual tears.

One such example is in the village of Zarvanystya (pro-nounced zar-van-eetza) in the district of Pidhaytsi, south-west of Ternopil. It is about eighty miles east of Hrushiv and the event that makes this otherwise obscure village noteworthy took place during the 13th century, when the Tartars were plundering cities like Kiev and ruining its churches. Many citizens were captured, induced into forced labor, or put to death. Few escaped. One of the survivors was a monk who, while fleeing the Tartars, came across a brook that was fed by a cool clean spring.

According to legend, the monk washed himself in the brook and then knelt by the waters to pray. That night, exhausted and in a deep sleep near the forest, he had a dream in which he saw the all-holy Mother approaching with a throng of angels. In the dream she presented him with a veil. Upon waking the next morning the monk noticed an odd bright light near the spring and approaching it discovered a radiant icon of the Virgin Mary. She was holding the Christ child in the picture. So powerful was his experience that the monk erected a chapel and although the Turks devastated it, the structure was subsequently rebuilt and many people, including a prince, were cured of disease by a visit there.

In a way, I felt like that monk. But now the oppressors were Communists, not Turks or Tartars. In 1960 they had destroyed the chapel at Zarvanystya and everything else they could lay their hands on.

For the moment, however, things were looking better. The Soviets were introducing certain ''reforms'' and once more I was on the way to freedom—miraculously sooner than my sentence dictated. They had taken me out of the Perm hospital at labor camp 389-37 to meet with the authorities. The other prisoners were separated so they couldn't talk to me. The commandant of the prison was there, and I was read my decree of release. What a glorious, unexpected moment. I was given an official pass so I could walk by all the guards. I knew that something very important had happened— heavyweight politics—because everyone was so full of fear.

A few minutes later the entry to the camp was opened and three civilians came, two of them KGB agents and the third a procurator who looked at his watch and said, ''Take him beyond the walls of the prison.''

The commandant informed them that I had refused to sign any documents.

''We don't need any signature,'' one of the KGB officers said. ''What the devil do you need a signature for? Release him.''

And with that I was led from Perm Camp 37. I was outside the barbed wire!

They gave me a train ticket to Moscow and said I could even hold a press conference if I desired. I had great difficulty believing all of this was actually happening. I feared it was some sort of provocation. I had a sentence of 12 years dangling over me and I had only served two years of it. I'd received almost no information from the free world and so I knew very little of the changes taking place in Russia.

They brought me to the train station in Chusova, where there were 21 other prisoners waiting. They were from camps 35 and 36 and still in camp uniform. I had dressed in civilian clothes.

"Josyp, how are you? Where were you this last while?"

It was like a reunion. They too were political prisoners, and we had been sprung as a result of the new attitudes in Moscow. It was evident that the KGB was very interested in us giving interviews to the foreign press. It was part of Gorbachev's new scheme of public relations.

But we decided not to go along with that. There would be no press interviews. We didn't want to take part in Soviet propaganda. While all of us were elated as the train moved through the dreary foothills, we still harbored apprehensions and great anxiety. The unfinished sentences hung over our heads like the sword of Damocles. We could be rearrested at any moment. And KGB agents, posing as ordinary passengers, sat in our car watching everything.

As long as we were in the Urals, our drab dress was not too different from the local workers. But when we got to Moscow the people on the streets massed around us. They could tell we were prisoners and some of them wept. Other Moscovites prodded us with questions. News of our release had been broadcast on the Soviet airwaves.

A group of women brought us fruit and flowers. "You're from Perm?"

"Yes, we are the political prisoners," I said. "I guess Gorbachev has some kind of special love for us."

An officer of the militia approached asking to see my documents.

"Let me see *your* documents," I retorted. "We are free people. We are free from the prisons where we were unjustly detained. I want to see your identification. You're a provoker."

I threatened to hold a press conference—and not the type Soviet officials had in mind.

The militia began to disperse but the KGB was still watching. We approached one of these "civilians" and I asked, "Why are you persecuting us? Why is the militia hounding us?"

"You're mistaken," he answered. "I'm not a KGB officer. I'm a civil engineer."

Sure. In a few minutes the KGB openly came out from the shadows and began dispersing the crowd.

We boarded taxis and I felt very ill. I still had problems with my heart. Before heading for Carpathia, I decided to rest for a week in Moscow, at the home of a Jewish woman who was a friend of the family. I telegraphed Olena, who couldn't believe her eyes. The father of her three children was coming back to Dovhe.

That evening Radio Free Europe, Voice of America, and BBC said an additional 22 prisoners were also set free that day. Although it was the dead of winter, there was definitely a thaw in Moscow.

When I felt better, I took the train to L'viv for a visit with Archbishop Volodymyr Sterniuk. He and others had already heard the news and were waiting for me. When I stepped out of the train, a mass of friends was waiting. Among them was Stepha Sichko and Vasyl Kobryn. Kobryn was now chairman of our initiatory committee for legalization of the Church and defense of all faithful.

The crowd waved embroidered scarves and the Ukrainian flag. Intimidated by our numbers, the militia kept its distance. I couldn't speak. I was crying too hard.

We went to the home of one of the activists and that evening met with Father Budzinskyi, the Studite monk who had co-authored the letter to Marshal Ustinov. The very next day, we started putting together the next edition of the *Chronicles*.

In effect, we were throwing down the gauntlet and announcing our resurrection from the underground. Because my release was arranged in the Kremlin, I knew I had a certain leeway I never had before. The local and regional officials wouldn't dare arrest me without enormous reason. If anything, they would wait me out.

The young Catholics and the traditionally strong believers supported my decision to pronounce the Church's legitimacy but those weaker in faith feared that we were acting too boldly and they spoke instead about "evolution" and "progressive" change.

No! We were coming out. We had been underground too long. We had a right to exist. We had survived the Nazi and Communist forces and had proven ourselves. We were Catholics.

Next I went to Lavochne in the Carpathians. About 3,000 people were waiting for me there. It was all overwhelming, but it was just a stop on the way to my native Svaljava and then to our current home in Dovhe.

The children were sleeping. My wife and friends were there. Olena didn't know exactly when to expect me. I'd sent another telegram but it hadn't arrived. Everyone threw themselves at me and it was wonderful to see Olena after two long years.

Almost immediately I started traveling from village to village, reclaiming churches that had been turned over to the Orthodox. The parishioners had never given up their roots and began driving out the Orthodox priests. That greatly upset the Soviets. They tried to talk with us—the KGB and Party officials—but I openly continued my evangelization.

There were threats that I would be rearrested, or that my house would be attacked. When the officials came to see me I told them that if they didn't like what I was doing they could indict me, but until they did I was going to continue writing, preaching, and protesting. I complained about the inadequate pension the peasants were given, and soon they were forced to give these people more equitable compensation. Provincial authorities began to fear that unless I was stopped they would lose their positions, and that led to death threats against me.

Meanwhile the press stepped up its efforts to declare me a nationalist. Again, they said I was merely hiding behind Church activities. It was an effort to demoralize and divide us. They also referred to me as a criminal recidivist and a schizophrenic.

While the Soviets invented stories to discredit me, I had the opposite problem with my followers. They began exaggerating stories about my mystical "powers" and how holy I was. I had never considered myself a man of special powers and was shocked when, after group prayer, people claimed to be miraculously healed. They also spread rumors that I could bilocate, but I knew of no such phenomena except for my "flying" during dreams. My talent wasn't mysticism but in converting the people—evangelism. And even this was exaggerated. If I went into a village and converted five or ten souls, rumor soon spread that I had converted a *hundred* there. The people brought me their children to bless, and while I hardly considered myself a healer, I prayed constantly for them. They were swarming all over our home—the sick, the depressed, the needy.

At home we had a family altar because it is my strong conviction that families must pray together. And the children must be brought to church, no matter how disruptive they are. Small children need such exposure and should be taught short prayers. The first one we taught my daughter Kalyna was, "On the hill, on the hill, Mother Mary lives."

Prayer is the most important component but, as I have stressed, it must be coupled with action. We visited churches that had been destroyed and logged the ruins of cemeteries and monasteries. We circulated petitions concerning the Chernobyl disaster, demanding full disclosure of the damage and health risks. We also petitioned for Raoul Wallenberg and began to prepare the May issue—Number 16—of the *Chronicles*. It was a hurricane of activity.

All this was possible only because of the new policy of *glasnost*, but that policy did not seem like it would last forever and despite the face it presented to the West, the USSR was still intolerant of religion. At the end of April 1987, when the Basilian nun informed me of the events unfolding in Hrushiv (again the pronunciation is hru-shoo), there was the debate on whether we should go there. The fear was that such an event would be blamed on us Uniates. The Soviets would claim that we had invented it. But we decided that whether or not we went to Hrushiv, the press would still denounce the apparitions.

And the compulsion to go—to see that same loving face that had materialized at Vladimir 15 years before—was all but irresistible. Was this truly a major apparition, or a case of suggestive imaginations? Were the people exaggerating this, just like they embellished stories about my "powers?" Was it an historical event that would compare to the apparition at the Ukrainian town of Seredne?

Seredne, like Zarvanystya, was famous for a Marian miracle. The date was December 20, 1953. Actually it took place in a nearby village called Dubovytsya. In a vision during Mass, a woman named Hanya saw the hill of Seredne and a spot where there had been small wells of clear water. She saw it all vividly, even though she had never actually visited the hill. As the vision continued she saw the Virgin Mary and the Virgin began to speak.

"My daughter, my daughter, my daughter, you see what a fullness of grace I possess. But I have no one to give my graces to, for there are so many daughters and sons that have turned away from me and no one asks of me in this jubilee year. I wanted to obtain a great forgiveness for poor sinners. Disaster is upon you as in the times of Noah. Not by flood, but by fire will the destruction come. An immense flood of fire shall destroy nations for sinning before God. Since the beginning of the world, there's never been such a fall as there is today. This is the kingdom of Satan. I shall dwell on this hill from which I see the entire universe and the many sinners, and I shall distribute my graces through this well. Who comes to repent of his sins and receive this water with faith, him shall I heal in soul and body."

Then the Mother of God supposedly added, *"Rome is in danger of being destroyed, the Pope of being killed. Rome must be renewed and raised through the hill of Seredne. The Catholic faith shall spread throughout the entire world. The sinful world with its sinful people is in desperate need of renewal."*

She ended with a haunting question: *"How shall this renewal come? Through whom and when?"*

Because of this vision we perceived an understanding of God's labors on our earth and we received the strength to resist evil and to rebuild our Church.

While Pope Pius IX declared Zarvanystya as a place of indulgences, the hill at Seredne, which is in the Ivano-Frankivsk region, has never received similar recognition. The reason for that may have been the false rumors which the KGB had spread about the site, and they were now trying to do the same thing at Hrushiv. Although I didn't research the historical details until later, Hrushiv had long been known as yet another place of pilgrimage. And once more, the Mother of God was involved. The accounts vary somewhat. According to one, the Mother of God appeared in the middle of the eighteenth century over the spot where the chapel was subsequently erected—more than two centuries before the 1987 apparitions. To commemorate the apparition, townsfolk planted a willow tree. This tree, feeding off a hidden spring, grew large and beautiful. An icon was hung from it in 1806. It was painted by Stepan Chapowskyi. Pilgrims came singing, praying, and placing candles in honor of the Virgin Mary. During the next century an opening developed in its wide trunk, and as the tree began to rot, water began to flow from the hole. The water was said to be cool and tasteful, and people who drank it swore to its healing powers. They came from as far away as L'viv and the western borderland to experience the curative waters.

The local governing authorities were anything but thrilled with such homage. There was plenty of religious oppression during the reign of the czars. Around 1840 they contacted a local hooligan named Justin Kina to breach the fence around the spring and dump decaying fruit, vegetables, and other rubbish into the pure water. According to legend, the Kina family was soon after destroyed, and an epidemic of cholera swept across Hrushiv, killing uncounted dozens of residents.

Again, Mary appeared in a dream. *"My daughter,"* she told one of the women, *"death is awaiting you too, but I want you to live. I beg you to clean the desecrated well, and have a Mass celebrated in dedication to Our Lord, so that death will cease throughout the village."*

The peasants talked about this dream in the village square and did as they were told, cleaning the well and thereby bringing an end to the horrible epidemic.

In 1856 a chapel was built around the spring and duly consecrated. It was called Blessed Trinity (or the Church of the Three Saints) because, in yet another seemingly supernatural occurrence, villagers spotted three apparitional candles flickering over the well. By 1878 a new chapel was erected and the walls were decorated with glorious murals. The chapel was blessed on the feast of Mary's Assumption and within a quarter of a century the Vatican had issued permission to Bishop Constantine Chekhovych for a benefaction of plenary indulgences to those who traveled to Hrushiv on certain holy days.

The people continued to come in increasing numbers, singing, reciting the Rosary, seeking penance. Even back then the authorities discouraged these pilgrims, dispersing crowds. But 36 years after its erection, another apparition took place in the vicinity, the one I mentioned as being tied to Fatima. Some 22 peasants saw Our Lady there, and she predicted eighty or ninety years of hardship for the believers. This was in 1914. As at Fatima, from what I understand, she also warned that Russia would become godless and bring mankind precariously close to destruction. It was a significant link to what Sister Lucia of Fatima was told years later—if Russia did not return to Christianity, there might well be another world war and whole nations would vanish.

I believe it was no coincidence that these messages were given in the Ukraine, where Christianity took root 250 years before it spread through Russia. It's as if the Ukraine once again faced the task of converting its large northern neighbor. The apparition I just mentioned was on May 12, and it began as a light near the church, lasting for a day. The original visionaries were joined by hundreds of neighboring residents, who stared awestruck at the image of Our Lady. Suffering was at hand, she warned, and Ukrainians would experience persecution. She requested penance and active work for the Church. Most importantly, she said that some of the people would live to see three wars.

Terrible times were coming. And terrible times indeed came. But there was another prediction couched in the otherwise gloomy prophecies: in the end goodness and Christianity would return.

Hrushiv and many other shrines were all but forgotten after the 1946 synod in L'viv. And of course the little chapel was chained shut by the triumphant, arrogant Communists. Satan was sounding the bell of victory, and how forlorn the believing peasants must have been—trudging past the closed chapel after toiling for a pittance on the new collectives. Blessed Trinity stood as a lonely memory of better days.

Gone from view were the embroidered cloths and gold trellis. Farm dust accumulated on the unseen artwork and settled like pollen on the unwalked floors. For years no one set foot in the tiny domed chapel. Alone, the iconic angels prayed.

Chapter 18

ABOVE THE
CUPOLA

But the eighty years were almost up, and mankind was heading swiftly to the new millennium. As we drove to Hrushiv, these and other thoughts were racing through my mind. We passed through the road barriers and encountered the tremendous sight that I described in the first chapter.

Although the Virgin, looking upon us from the unprecedented luminescence, did not speak on the first day or in any way give auditory messages, she said plenty with her sad but twinkling eyes. The way the light encompassed the entire environment, the peace we felt, and the reverence of the crowd, especially older women who remained prostrate for the entire duration, was an experience that etched itself into my memory as no other experience could.

The Mother of God, silent, but appearing to the throngs.

The Mother of God, there above the cupola!

I was thrilled that we had decided to come and experience part of an event that continued for three whole weeks. The Virgin remained for hours at a time; we would pray, study her, and then tend to business somewhere else, only to return and find that she was still visible.

I had known I was in physical danger but had felt secure beneath the umbrella of grace. Besides, many of the militia and KGB were busy trying to explain away the phenomenon

215

or, failing that, were on their knees questioning their consciences.

While it had been an excruciating disappointment (not seeing the Virgin at first), once she appeared, all my frustrations and anxieties burned away. I had luxuriated in her majestic simplicity, in her wondrous style, in the beguiling smell of fresh warm milk.

The Queen of Light, and also the Queen of Warmth. The same celestial woman who had lit up Cell 21—who had pressed her palm against my freezing head—was now arrayed in full splendor. It was so bright at times that you could see a needle, and it was neither the light of day nor that of night. We counted 52,000 people one day because there were 52,000 embroidered towels left as tokens of reverence and love. But how many had come without towels? People who didn't even know how to make the sign of the cross were learning the Rosary, which was said around the clock. One group ended and another began.

I am convinced that the Mother of God comes only to those places where there are devout people and where she is needed the most. Earth and Heaven are united as a child with its mother. Heaven is God. I wept when I saw people there who traveled from thousands of kilometers away.

My personal experiences in prison had built up to this moment, just as her previous appearances at Hrushiv (in the 1700s, and then in 1914) also seemed to have been a mere prelude to the great miracle of 1987. But why wasn't the Mother of God saying anything? Perhaps I was not worthy to hear anything. I didn't know. I had looked around and seen others rapt in conversation with her. Some, it seemed, heard a voice but did not see her. I made a mental note to collect testimonies as to what they were experiencing.

I don't know why, but after the first apparition, the strong sense welled within me that the persecutions were only beginning. I felt need. I felt want. And my head was humming with questions. Who was sending me these thoughts? Who was leading us along this way? Why did some suffer for the sake of the Holy Gospel while for others it was empty words?

She was silent that first day, May 9, but for the next week the Mother of God spoke many words filled with wisdom and warnings. It was the same luminosity day after day. She materialized in the smaller light as the oval hovered above the chapel and grew in intensity.

At other times the light, and the Virgin in it, appeared instantaneously.

Upon departure the light would intensify around her and you could barely see her outline.

For the first three days she remained garbed in flaring colors. Others saw her somewhat differently. Some saw her with a crown on her head or a ring on her finger. But when she was in black, holding the Infant, everyone saw exactly the same thing. She often started out with the words, *"Praised be Jesus,"* and when she mentioned His name, she looked skyward. She often had her hand raised with the Rosary hanging from it. It was not like Fatima or Lourdes, where there was a set or limited time-frame for her appearance. The Virgin showed up at various moments throughout the day. Not everyone could see her, and even some priests and nuns failed to witness the apparition. But the better part of half the crowd caught a glimpse of her, and those who didn't were left, nonetheless, with an undeniable sense of her presence.

The light was often exquisitely subtle, and its power pulsed, grew, waned. Suddenly it was as if the modest and obscure wood chapel, set hard by a narrow country road, was the center of our planet.

A beam of God's all-powerful grace was piercing mankind's great darkness.

There were those in the crowd who were told by the Virgin to pray at a specific time for her similar appearances in Yugoslavia. When later, after moving to Canada, I learned more about the apparitions in Medjugorje, it struck me that, just as many but not all see the miracle of the sun, so too did many but not all see the Mother of God at Hrushiv.

Unlike most Marian sites, Hrushiv had to contend with threats of violence. There were soldiers who had served in Afghanistan and that experience had so embittered them to the Soviets, that they would brush against a militiaman and ding him in the side with a knife. The police were terrified of such soldiers, who after their little assaults would then pray piously.

I had slept my first night at a home in a nearby hamlet. Other nights I went into Drohobych. There were no hotels in Hrushiv itself, and very few facilities. Yet, so many people had converged on it that the surrounding hills, meadows, and fields were badly trampled. The earth was hard as a rock, the potato crop smothered.

While most of the potatoes were ruined that spring, the following year, as if to make up for it, the crops came up with five times their normal abundance.

No way could I sleep that first night. I would lie down for an hour and then get up and pace—praying, thinking. People find it hard to believe how little I slept, but nobody could sleep after these experiences. We asked some trustworthy doctors whether living in such a constant state of excitement might affect our health. Mine was already in bad shape. The older women put packs on my back, which ached from the beatings I had received at Uzhhorod.

Prison was still on my mind, especially since I harbored an unfinished sentence. Once away from the protective crowds, I snuck about like a hunted animal. I especially avoided situations that would lend themselves to assassination. Except for preaching, I tried not to meddle in the events. I wanted to let everything occur spontaneously. I did not even meet the original visionary, Marina, who was maintaining a low profile.

Nor did I seek to document every miraculous claim. It is the Church and Church alone that holds such a responsibility. Not only must the Vatican authenticate the supernatural nature of such apparitions but, succeeding in that, must then make sure it is not a delusion contrived by Satan.

Why would Satan come disguised as the Virgin Mary? Obviously to confuse us and lead us astray. In the end times, in the era of the anti-Christ, we have to be very careful because evil forces are trying to dig in everywhere. Christians must remember that Satan is very powerful and he acts in mimicking God. The Church took a long time to decide upon the authenticity of Fatima; any time there is an event that appears supernatural we must always be on guard against demons.

I was also cautious because I didn't want anything to compromise our campaign for the Church's legalization. There was still constant interrogation and persecution. The KGB was trying to shadow me, but I kept melting into the crowd and slipping from their sight. The pilgrims arrived in a procession that was ten-people wide and the chapel was like an island in a human sea.

The KGB photographed everybody, especially students who came to see the miracle. There were also several Orthodox groups, including monks walking in the procession. One of these Orthodox monks, Ivan Kowalchuk, left May 10, my second day there, a Catholic. He converted. I decided to stay as long as I could. The apparitions had been going on for two weeks (since April 26) and I wanted to soak in as much as possible before they ended.

In the morning we walked to the chapel and approached the little byzantine building through the fields at the lower end of town. There were sounds I didn't like—the sounds of fire sirens. Sirens meant government, and government meant Communists.

Sure enough, several fire trucks were arriving with policemen. I didn't know what to make of it. I wondered if the Communists had decided to use force.

A man we knew approached by motorbike. He had recently returned from duty in Afghanistan. "We have to go," he announced. "The people are waiting."

There were thousands of people there already. With me were two Basilian nuns and a Basilian priest, Father Mychailo. Also with me was my constant companion, Sister Iryna. They had begun to organize the people for my arrival. Any appearance of mine had to be conducted in such a way that I was protected from the KGB and militia. Although they had not apprehended me the day before, no one knew what would happen now. I saw KGB from Uzhhorod and L'viv, and I could tell they recognized me.

One of the agents walked to a government vehicle, probably to radio that I was present. When he returned he strutted in my direction and was obviously going to speak with me. We were getting ready for a Mass.

"Josyp Mychailovych," he began, "Lieutenant Colonel Korsun would like to speak to you after this."

I was brusque. "Why didn't he come himself? Tell him I will not go anywhere or see anyone."

Korsun soon approached with Colonel Bogdanov of the L'viv detachment, whom I had spoken to the day before. Bogdanov again issued a warning. "Josyp, there are to be no speeches or rallies. Say your prayers and take off. You shouldn't have come. You were here yesterday. There are too many people as it is. Just pray and make room for the others. And know," he added obliquely, "that every suffering has an end."

"I don't understand what you're saying," I answered. "Is that a threat? With all the militia, I thought you had things under control."

"Where do you see all the militia?" Bogdanov said.

Many of the police were disguised as civilians. Those who weren't roamed about with their brown and red caps.

Again I asked, "Are you threatening me? I don't understand you."

Bogdanov was quickly losing patience. "No, we're advising you to say your prayers and leave. The fact that you've been released from prison doesn't mean anything. If you disturb the peace we can still incarcerate you, understand? You have no right to be here. You're from a different region. Pray for a while and then leave."

I wasn't in the mood for courtesies. "Listen, you Russian. You know full well that I am not going away. These are my people and I'll start telling my people who it was who tortured me all those years in camps and prisons for my belief in Christ. Those times when you ravaged the faithful and even little girls, those times are now gone!" I accused Bogdanov of raping a girl at regional Communist headquarters.

"That's a lie!" he said indignantly. "It was the Banderites who set that up."

Korsun intervened. "Listen, Terelya: no one is chasing you away. But I warn you, no speeches."

As I had on May 9, I raised my voice to the people. "Brothers and sisters!"

Korsun hissed. "Are you mad!"

But Bogdanov had enough. He was getting nervous. "Terelya is a fool," he sneered. "Let's go."

They left, and led by Basilian sisters, we began praying the Rosary. There was a statue of the Virgin and two crosses in a courtyard. Prayer and Masses centered around them. I could tell there were many people from the eastern part of the Ukraine because of their clothes and hairstyles.

A Mass began, and the sight of all the pilgrims was intoxicating. There were so many embroidered towels that the road from Hrushiv to Kiev could have been covered with them. I said a few words to the people and once more asked them to pray for those in the camps. It didn't take much to inspire fervent prayer; just about everyone knew someone who was still in prison.

Except for those who were taking photographs, the militia was no longer such a presence. We resumed the Rosary after Mass and directed our prayers to the well-being of our nation, the Ukraine.

It was around then that the converted monk, Kowalchuk, informed me that we were wanted in the next hamlet, where there were people who had come all the way from Central Asia. "They want you to say a few words," he said.

That was the way it went for the next week, my time divided between Hrushiv and the surrounding villages. Sister Iryna came with me and we were careful not to let anyone see precisely where we were heading. One young man led us across a field. On the other side a car was waiting. It was about an hour trip to a house where thirty or forty Uzbeks and Tadzhiks had gathered. "Peace be with you," I greeted them.

Many of these people were Communists who needed someone to talk to. They were perplexed and overwhelmed. They too had been to Hrushiv and they too had seen the Mother of God.

They were full of anxious questions. What did such visions mean? What should they all do now that they had experienced the supernatural? Should they tell others, or keep quiet? What were the consequences for the Soviet Union?

There were people from a sanitorium and they had been forced by the militia and KGB to sign a document stating that they would not relate their experiences to anyone.

It was a desperate tactic by the Communists. Failing to halt the apparitions, they now were trying to control the damage. Even KGB officers were warned not to relate what they saw, and officials went through the countryside trying to find out who had seen the apparitions and what they were saying about them.

My meeting went on for hours and when it ended we were all friends. I prayed with them in Russian, so everyone could understand what I said. I prayed for all the nations enslaved by Moscow: Byelorussia, Georgia, Armenia, the Baltic states. "Oh God," I intoned. "Give us the strength to endure and to survive until those times come that will be joyful for all of us. Give us the unity and strength to defeat Satan, the wisdom and strength of spirit so that all together we can rise up against our common enemy and defeat him."

I asked forgiveness for our persecutors and vowed an unending quest for freedom. The powerful signs at Hrushiv, I said, were not just favors from God but also the path toward His truth—an urgent call to follow in the footsteps of the Apostles.

"Please, oh Lord, our great and only God, grant freedom to the Tadziks, to the Uzbeks, to the Kazakhs, the Kirghiz, to the Ukrainians!"

When we returned that evening to Hrushiv, it was the same surreal sight. There was the sea of candles, reaching heavenward with their small licking flames, casting shadows on the old women who had quietly passed on the Catholic Faith to their grandchildren and had prayed secretly for decades.

Mass was celebrated by Father Mykhailo and another priest named Mykola. I read a meditation while young people handed out leaflets calling for Christian unity.

The militia were trying to move people out but many refused to budge. There was singing and continuous prayer. Every once in a while a group of people would spot the Mother of God and others would look that way. The light was the same as on the first evening.

I saw her as a human countenance, like an actual person there. The first three days she had on the fiery garb, but not everyone saw her this way. Sister Iryna described her as wearing white clothes. Everyone had their own experience.

Almost all the pilgrims had rosaries and almost everyone was looking towards the cupola. The people didn't lower their eyes. The unusual light grew more intense. Each leaf and blade of grass was electrified.

In the heavenly radiance even the most homely people looked like beautiful angels. It was as if we were transfigured that day and evening. Many people wept or smiled with tears in their eyes.

I was so moved I could hardly speak. It was then—I don't know how—that I again saw the Blessed Virgin in the flaming dress, a Rosary in her right hand, her head covered by a blue veil.

Her garments were so delicate you felt you could reach up and crunch them in your hand. What's interesting is that she was looking directly into my eyes. I later asked others what they saw and it was the same thing: Mary looking straight at them. How, except by supernatural powers, could she look at everyone in such an individual way?

People shouted. Others fell prostrate. "Dear Mother of God! Look, people!"

At that moment we felt so powerful that it was as if we were capable of superhuman feats. The glow above the churchyard was celestial and the ensuing silence was pleasant, majestic, awesome.

In the ecstasy was the firm feeling that we were now so strong that we would win our freedom. The Mother of God was not just looking at us but was also imparting such strength that no one would be able to defeat us. There was also the feeling that we were part of a divine mission. The mission is to convert a dying world. The mission is to turn humans to Christ the King before the chastisements.

She extended her hand over the head of the infant Jesus and disposed of the cloak over her shoulders. Then she began to speak: *"My son, my children, I rejoice in you and am happy in you. I'm telling you that from today I am with you and over you. Go and be not afraid."*

Not everyone heard her, but those who did experienced the same sensation—as if the voice was surrounding them. It's hard to explain in any other way. When I speak now you hear me directionally, but the voice at Hrushiv wasn't like it was among us. There were many people of different languages yet she spoke to each in his or her own tongue.

The Mother of God talked at length about penance and conversion. She urged us to pray to Christ the King. She told us to pray for the deceased as a precondition for entering the path of love—this is very important and bears repeating, praying for the souls in Purgatory—and she likewise mentioned our duty to convert unbelievers. What good is it only to speak of God among ourselves? We must go among the humanists and atheists.

Many people heard the same message but she also spoke on a very personal level. There are some private matters I do not wish to recount. Again she told me about my life, and where I was heading. She mentioned that I would find myself beyond the borders of the Soviet Union but that she would send people to help me. Then she began to give me certain secrets and messages concerning the world at large.

Kelechyn Area—Birthplace of Josyp Terelya

Father Mykola Symkajlo Hears Confessions
In The Forest—1979

226

Drawing of Raoul Wallenberg

Solitary Cell 389-15—Perm Camp

Perm 35—Concentration Camp

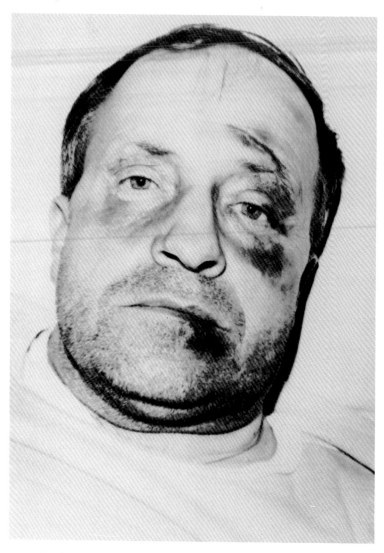

Father Petro Zaleniuk—Beaten by the KGB for Celebrating Mass in the Ukrainian Catholic Rite

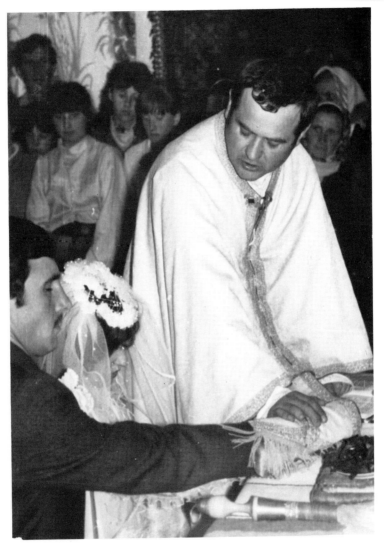

Underground Wedding

October 28, 1990—Kiev—in the Square of St. Sophia—Special Soviet MVD Riot Police Block Access to St. Sophia Cathedral

Kiev—Destroyed Chapel. Church in Background Converted into a Museum

Camp 315-30, in L'viv

1983—Divine Liturgy in the Catacombs, in the Forest of Zarvanytsia. Mass is being celebrated by Bishop Pavlo Vasylyk

July 1989—in the Hoshivskij Forrest (in the Carpathian Mountains, Near the City Dolyna)—22,000 Ukrainian Catholic Youth Participate in the Divine Liturgy. This Underground Mass was Celebrated by Father Yaroslav Lesiv.

October 7, 1990—City of Ternopil. Column of Ukrainian Political Prisoners, Moving in Direction of Headquarters of KGB

The Excavation Begins at the Mass Grave in Dem'yaniv, 1989

Hundreds Had Been Executed in the Past for Their Religious Beliefs—Shot in the Head

A Funeral Liturgy on October 29, 1989,
was Attended by Hundreds of Thousands

Josyp Meets With Pope John Paul II

Blessed Trinity Church, Hrushiv

Josyp With His Three Children

Josyp Speaking to Pilgrims at Hrushiv

Blessed Trinity, Hrusbiv

Inside Chapel at Hrushiv. (Miraculous Well in Foreground)

Pilgrims Arrive for Mass at Hrushiv

Activist of Ukrainian Catholic Church (extreme left in the photo) Dr. Stepan Khmara during an interview with foreign and Soviet media three weeks before his arrest in 1990. Dr. Khmara is currently imprisoned in Kiev. His trial was to take place on January 11, 1990.

Marina (Seer at Hrushiv)

Chernobyl

Prison Camp. (Two Paintings By Josyp)

Demonstration for Legalization of
Ukrainian Catholic Church

*1988—Josyp and Olena Terelya During Communion
From His Holiness Pope John Paul II at the Vatican*

Paintings by Josyp
Showing the Communist Menace to the World
252

і за ім'я Моє будуть вас ненавидіти...

1946   1986

Painting of Josyp Terelya

253

The Underground Church Confronts KGB Agent—1988

The Underground Church Comes Out—1989

Photo Courtesy of John Riddiford

The first monument to Our Lady of Hrushiv outside the borders of Ukraine on American soil—in Elmira Heights, N.Y., U.S.A. The monument was blessed and unvieled April 26, 1989 on the anniversary of the Chernobyl disaster

Chapter 19

'MY DAUGHTER UKRAINE'

It was overwhelming and everybody was so caught up in the events that no one wanted to eat or sleep. That night I went to stay with some nationalists. The older women washed our clothes and brought straw in from the barn, covering it with quilts.

But who was ready for bed? We talked nonstop, remarking on how pleasant Our Lady was and sharing our experiences. When I think back on it, the events of certain days run into each other. It's difficult to precisely recall what transpired at specific times on specific days. It was a floodgate of emotions, revelations, and sensations.

On the following days I did much the same as I did on May 10, commuting to Hrushiv while I was staying and preaching elsewhere. A boy arrived around nine o'clock on the morning of May 11 with a note for me to meet with a group of young people in the village of Oriavchyk, which was a couple of hours away. The group included Basilians and a brother from the Studites. I entered and said, "Praise be to God!"

We sat at a table and the Studite blessed a meal of sour milk. We talked about the issues facing the Eastern Rite Church, and afterward I was handed a letter from Olena, who was worried about me. Naturally she wanted to know when I would be returning home. She mentioned a priest

257

named Havryliv and inquired as to his whereabouts. No one knew where he had gone and we feared the worst. In the Soviet Union, people were still disappearing.

From there I went by truck to Tyshiv. I was to be dropped off and then they were to go back for my friends, taking them to the station in Hrebeniv because there were fewer militia along that particular route. Hrebeniv was on the rail link between L'viv and Mukachiv, south of Hrushiv. While that area was relatively free of congestion, other routes, especially beyond Smozha, were jammed with pilgrims. The crowds were a spectacle to see! And the militia was impotent to do anything about them. They were heading for the city of Stryy and from there west to Blessed Trinity.

Pilgrims were hitching rides in cars and trucks or packing inside unending bus caravans. The police had orders to deter anyone from the uplands heading in the direction of Skole (which was before Stryy), but there was simply no stopping the faithful. The thought of seeing the Mother of God had put determination in their eyes.

We got to the place where the meeting was supposed to take place but no one was around. That set off an alarm. In the underground, there's an ironclad rule: if someone is late, you wait just five minutes and then hurry out of there. The tardiness may be an indication that the authorities are on to you.

Soon, however, I was met by a farmwomen who directed me to the right house. Inside was the group I was to meet and we began to exchange information. They told me the authorities were already passing around word that we Uniates had concocted the Hrushiv miracle—invented it to buttress our cause. Terelya the ''fanatic'' was stirring things up; I guess there had been a public lecture about it. Word was that I would soon be thrown out of the USSR and would spend the remainder of my life in the ''garbage bins'' of America.

I returned to Hrushiv with a man named Vasyl. We traveled a road that coursed by the village of Truskavets, one of the places I stayed overnight during the apparitions. The road was lined by huge trees that looked to be two or three centuries old. We saw a small crowd and I spotted a policeman I knew. He was from Falesh. I wondered what was going on and he told me the militia had orders to cut down one of the trees and block traffic with it. They were trying everything to staunch our pilgrimages. They acted as if their concern was for damage to the crops and they tried to scare people into thinking there was contagious disease spreading through Hrushiv.

But when we got there it was obvious such tactics had miserably failed. In some spots, the pilgrims had piled so much money—large bills of up to 100 rubles—that it was ankle-deep. The flowers were even higher. Rich Georgians were constantly tossing money and many people were still stuffing cash into the crack above the window. About thirty men arrived in government cars armed with machine guns.

Included in the contingent was the chairman of the local village council, the secretary of the local Communist Party, and the regional procurator. The police collected all the offerings and dumped the money into potato sacks. Then they tore the board off the chapel's back door and scooped up donations that had been dropped inside. Later, they said they had collected 30,000 rubles, but that's ridiculous. There was much more than that. Some went to the village council but they split most of the money among themselves.

On May 11, hordes of children came to Hrushiv and the school directors followed in hot pursuit. But the teachers and principals had little chance of weeding their wayward students out of such a large crowd. The authorities were especially concerned about students from the technical schools and universities. There were thousands of young people, including a group from the art college in Dnipropetrovs'Ke.

The young people walked in a procession around the chapel, singing hymns and reciting the Rosary.

When we reached the chapel there was the by-now familiar glow in the sky. We made an altar out of a small table and a priest named Ivan said Mass with 11 other members of the underground clergy. Actually, it was a simultaneous celebration of nearly a dozen liturgies. So that more people could participate, priests split up and said Mass in 11 spots. The people surrounded them so the police couldn't see what was transpiring. The Eastern Rite Mass, after all, was illegal. I assisted at the liturgy.

There were many people from Eastern Ukraine and a guide who explained the rituals to them. Government officials were running here and there but couldn't see or hear what we were doing. We were crowding them out and singing too loudly. There were also a few hundred Georgians who stayed despite the best attempts of the Soviets to send them back to their home republic.

The Mother of God appeared as we began celebrating the afternoon liturgy. It was as if she was looking down and praying with us—taking part in the Mass! At one point on this day, she had her left hand on her heart and tears filling her eyes. Once more I heard her voice, and she began to relate information that I felt was pertinent to the end times. It was as if she was coming to give us strength. She wanted us to go and proclaim the Gospel. She asked us to forgive our enemies and go to them with love.

It's through suffering and love, she emphasized, that we will be released from Satan's bondage.

The Mother of God emphasized that now was the time of labor. Soon the harvest would come. She said that even in the most difficult times the true Christians will find the strength to stand up to the prince of darkness. If we follow divine truths, she said, we will be girded and strong.

She also implored us to pray diligently. She mentioned that the *Creed,* the *Our Father,* and the *Hail Mary* should be said daily. And she lamented that the prayers to St. Michael has been so woefully neglected.

She suggested that we carry a Rosary or even wear it around our necks.

She said difficult times are coming and that the Rosary is a powerful weapon against spiritual adversaries.

"Convert the unbelievers," I heard her gentle but firm voice say.

"Proclaim the Word of God among those who have denied His Son. Pray! Pray for those who are leading immoral lives. Pray the Rosary. Teach your children to pray the Rosary. It is powerful against the anti-Christ. Stay clear of sin and offer up your prosperity, your tranquility, your life. Sacrifice is a chief commandment declared by Jesus Christ. Remember that sin is the forbidden luxury and that sacrifice allows you to become a sincere participant in the

sufferings of Jesus. It is through this that you will save those who have fallen. Do not doubt. Do not have fear. And pray. Pray constantly and everywhere. Openly bring witness of Jesus Christ and do not be ashamed of the sign of the cross. Use it, and prepare for great persecutions and new sacrifices."

It will be through the Church, she said, that justice and peace will prevail.

"Lead a pure and sinless life," she said at another juncture. *"Do not overindulge in drink, do not smoke, do not go to sinful dances."*

When her voice stopped I felt so peaceful it was as if I was listening to the ocean or to rustling leaves. At one point her lips were moving but I couldn't hear her voice. When it returned she elaborated upon the initial messages:

"When you pray during Mass use the sign of the cross 33 times. During the liturgy all the people should be blessed with holy water. In this way you will overcome their unrest and fear. Those who are closest to you will avoid you. Due to the unfaithfulness of priests, you will even be tempted to leave my Son and accept paganism. But suffering and prayer will overcome everything. A great task awaits you. There is a greater need for lay apostles than ever before. Help the Pope and the third secret of Fatima will be revealed to you. We are living in the times of the Father. The third secret is all around you. The times of God have begun."

Our Lady went on to urge that we remember the Pope. *"Pray for the Holy Father in great numbers. This will help him. Pray together at one time, for prayer will be especially helpful then. Show your loyalty everywhere to the Pope and Church. Do this publicly and constantly. Do not follow the modern priests. Listen to God and love God. Pray for the children, and prepare for evil times—much worse than you are now witnessing. Pray the Rosary daily, especially for the deceased, and remember that I am with you. Do not pay heed to the difficulties that surround you. I come to lead you to my Son."*

When Our Lady stopped speaking I experienced strange physiological effects. It was like a tension or stress swelling in my ears. My blood pressure rose and later I felt like there were needles behind my right ear. But there was also the soothing sound of the ocean. It was as if nature was speaking. And some also heard what sounded like a harp.

The Virgin spoke normally but not the way we understand it. I know that seems confusing, yet I can't find another way of describing it. Her voice welled up around us. On the 11th she spoke about the prophets and apocalyptic times. I will describe more of this in a moment. What the apostles and prophets have prophesied is now happening, she told us. Those times announced by the prophets of old are now upon us.

Some of the people came to me and asked why God was testing us so severely. I would answer them with a flurry of questions. "How much have you prayed lately? What good deeds have you done this day? How often are you sorry for the evil you have committed? How often as you enter your workplace do you ask for God's blessing?"

Unknown to the higher authorities, a good number of militia were secret worshippers and some of them even came to hear me talk. Following Mass we formed a wide circle around the stone cross. I was given a megaphone and began to speak. It was like Our Lady gave me the words. I spoke about how the power of God had brought us all together and proclaimed that we were on the way to freedom. I spoke about our new brotherhood. I spoke about the need to love each other.

"The darkness sown by Communism has swallowed neither the heart nor eyes of our God-fearing people. Yesterday, when I was in Russian bondage, I was told that after the death of Vasyl Stus (another political prisoner), it was my turn. But look what happened. As you can see, I am with you."

Addressing the issue of why God allowed good people to suffer and die, I pointed out that it was the blood of martyrs that purchased peace, just as the blood of Christ purchased our salvation. "Not a single effort or death has been wasted for our cause and for our people."

Even in the worst moments, I pointed out, we must believe in the goodness of God. Toil is followed by the harvest. The best things do not come easy. I urged the people to pray again for those in the camps as well as for the persecutors.

And I also urged prayers of thanksgiving. We needed to thank the Virgin and her Son. "They are immaculate and blessed. They have given us a great love for our fellow man and the strength to oppose evil and emerge victorious." Many of those who were traditional believers said they saw the Mother of God dressed in black with the Child in her arms. They would ask why she was in black and she would say, *"There's a great tragedy in the world today. People have left my Son."*

To the Communists and even many Orthodox, of course, the concept that a supernatural messenger had arrived in the Soviet Union was perplexing, overly coincidental, and crazy. Can you imagine an atheist watching thousands of people carrying on a long dialogue with thin air? As for the Orthodox, I think many of them felt uneasy that the miracle was occurring over a Catholic chapel.

No doubt some fundamentalists and Pentecostalists also wanted to dismiss the events. They tend to attack Marian phenomena and I have the feeling Christ is unhappy with such disrespect for His mother. Their argument is that Mary's role is not explicated in the Bible. I have the greatest respect for the Bible and know it was the work of the Holy Spirit. But it is a book nonetheless, and any book has its limitations. It does not contain all of God's workings. No book could. The Holy Spirit did not stop working wonders or giving us messages once the last Gospel was written.

Others were uncomfortable with the apparitions because our materialistic world teaches that such phenomena are psychological aberrations. If Hrushiv was a case of mass hallucination, however, how could so many onlookers describe the same thing without talking to each other during the apparitions? Yes, at times she appeared somewhat differently, and many saw phenomena on a much smaller scale, but the essential experience—and many of the messages—were identical.

The militia and KGB knew in their hearts that something inexplicable was occurring. There was one policeman who took off his uniform and stated that he didn't want to wear "the mark of Satan" any longer. Since they could never hope to rule such a crowd, even with hundreds of men,

they resorted to their typically dirty tactics, such as sending in drunks to disturb our prayer or otherwise trying to
sow fear, discord, and confusion.

On May 10 or 11 one officer who had been drinking too
much spotted the apparitional light and fired a shot at it!
It was an act of mindless bravado. I didn't actually see it.
I just heard what sounded like the crack of a whip. The
officer was immediately struck unconscious, collapsing to
the ground. His arm turned black, as if he had been electrocuted. Some people assert that a ray of light materialized
from the area of the chapel—a shot of light—and that this
is what knocked him down. It was the living force of God.
I didn't see the light but I did see the officer. He was unconscious for a long period of time, and when they revived
him he could remember nothing.

Although there were rumors that this officer then converted and became an evangelist who roamed penniless from
village to village, I have since learned that he was simply
sent away from the Western Ukraine into another region
of the USSR.

Other scenes at Hrushiv were more pleasant. I saw plenty
of non-Christians converted instantly. It is sometimes easier to convert Communists than to convert the Orthodox
atheists. I was witness to a Russian officer—a captain, no
less—stating uncategorically, "There is a God." There were
many stories like this, but the most dramatic may have taken
place on May 12. It was an event that once again demon-
strated that no person or government can alter or in any
way halt God's work.

That morning, I was on my way to see a priest named
Father Zenko in another nearby hamlet called Morshyn. He
was going to help me arrange for a car. I needed the vehicle
to go to Pidberechy, where there was a rendezvous planned
with a bishop who would then return with me to Hrushiv.

As we drove I spotted the police cutting down a tree,
just as I had been told they were going to do. They were
still intent on creating a roadblock and thwarting the pilgrims. Young cadets were there from L'viv.

Nearby were police cars and two fire engines. The wind
was howling that day, with a mourning sound.

We stopped and I went up to the policemen. What I wanted

to know was simple: Why are you cutting this large lime tree down?

They answered me with silence.

"I know why you are doing this," I answered for them. "Colonel Bogdanov gave the orders and you are happily carrying them out."

I spotted a captain I knew named Dmytro. He was from Horodka and we got along. "Dmytro," I said. "Have you lost your senses, cutting down a tree like this?"

The wind was blowing so hard it was difficult to hear each other. They had the tree about halfway cut and took a break. Dmytro turned to them with a smirk. He asked the cadets if they wanted to see the true-life nationalist Josyp Terelya, about whom they had heard a lecture on February 2. "Here he is in person," said Dmytro, his mouth forming an ironic smirk. "Right in front of you."

They walked a bit closer, studying me, not knowing quite how to react. "Look," I said to one of them, "you're cutting up the Ukraine just the same as you're cutting down that tree." I then told them how the strategy made no sense. So what if they blocked this one road? The pilgrims would simply find an alternate way to Hrushiv, or walk around the tree. Cutting down a tree was the measure of their bewilderment and desperation.

The cadets wanted to know how I had been released and if it was true that the Eastern Rite Church had conspired to create the Hrushiv "miracle." I asked if any of them had been to Blessed Trinity and they told me that they weren't allowed. I suggested they sneak there and see for themselves. I told them to go singly and meld into the crowd.

My "friend," the captain, stood by pretending he didn't hear anything. Soon two more cars pulled up but the militia stopped them from going through. In one of the cars was an old nationalist named Ratush, who shouted, "Josyp! God's might is with us!"

The cadets were almost finished cutting through the tree when the wind stopped very suddenly. It was like the earth had ceased its rotation. It had been constant up to now, but suddenly there was an eerie lull. Although it was cut, the tree managed to stay upright for a few seconds before it began tilting towards the road.

But all of a sudden the wind shifted and a huge gust
pushed the tree so that it fell onto the militia cars, the
branches crashing and crackling and sending pieces of the
vehicles flying in all directions. Instead of blocking the road
they had ruined their own equipment.

The police stood there, mortified.

Later that day several of the cadets snuck into Hrushiv.
We left and went to see Father Zenko in Morshyn. He
wasn't home. So we decided to head back to Blessed Trinity.
I walked through the village and was surprised at how few
police and soldiers there were. I was elated at what divine
providence had accomplished, but at the back of my mind
was still trepidation at what the authorities might try next.
Near the municipal building was a taxi with L'viv license
plates, and I started speaking with the driver, another young
lad who had just returned from Afghanistan. He informed
me that a reporter and photographer from the *Literary
Gazette* were in town. Based in Moscow, the *Literary Gazette*
is a prestigious national publication, similar to the *Wall
Street Journal.*

I arrived at Blessed Trinity around noon. The crowd was
quiet and peaceful, staring towards the balcony and cupola.
I looked up and saw the Virgin immediately. Her eyes were
aglow. She looked at me and began talking without moving
her mouth.

*"You will climb to the top of the ladder and will not
fall. The Infant is protecting you and I am giving you grace
and strength so you will be able to travel your path to the
end. In ten years your people will be free and your enemies
will never defeat you. You will be invisible among them.
Serve Him and I will always be with you."*

In the Ukraine there is an old legend about a man named
Shuhay who was given some herbs by an old woman and
afterwards became impervious to bullets. I felt like Shuhay,
but my "herbs" came from the Mother of God.

Others felt the same way. There was an unprecedented
feeling of daring and boldness. And the media was arriving
in force. I met the reporter from the *Literary Gazette* and
asked her about her own experiences at Hrushiv. Her answer
was surprisingly candid. "I see the Mother of God!"

"Will you write that?" I asked.

"I already have instructions as to how I am to write this article," she answered.

"Do you really think there is mass psychosis among all these people?"

She said there was no evidence of psychosis, just a sense of love and goodness. And when her article came out it contained the expected explanations of mass hallucination but also contained phrases that implied her belief in the miracle. Readers in the USSR know how to read between the lines.

On May 12, a television crew from Kiev was also there and while the news editors obviously had seen nothing unusual in the tape, when they showed the footage on their evening broadcast, people watching at home spotted the Mother of God. Naturally they stopped showing that particular footage. But it had already raised quite a clamor. A dozen newspapers jumped in to attack us, claiming that the miracle must have been contrived on orders from the Pope himself. A special commission was organized to study the situation, composed of Communist committeemen, psychiatrists, philosophers, medical doctors, and Orthodox priests. Soon they would travel throughout Carpathia trying to convince people that it was mass hallucination or a hidden projector supplied to us by the CIA. They implied we had gotten our hands on the most recent Japanese technology. There was also a rumor that I had been given three million rubles by the Vatican to contrive the Hrushiv events.

The reporter from the *Literary Gazette* had marveled at all the children who were there. She couldn't understand how after all these years, the youngsters hadn't been totally brainwashed. Indeed, I believe it was that day, in the village of Truscavets, that a high school teacher was conducting biology class when her students began talking about God. It was obvious that despite official admonitions a number of her students had been to Hrushiv. She was a Communist and Communists were forbidden from going there. Still, she was curious. She wanted to know what the people in Hrushiv were saying.

The students were afraid to answer her questions. They knew the school director was searching for anyone who had been there. But finally a girl let it slip that she had experienced the miracle. Soon it was obvious that a boy in class had also been there. In short order it became apparent that just about everyone in the class had snuck into Hrushiv at one time or another since the apparitions began on April 26, and after class these students, along with many others, decided to troop back to Blessed Trinity together. It was a defiance born of supernatural strength. The director was helpless to stop them. He didn't want to make a big scene and have his superintendent find out that he had lost control of the school.

But it so happened that the regional inspector of education was driving through this area and saw the hundreds of students heading towards Hrushiv. When he stopped to ask where they were going, they answered, "To see the Mother of God!"

Afraid to confront so many people directly, the local authorities continually resorted to foolish tactics similar to the tree-cutting. On the 13th or 14th they placed a canvas on the roof of the chapel to try to cut off the light, and attempted to drown it out with search beams. To no avail. The force behind the illumination was a force greater than anything man-made, certainly greater than electricity. They also covered some of the incoming roads with garbage and indicated that there was a plague of hoof and mouth disease.

Although very little news of Hrushiv reached the West, where the press is about as warm to miracles as the Communists are, it was a truly major event, an outbreak that, in crowd size, was reminiscent of the early Solidarity gatherings at the Polish shipyards. While the Polish drive for freedom was fueled in part by Pope John Paul II, the Hrushiv events were fueled by the Mother of God herself. The authorities sent in trucks to haul children to the collective farms, but that didn't work either. The children would do a little work and then be carted back to Hrushiv by drivers who also wanted to see the miracle. In other words, people were being transported to Hrushiv in government vehicles! Those at the local collective farm, which was named in honor of the Communist Zdaniv, expressed disgust that people were leaving their jobs during working hours. They referred to the faithful as "hooligans."

But Our Lady's words were the only ones that mattered. To her we were certainly not hooligans:

"My daughter Ukraine, I have come to you because you have remained faithful to me amidst this desolation, and devout people will spread news of me everywhere. I know best where I am to go. I go where it is better for my Son," she said.

To me personally she said: *"Do you love life? Are you always walking the road of life? You are very disturbed. You are not at peace. You want to do everything at once, and to convert everyone to my Son. But only those who possess and understand love will convert. Do penance and make peace with your shortcomings. Be at peace. You are not at peace. You are filled with fears and apprehensions. You know what is to happen, but it is almost impossible to avert this."*

When the Mother of God looked into the future, she said, *"I see fire. The villages are burning. Water is burning. The very air is on fire. Everything is in flames. If people do not convert to Christ, there will be war. There shall be a great conflagration."*

The Mother of God said, *"All you who have heard me today, you must go into the world and witness about what is to come."*

One also got the sense of famine and earthquakes. But after that will come spiritual renewal.

On May 13, we arrived with Mass already underway near the chapel. I brought a wooden cross that had been presented to me by a well-known Ukrainian artist. As I looked over the crowd, I felt their souls filling with the sincere love of Jesus Christ. And at that wonderful moment, I could envision the creation of a single apostolic Church in the Ukraine. I could feel that we were indeed in famous historical times. The people were singing a hymn and praising Mary and Jesus and after the hymn there was a great silence. I looked up at the cupola and allowed my eyes to again feast upon the supernatural field of light that seemed to subtly illuminate half of the sky. There were tears in our eyes—tears of joy, tears of inspiration. I myself was overflowing with jubilation. I knew the pilgrims were waiting for someone to speak. But I felt at a loss for words. What was I to say to them?

"Glory be to Jesus!" I finally began. I couldn't stop myself. I felt propelled by transcendental energy. "Dear brothers and sisters, today we are together to mutually praise the Mother of God and Our Lord Jesus Christ. Although not everyone sees the Mother of God, we have all tasted her goodness and her gentleness. We have all realized that we have not been abandoned. Here today, the whole of Ukraine is creating its own image. I can tell this by your smiling faces and your sincere prayers. Prayers and good deeds can conquer the world. A year ago our people suffered a terrible calamity, the accident at the Chernobyl power station, but help has arrived from the Queen of the Ukraine. She gives us hope and strength..."

I also mentioned another nuclear accident that had occurred just a few days before. On May 5 there was a leak at a station in Rivne, which is only a hundred miles or so northeast of L'viv. It had been built hurriedly (to win financial bonuses and awards, like the Order of Lenin) and it was erected on soft turf instead of a proper foundation of granite. As a result, two reactors sunk into the bog.

The authorities were concealing information about the accident but we had received reports of strange ailments. Workers were trying to contain the radioactivity by pouring fiber glass into the holes.

"What is this?" I asked. "Has the enemy found a new way of destroying and exterminating God's people of the Ukraine? The KGB is spreading rumors and false information that all this has been caused by the Jews, because it was they who were responsible for building the nuclear power stations. Remember, the Russian Empire has always had three internal enemies: Ukrainians, Poles, and Jews."

I mentioned that there were many Jews converting to Catholicism. "Remember that only Christians and Christ's teachings will save the world from another war," I said. "That is why we must go among the wolves in this world and bring love and God's truth to everyone."

I then expounded upon more of Our Lady's messages. She emphasized praying the Rosary because Satan loses power during that prayer. She had said: *"Who wants to receive the grace of God should pray constantly and take upon himself voluntary penance. Be merciful. Remember that the Rosary will preserve mankind from sin and perdition. Pray for ravaged Russia. You can save the world by your prayers. How many warnings must mankind be given before it repents? The world continues on the road of self-will and hedonism. Russia continues to refuse to recognize my Son. Russia rejects true charity and continues to live a demonic existence. Did I not ask for prayers for the lost Russian people on other occasions? If Russia does not accept Christ the King, the entire world faces ruin."*

Then Our Lady granted us a prophecy that she would greatly expand upon a couple days later. But this is what she said for now: *"I see a large field in flames and upon it are many nations. There is not even time to dig graves. There is no water. The heavens and the air are on fire. I beg you to beseech the Eternal One to forgive you and accept you under His wing. In the past, God's plan of salvation was given to mankind through His prophets. Why don't you follow the path set by the Holy Father, the Eternal God?"*

But it was hardly as if Mother Mary was there solely to admonish us. *"My faithful people,"* she also said, *"what a joy it is for me to be with you, for I see faith and strength in you. I see that you have preserved your fidelity to the Church, even when it appeared that faith was at an end. This is why I turn to you and ask you to forgive your enemies—to be a beacon in the dark. Through you and your martyred Church will come the conversion of Russia, but hasten and pray very much, especially the Rosary."*

There were unique images in the light over and around the chapel. At one point the Mother of God said that when there was a question of faith, I should always give witness fearlessly. Her mouth moved normally, like any person's would. She told me I had only finished part of my work and that there was still a long way to go. *"The road you have walked is only a part of your walk. Look to your right and you shall see those who want the Church to collapse."* She pointed. *"See those who are persecuting the Ukrainian Church."*

When the Mother of God said this she began to recede and a more brilliant light appeared. To the right of me, up there above the chapel, a misty screen materialized. I believe it was May 11. On this "screen" I saw 19 faces. I knew

certain of these people. Some were governmental officials
I had already met, some were KGB and high-ranking authorities, but other of the faces I was totally unfamiliar with and
didn't come to know until later. The gallery of faces included
priests, and even a cardinal. I subsequently met this cardinal at the Vatican. I cannot reveal his name. The Virgin
told me to keep secret all the faces I was seeing. It was
like looking in a mirror with a mist rising before me. None
of the faces on the screen were those of normal people. Their
faces were contorted. Though they wore smiles, they were
frightening smiles. Their eyes were anything but trustworthy. I felt within myself as if I was walking through a forest
and a snake had darted in front of me. I broke into a cold
sweat. It wasn't fear, but terror.

"Keep the secret," she reminded me.

When I came to, I began to understand the great peril
facing the Church. There were many faces I never expected.
I knew some of the people and never felt they were a threat.

On May 14, with the apparitions continuing into their
third and last week, a newspaper called *Road to Socialism*
printed an article with the headline, "Doubts of the Silhouette." Underneath was a subhead: "About the so-called
miracle in the Drohobych area." The writer tried to explain
away the apparitions as the result of corroded glass reflecting lights in a freakish way. "The only thing you need from
there," said the article, "is a good imagination."

The article continued: "During the last several days, very
many people from Drohobych, mainly the faithful, have traveled [to Hrushiv] and all the bus routes were packed. Why
are people traveling to the old village? Some people have
spread the rumor that if you look at the balcony from far
away you will notice something like a silhouette that fades
away when you come closer. At the same time, during this
unusual happening, if you look into the window you can
see silhouettes of the Holy Mother and saints on this glass.
It is odd how people who are not faithful also fall into these
silly conjectures. Everyone is traveling there out of curiosity. The faithful people stand by the chapel and kiss the
wooden walls and the cross someone has brought. Among
those who flock there are those who want to experience
spiritual ecstasies."

If only they could have seen the luminescence. The light always appeared unexpectedly, and even on a bright clear day it was discernible. Towards the end of the apparitions a fringe of violet would surround it. Before her appearance, many people saw the smaller inner white light, but I did not always see this. Observers standing on one side of the building tended to see an illuminated cross, while on the other side people saw the figure of a woman. But the cross was there before and after she came. Some pilgrims saw the crucified Christ. I learned later that five Polish and German priests came incognito and they too saw the cross.

Masses continued almost without stop. After one sermon, Father Anton and I left to meet several Russian and Jewish families who wanted to be baptized. That year (1987), several thousand Jewish families converted to Christianity. They renounced other Jews who served and still do serve in the upper echelons of the Communist Party. After the Baptism, we headed back for Hrushiv. There were 54 of us traveling together.

We got to Blessed Trinity after lunch. I would estimate that there were about 20,000 people around the chapel. The excitement was at a fever pitch. The Basilians were saying Mass for every arriving group, and the militia had given up the routine of asking for everyone's identity cards. I conducted some business with Father Petryo Zeleniukh, a Redemptorist, and then I looked to the chapel and again saw the Virgin.

On this day the Mother of God was visible just about the whole time I was there. The thought occurred to me that Catholicism is continually growing and expanding, revealing the secrets of its existence and in those secrets, revealing itself.

That night we prayed for the conversion and unity of the Ukraine. It was an emotional moment. People shed tears and embraced. It was warm and sultry and the first stars began to twinkle in the full sky. The moon gazed down on us happily, as if it were singing to itself.

But the most joyous light was still the one encompassing the vicinity of the chapel. It greeted us and bathed us and it seemed like everyone saw Our Lady that day. She held the infant Jesus and with heavenly humility bowed to us.

Her face was widened into a smile and she looked everyone in the eyes, like we were all one large entity. It was ineffably beautiful. Suddenly the rustling and whispering stopped and a deep silence fell upon the area. Again Our Lady began to talk.

"My daughter Ukraine," she said. *"I am interceding and praying for you, for your children, and for your future. The time is here when this nation of yours that loves God shall attain its statehood and become a haven for those who remain faithful to Jesus Christ. But the anti-Christ is very powerful and is opposed to the will of the Eternal One. Russia continues to involve itself in division and war. It continues to reject the call to love and the Eternal One, the call issued by Our Lord and Savior."*

She continued: *"My heart is turned to the Ukraine because of her faithfulness. There is no special merit in remaining faithful when no one is persecuting you. Heroism and a true heart are needed where faith is being destroyed, amidst persecution. This is why I have come to you. You are dear and precious to me, my beloved children. But all of you must say this prayer: 'O my God! I am heartily sorry for having offended you and I confess all my sins.' My children, keep all the prayers that I have entrusted to you for your correction and the preservation of your souls. Do not neglect your prayers to the Archangel Michael. Teach the children, for this will save them from the anti-Christ. This is your heavenly defense."*

It was a long message that I wrote in my diary. She went on to say, *"My children, all of you present are dear to me and please me. I do not make distinctions as to the color of your skin or your religious faith. But here today you have received the knowledge of the one true Church, and by that same token you have received the way to Heaven. You must follow this path, a path that is not an easy one and is not accessible to all. But whoever steps from it shall be rejected, for he will no longer be able to make the excuse that he doesn't know the true way. Pray always for the deceased. Do not forget them. Pray especially for the deceased who did not lead holy lives. Through my prayers and the prayers of thousands of faithful, the innocent victims of the great holocaust in the Ukraine and the victims of the disaster in Chernobyl are now in Heaven. Woe to him who has forgotten those who were killed and does not remember them amidst daily routine and troubles."*

"Love is longsuffering," she continued. *"It was because of the envy of Satan that death entered into the world, and everyone who is now serving him will receive death. The anti-Christ is sowing envy and dissension. Many lies are being proclaimed today against the truth. The innocent are condemned. The seal of the devil has been placed on the foreheads of many. How many there are that have been crucified on the red five-pointed star, the mark of Satan. Their deeds are evil and are known to God. The wicked world is gorging itself on depravity and impurity. The people are falling into the hands of Satan. They are blinded by unceasing idolatry. How many come as false messiahs and false prophets! So I warn you to be diligent and circumspect, for happy are those whose lives are blameless, who walk according to God's commandments.*

"But these are few, and everyone must be careful to use these symbols wisely in order not to fall into the trap of the anti-Christ. Cast from your shrines any signs of Satan that have been forced upon you. The churches are weeping and perishing. Lead a pure and sinless life. The Kingdom of Heaven-on-earth is at hand. But it will come only through repentance and penance. You can achieve the destruction of all the arms that have been arrayed by the unbelieving nations through prayer and fasting, through the action of all people who have accepted Christ. The Eternal God is calling out to you and is asking you to turn from Satan before it is too late. Ukraine, this is why I have come to you, for you were among the first of nations to become mine. You alone have not lost hope and love, though you have been inhumanely persecuted."

Then her sweet voice said, *"I pray for you."*

On May 15 I didn't see Our Blessed Mother. I spent much of the day in the village of Kozeva, kept vigil at night, and prayed the Rosary until morning. She appeared again on May 16, 1987, my last day in Hrushiv, and the visions she showed me will haunt me forever.

Chapter 20

PILLAR
OF FIRE

I had no inkling of the sights I would soon see. The day began normally enough, if one can call a day spent with the Mother of God normal. I had a very strange feeling that I was spending my last days in the Ukraine. I arrived at Blessed Trinity in the morning and the crowd was especially dense and expectant.

The main liturgy was celebrated by Father Yurko, from Dora, and a priest from Transcarpathia. The crowd divided into smaller groups for individual celebration. Father Ivan Senkiw presented a sermon about persecution and told the people I would be speaking after the liturgy. A group of women from the area of Kirovohrad approached me and one of them gave me a loaf of bread and asked that I pray for her sons, who were in Afghanistan. Tears crept into my eyes. These were such devout, good people, truthful and humble people, and they had endured catastrophe after catastrophe.

I began to pray the Rosary earnestly. Then I began my talk. Only God could have given me the words and strength: I spoke to the people for about five hours. Before we knew it, it was evening. The sun was touching the horizon. It bounced and fled to Transcarpathia.

The crowd was staring at the dome of the church. All of a sudden someone called out. "It's her!" The Virgin had once more returned. Really, it's hard to relate the light in terms of colors. The aurora was pleasant and alive. Truly alive. And from that aurora a brilliant light had distinguished itself. It began to move and stopped over the church. You could see the form of a human figure. The light expanded and in the brilliance over the cupola appeared the character of a woman. She held a child in her arms. It's hard to describe the countenance and hands of this woman. I paid more attention to her garb. I felt as if they were flames of fire. I repeat, it's impossible to describe her beauty. Her smile was quiet and joyous and at the same time sorrowful. I don't know how the others felt, but I began to experience a new strength, new physical strength. The woman bowed twice to us.

Most people prayed and watched the apparition while those who saw nothing milled expectantly about. It was the Christ child she held in her arms, and her garb consisted of flares of many colors. She looked at me with great tranquility, as if to say, "I am with you." I felt another surge of awesome strength. I felt bold. I felt love. I felt unconquerable. Then a nun named Sister Josaphata whispered, "The Mother of God is about to speak!"

I waited in unreal anticipation. There was a great feeling of solemnity. Our Lady moved gracefully with the Infant and stood over the dome of the chapel. A light pierced all our souls. We were holding our collective breath. Then the Mother of God raised her left hand and kissed her Rosary. Everyone who saw her heard the following words:

"Repent and love one another. The times are coming which are spoken of as the end times, as has been foretold. See the desolation that surrounds us, the sloth, the genocide, the many other sins. I came to you in tears to implore you to pray, work for good, and labor for the glory of God. The Ukraine was the first to acknowledge me as its Queen, and I have received her under my care. You must work, for without work there is no happiness, and no one will gain the Kingdom of God without working for it. If you work for God, you shall win my heart and you will be able to love in unity. Follow the leaders of the Church boldly and you will win your own country, gaining love among the nations of the world. I love the Ukraine and the Ukrain-

ian people for their suffering and faithfulness to Christ the King. And I shall protect the Ukraine for the glory and the future of the Kingdom of God on earth, which will last for a thousand years."

The Virgin also had some personal messages for me. *"What is difficult is worthwile. You are troubling yourself again with doubts, and you are hoping for help from afar. You will not receive such help. Help comes only from my Son. A long and sad road awaits you. You will find people to help you, and I will never leave you. But change your attitudes. You are not at peace. You must not fret. Do not become angry. You are often angry with human presumptions, but you must not be that way. Prayer and the Rosary will save you. The anti-Christ is doing everything to break you. . . Suffering and peace."*

What did all of this mean? I had been told there was a bright road before me, but that it would also be a sad road. Our Lady was speaking of the "anti-Christ," and it was as if she was talking more about a spirit than a single man. Could it be that there have always been men imbued with the spirit of anti-Christ? If so, there are many anti-Christs and an anti-Christ is simply a person who stands up against God. Perhaps atheists are anti-Christs. Perhaps, as I explained, Lenin personified the anti-Christ. He was certainly out to challenge the Eternal One.

The visions I saw on May 16 I have never revealed before. They happened amidst that backdrop of silvery-blue light. I was watching and waiting, not knowing what I was waiting for. In the distance the clouds were blackening—rolling and piling up. The clouds began to tumble over the upper half of the village, right above the church, and I saw a thin light around the palm of my hand. I felt as if everything had stopped. It was as if time had halted.

Then I heard the voice again: *"Pray to the Sacred Heart of Jesus. Fall before the feet of the Blessed Trinity and ask the Father, Son, and Holy Spirit that sins be forgiven. Look."*

I looked in the direction she was indicating and I saw a vast ocean. Half of the ocean was quiet and pleasant, the waters very calm and transparent. I saw the fish and other animals of the deep. The other half of the ocean was dark and stormy. The lightning was cutting through the horizon and an awful noise rumbled over the ocean. And in these flashes of lightning I saw the heads of people who I couldn't initially identify. Then I saw Lucifer. He appeared as a handsome, swarthy man in a dark suit. Everything about him was beautiful but his eyes were red. I had the impression that he was blind. Three boats appeared in the ocean and when the storm drove them closer I saw that these were three large books—one red, one black, one brown. They were Talmuds and they floated like three large boats. On each of these Talmuds was a large head. I was filled with consternation but I heard the voice of a woman say, *"Do not fear. I am with you."*

On the red book I saw the head of Marx and around the head of Marx were eight corpses missing their heads. On the black Talmud I saw the head of Lenin and around him six black cadavers. They too were headless. On the brown Talmud I saw the head of Hitler and around him four brown, headless cadavers. All of a sudden a crimson cross appeared over the ocean and the ocean subsided. A strange light covered the entire earth. The voice of the woman, who seemed to be by me, said, *"Lucifer is losing strength. To maintain himself on the throne of darkness he began to portray himself as repentant, but this is not true. Lucifer is cunning and clever. He is preparing a great deception for all of God's creation, and especially for the people of God. For a short time a godless kingdom shall maintain itself from one end of the earth to the other. This kingdom shall be given birth by a lascivious woman. From her womb will come the spirit of godlessness. The godless spirits are the servants of anti-Christ. They will begin to deny the existence of the human soul in order to destroy religion and morality. The anti-Christs have strong reason to deny the immortality of the soul, because depriving man of the soul, they shall have an open and fertile field for the seed of disbelief."*

Lightning began to flash again and the clouds continued to roll. The woman began to explain that the tempter was raising this against her so that she could not speak about the anti-Christs and their father, Satan. The ocean again subsided. A light covered the entire earth from end to end and at this time an awful noise extended over the face of the planet. From the ocean emerged an immense, fiery column. From a distance it looked like a fiery dragon. The head was white like light. Around his neck was a golden cincture. His chest was reddish brown and his feet bloody rod. He grew larger, at a fast rate. Again I was filled with fear. I almost felt paralyzed. My mouth was dry and bitter. The voice of the woman continued: *"This is the beast, the servant of the anti-Christ, and himself an anti-Christ. But do not fear because he is not for you."*

The beast began to shrink and fade away. And from his mouth came seven flags. I recognized six of them as the flags of Czechoslovakia, the USSR, Romania, Hungary, Poland, and East Germany. The seventh was either Yugoslavia or Bulgaria. I believe it was Bulgaria. A large white dove flew over and began to collect the flags of these nations but did not have the strength to keep them in its beak. I saw myself among a large number of dogs—red, black, and white. I heard a voice. *"Tell no one what you have seen about yourself or else it will not take place."* I knew it was the Mother of God.

An immense earthquake began. The sky turned red. The black clouds filled the horizon. The white dove I noticed had great eyes and I saw in him Lucifer. Above the ocean he grabbed a red banner and on this banner were the faces of Marx and Lenin. The heads were waxen yellow. They appeared dead. It was very unpleasant to look at them.

Again the voice spoke. *"In two years you won't be here. But you shall receive the church at Hrushiv into your dominion. Remember the red beast with gleaming eyes. It is watching by day and night. He wants to destroy life on earth. But those who know this will not die."*

I then saw a Russian soldier and over him three large green rockets. I felt they were almost alive. The Russian was standing on a map of red color. It was a map of the earth. And I saw from the Soviet bloc a large hammer and sickle and from the point of the sickle flew the red flag. On the other side, from North America, rose a large blue rocket, and from it the flag of the USA. Then I saw a large open book like a building. This building was divided into five stories. Each of these stories was colored with the flags of ten socialist countries. The paint was fresh and did not adhere too well. On the fourth floor all the windows burst into flames and I saw the destruction of a large concrete wall. This was in Germany. And on the map of the Ukraine, I saw many black and gray blotches. Then the Ukraine was divided by an immense red river. I was surrounded by the dogs. A part of our people covered themselves with gold cloth and the others with a brown-red cloth. Under this brown-red cloth I saw sin. And on the clothing or garb of those under the gold cloth I saw crosses. Many people were laughing and bore the cross of our Savior without faith and love. For some unknown reason, I saw meetings and gatherings in the great cities of the Ukraine and over them the anti-Christ himself, who smiled at them gently. Chaos filled our country. All the atheists went to the churches. I was very disturbed. Their eyes were strange, with a red gleam.

I saw that our faithful again gathered in the woods. I saw many of our priests with unkempt beards and hair. They proclaimed strange sermons with their blackened lips and on Fridays they ate meat and drank wine.

I saw Rome and the Pope. We were sitting together in the palace of some church. And I'm giving the Pope the pictures and papers of our Church. The Pope looked at this somewhat dryly and I was disturbed in my soul and the Pope asked me whether I realized or knew what my future would be—how the road of my own life would unroll. I answered, "I somehow experienced it but I don't know." The Pope then said, "Believe me that I will always be with you. There will be many rumors that I have renounced or rejected your Church, but do not believe stories. You'll hear rumors that the Pope has bowed down to Satan, but do not believe them. You shall see two triumphs of your Church. In one year you will be witness of such an event in Rome as has never taken place before, and three years later you will be witness to still another great event. Here in St. Peter's Square, a great act of consecration will take place. In this very room, you, your wife, and children shall pray for purity and love."

My eyes passed over the ocean and I saw a large city. I heard the woman's voice. *"Josyp, look. To your right, you will see the one who has the scales of justice in her hand."* I looked and I saw the great Statue of Liberty with a torch that burned very brightly and in the left hand were the scales.

I saw that this was the hand of a righteous judgment. The voice continued: *"You're surprised that the one who has the scales is in America. There is also much evil there, evil that will be found in the Church of my Son, but there will come a time that a white rider on a white horse will kill the red dragon. Here you shall see that the people of this nation are good and devout. This people will pray more for the conversion of the Ukraine than Ukrainians themselves. There shall rise many new pseudo-Christian rituals. They shall all claim to be Christians, but they shall live a life unworthy of my Son. For a short time we shall see the rule of a living faith in the Ukraine, but with false pastors with the false cross on their standard. This new faith will begin to spread paganism, concealing or masking itself with false flags. The name of Christ will be invoked only to keep the people in its grasp. You will call out and not everyone will hear your voice, but he who hears you will follow you. You will fall into moments of questioning your faith. You will persevere and rise again. As the human soul is immortal, so you will see my words come true."*

Then I saw a large city, burgeoning with red flags. The city of Babylon the Great. I believe it was Moscow. Parts of the city began to sink into the earth. Around the city I saw another map of nations, cities, and villages. I recognized Russia. The earth itself was polluted by the Russians. They received this technology of degradation from the West, and conveyed these anti-God ideas through the entire land. I heard the woman's voice: *"Pray for Russia. Russia will be converted only when all Christians pray for her conversion. All Christians should repent and, through purification from sin, stop the godlessness in Russia from continuing to spread through the world. Pray in brotherly love for the conversion of the Russian people. The believing Ukrainian Christians will save their own nation. Until the West acknowledges its own guilt before the East, Russia will not be able to receive Christ the King."*

Again I saw the ocean and floating in it was the globe of the earth. Billows of black and red smoke were spreading over the horizon. Over one part of the earth I saw the inscription "SOCIALISM." It was written in Russian and was like blue on red. A mass of people were walking along the earth carrying red flags. In the first ranks, the red flag had the inscription "Peace." From the ends of the globe appeared the figure of a man and it began to grow. He rose to the heavens. And in his hands he carried an immense red flag with the insignia of the anti-Christ. The insignia included the heads of Marx, Lenin, and Engels—again, yellow and not alive. This man became as a statue. I heard his voice. "It has been given to me to take peace from the earth."

I experienced and felt the earth shaking. I was filled with fear. It wasn't really fear but something deeper and worse. The woman said, *"Do not fear. You see the anti-Christ in three persons but he can no longer do anything to you. He will not bother you anymore."*

I saw a map of the Ukraine and the bloody river began to dry up. The earth in many places was scorched and took on a black-gray color. This was the color of death. But amid the black-gray ashes I saw grass sprouting. It was very tall. I saw the people kneeling and crying but I knew these were the tears of joy and salvation. I saw the new Babylon, the red city, that was falling into the earth. In that city, under a Christian temple, was a secret hiding place. There were eight men there—eight rulers, all eight waxen yellow. They laughed horribly and bared their teeth. Gorbachev told me it wasn't he who was in charge of the state. I saw the real leader of the USSR behind a yellow screen: It was Lucifer himself, in the figure of <u>Yeltsin</u>, his eyes red and his face blushed. I looked and from the earth of that city, immense dull red rats, large as dogs, began running. These animals were awful. I knew they were poisonous.

I heard the voice of a woman full of love and goodness. She said, *"You have seen the godless East and West. The difference is that in the West godlessness is not officially recognized. But the goal of godlessness in the East and West is the same. In order to save Russia and the whole world from godless hell, you must convert Russia to Christ the King. The conversion of Russia will save Christian culture in the West and will be a push for Christianity throughout the world. But the kingdom of Christ the King shall establish itself through the reign of the Mother of God."*

I heard the pleasant singing of angelic choirs and the words, "Most Holy Mother of God, save us."

Chapter 21

AFTERMATH

Although the major apparitions halted at Hrushiv after about three weeks, from time to time there were additional sightings and to this day, in addition to occasional apparitions, there are phenomena on a smaller scale. Many of those who make the pilgrimage report seeing silhouettes of Our Lady in the window glass or on the chapel's balcony. The crowds are much smaller but Our Lady still hints at her presence. The little clues have been left as sort of a permanent sign.

I left Hrushiv to carry on the mission of converting my fellow Ukrainians. I visited as many villages as I could and preached for an entire month. In that single month, 34 Russian Orthodox churches were converted to Catholicism. Around the same time, Bishop Pavlo Vasyluk converted five Lutheran parishes in Estonia. Entire villages accepted the apostolic Church. The authorities accused me of creating inter-church strife, but I felt strongly about my convictions. The KGB would try to follow us but we were able to keep out of their view in a way that was nearly miraculous. It was as if we simply disappeared when they followed us through the glens and forests.

The powerful encounter in Hrushiv stayed with me and gave me inspiration. At the time we saw the Mother of God, our focus was entirely on her. We were cut off from all other experiences. And afterwards I remained totally under the sensations felt during the apparitions. This is why I'm skeptical of people who claim to have seen the Mother of God and then after their vision go about with other things. When I saw her, I was so taken by her that she was all I spoke about. The bishop of the diocese has still not accepted the Hrushiv apparitions and priests and nuns from that diocese are therefore reluctant to go there. Some of the reluctance was because Church authorities feared the commotion caused by Hrushiv would jeopardize the Church's fight for legalization. But believe me, plenty of priests and nuns make the pilgrimage quietly. Besides the Mother of God, I saw certain lights that were probably angels. I can't understand how I knew they were angels. But this much I do know: Hrushiv was only a part—a big part, but only a part—of a larger outbreak of heavenly phenomena. During the same period of time, she also showed herself in, above, or around other abandoned churches or holy grounds. After midnight near a cemetery in L'viv, towards the end of June, three of us spotted five luminous crosses moving in the sky. They were silver with a blue edge. At first we wondered if they were part of some kind of cosmic experiment by the Soviets, or UFOs. We watched for about an hour and the next day, when we went to search a woodland where they seemed to have landed, we found nothing. I am now convinced that when people see UFOs, they might well be seeing good or evil supernatural wonders—not the vehicles of spacemen.

In addition to Hrushiv, there were at least 13 other places where spiritual signs were noted. During June, near Hoshiv, which is about 27 kilometers from Hrushiv, people saw strange celestial spheres and thought they might be connected in some way to nearby missile silos. But then the Mother of God was also spotted, and though she couldn't be seen from up close, she was apparent for those who were a couple kilometers away. The light itself was visible for a couple dozen miles. She appeared to be standing over a hill where a ruined monastery was, materializing in the sky at daybreak or in the evening. The old monks interpreted the event as a warning.

Our Lady was also reported in Buchach, Ozerna, Kaminko-Buzsk, Berezhany, and the old Marian site of Zarvanystya, where the monk was given the miraculous icon in the 13th century. We stopped to investigate some of these reports and in a few instances witnessed phenomena. Five of us, driving near the hill of Hoshiv, saw the silhouette of a woman in a moving light. Father Yurchysyn was with us. A bit lower and to the right of the monastery was the contour of another person giving out light. Father Yurchysyn exclaimed, "The Angel of the Ukraine!"

At these and other sites, it was said that the Mother of God turned to the priests and warned that they must correct their lives. She also repeated her call to pray for the dead and to always remember the Rosary. She also tells us, at these various sites, to pray in large numbers for the Pope because he is going through difficult times.

It was no accident, in my mind, that the Mother of God spread her wonders to sites of worship that the Soviets had destroyed. For example, the church of Ozerna, where apparitions were later seen, had been totally broken, the doors smashed, the walls caved in, and the grounds covered with garbage. Silhouettes of the Madonna were also witnessed at hospitals, on the walls at schools, and in the windows of stores. In Ternopil, she was supposedly seen on the wall of the Church of the Nativity, which had been closed in the 1950s. According to *The New York Times,* which printed a front-page story about the apparitions on October 13, 1987, one man saw "a mist—well, more of a shadow, something dark" that flickered along the gray stones. When one observer shouted "I see!" a second time, he was fined for the outburst, according to the *Moscow News.* Was this the power of suggestion, or an ingenious conspiracy, or simple pranksterism?

The Soviets took a predictable stance. "For every miracle there is a director, a stage manager and a crowd," said Mikhail Y. Babi, committee secretary for the Ternopil regional Party. "The question isn't about believers; it's about how to exploit people, which is really a pity." The purpose of all these sightings, said the Communists, was to pit believers against atheists.

At Zarvanystya, the apparitions were of a woman in white garb. She spoke of the possibility of war, that the world was so sinful it would be hard to prevent. And she seemed always to mention the conversion of Russia.

As I write, she is reported in the eastern part of the Ukraine.

There were so many of these events we couldn't pay attention to them all. If you wanted to document such occurrences, it would have been a full-time preoccupation. One of the most intriguing phenomena was that of a mysterious old woman, or nun, who would approach pilgrims, speak with them a short while, and then wander away and disappear from sight. Those who encountered the woman were later convinced that it was the Mother of God. At Hrushiv, the visionary Marina told the account of meeting this older woman for herself. The woman told young Marina to come to Blessed Trinity and pray. "But the doors are chained and locked," Marina answered.

The woman responded, "There is nothing locked to me."

When they got there the door was indeed open and the woman entered, praying with her hands raised.

On other occasions, pilgrims reported looking through the keyhole of the abandoned, locked church and seeing the entire interior strangely illuminated, with a woman inside, praying.

Yet another time, a woman from Buchach crawled through a small opening into Blessed Trinity to get some water from the well. It was for a child who was ill, suffering from internal swelling. Suddenly a beautiful young woman appeared next to her, dressed as a nun. The woman said softly, "You have a sick child." She then handed the woman three small pebbles. "Here, put these in a glass of water when you get home and have the child drink it." They also prayed the Rosary together. When she returned home the woman did as she was told and the child recovered.

There were all kinds of cures: from cancer, from eczema, from psychological disorders. I myself didn't have the opportunity to conduct investigations into all the miraculous cures and now I regret it, because many of our good people can't understand the immense importance of all this. Let us imagine that what happened at Hrushiv was just a hoax. Why, if it was a hoax, did the Communists demand that all their people who had been at Hrushiv during the major events sign a declaration stating that they had seen nothing?

News of events such as Hrushiv flew throughout the Carpathians. The Soviets knew that they were powerless. After I left, detachments were withdrawn from Hrushiv and so were road barriers. The only police who remained were there to help direct traffic.

After Hrushiv, the villagers everywhere were much more willing to risk putting their names on petitions about matters such as Chernobyl, or to request extended broadcasts from Radio Vatican, which up to then had lasted only 15 minutes (and still haven't been lengthened).

I felt unworthy of what I had been favored to see. And I felt unworthy as a preacher. The dangers were secondary to me, but they were always present. When we went into the countryside, the KGB tried to track us with radio equipment and dogs. We walked from village to village, a mass of us strutting through the forests or along the streams. Yet the authorities kept losing sight of us. People listened to our accounts of Hrushiv and some would convert, while others were more obstinate and threatened to call the militia. It was the beginning of a great struggle that has yet to reach its crescendo. There will be renewed persecution and martyrdom.

In July, 1987, eleven Orthodox priests visited Hrushiv and by the third day, five of them had expressed their intentions of converting to Catholicism and leaving the Russian Church. That same month, according to Father Michael Vasko, peasant children who were driving cattle to pasture saw an apparition of the Virgin. I believe the date was the early morning of July 28 or 29. Father Vasko himself saw the illuminated cross with Christ crucified and when it faded Mary appeared, dressed in splendiferous white.

Why does Our Heavenly Mother appear in such inconsequential villages as Hrushiv? Why does she not appear to atheists and unbelievers?

Because the atheists, who are not so much disbelievers as *anti*-believers, would never spread the truth of what they had seen. And also because they do not operate with faith. God often reveals Himself to those who first reveal their faith to Him. Many of our so-called leaders and intellectuals prefer to dismiss supernatural events not only because such occurrences are physically intangible, but also because these people privately seek to establish *themselves* as little gods. They seek the power to determine when human lives should begin and when they should end. They seek to control our thoughts. They seek to prove their own omniscience. Socialists are especially prone to such thinking.

The messages from the various shrines were the same as Hrushiv, and it was making the authorities very edgy. Besides forming a "scientific" committee to denounce the apparitions, Soviet officials began another religious crackdown. On June 8, one such administrator paid a visit to Father Yavorsky, a priest in Drohobych. There they conducted a search for "religious literature." They also tried to get Father Yavorsky to sign a declaration stating that the activity of the underground priests would stop. Once again they were trying to forcibly merge us with the Russian Orthodox. The priest refused and they began threatening him. They also wanted to know about Hrushiv. In fact this was probably the main purpose of their visit. They wanted him to sign a declaration dismissing the miracle. Again he refused and the administrator, a man named Gertz, threatened the priest with punishment if he made another visit to the site of the apparitions.

Meanwhile, the article in *Road to Socialism* personified the way Soviet "journalists" approached the baffling issue. The reporter of that particular piece related how he arrived at Hrushiv with a taxi driver, and how the taxi driver started to point to the balcony, claiming to see something. The writer denounces his driver for daring to believe. "I squinted and looked to where he was pointing," recounted the reporter. "I saw rabbits from the reflection of the sun, and yes, I could see the crosses and the old icons behind the glass in the church but I didn't see anything. I told him it was just the old icons in the church. 'Oh,' the driver said, 'you don't see because you are not faithful.' He waved his hand at me. Later I was told this man was not good; he had been head of a Communist committee for car pools and believes in neither God nor the devil, but came here among the faithful to gather money for a so-called charity."

In other words, any good atheist who thought they saw something at Hrushiv was making such a claim only to collect money. He pointed out that part of the chapel near the balcony had carvings and that with certain refractions of light, people could imagine heavenly images. He also said a false priest tried to organize Mass at Hrushiv and had also conjured miracles in L'viv. He indicated that such schemes had their roots in nationalism. The reporter went on to say that "there is always someone who claims to see a silhouette" but that it was a product of suggestion and imagination. "People talk and gossip," was the way he put it.

In part, the press was writing so much about the apparitions in an effort to undermine a new local Communist secretary, who was a Gorbachev man. By making the events so well-known, it left the impression that matters were getting out of control in the area. And that played into the hands of anti-Gorbachev forces.

The press found it highly coincidental that the events were taking place during what the Pope had declared as a "Marian Year." The implication, again, was that Hrushiv was a plot by the Uniates and the Vatican.

The Soviets were especially disconcerted because up to 80,000 people a day had gone to Hrushiv, and yet, the press had declared that Catholics no longer existed except in the minds of people like myself. During 1987 there were dozens of articles and pamphlets that denounced the Eastern Rite.

And the newspaper articles continued for years. As recently as May 13, 1989, the newspaper *Free Ukraine* printed a piece headlined, "For Whom Is The Miracle In Hrushiv Convenient?" It recounted the "very odd and unusual rumor" sweeping the area. "On the cupola from time to time it was said that an icon of the Virgin Mary appeared," said the article. "From close up nothing could be seen, but if you stepped back a hundred meters and squinted, then the Blessed Virgin will sort of appear. Information about these happenings began to grow larger and people began to say that on the window panes of the church, and on the metalwork, you could see silhouettes of the Holy Mother and also of various saints. Talk about the so-called miracle in Hrushiv was brought to the attention of surrounding villages. Among those who came to see the alleged miracle, unfortunately, were even the young people. They crowd around the church, they pray, and they look through the windows. Normally they don't see the miracle, although some people who gaze at the weathered glass and panes suddenly cry out, 'Look! Something flashed!' Something like an icon of the Holy Mother appeared.''

The article disdainfully reported how old men prayed and read psalms, seeking religious ecstasy. It also said that miracles and devotions pertaining to the Mother of God were a time-honored Catholic tradition—''the aim of which was to strengthen faith and discourage the masses from fighting for a better life.'' It called our Uniate Church ''a synthetically formed hybrid'' and said that we divided the Ukraine spiritually and politically. The article accused Eastern Rite Catholics of supporting Hitler and said our leaders ''ended up in the garbage bins of the West.''

The article went on to attack Marina's mother, Myroslawa Kizyn, as well as her husband. ''People were told by her young daughter that the Holy Mother appeared to her,'' said the reporter. ''It is self-explanatory that without her mother's coaching this would never have happened. The mother and father encouraged people to look closer at the balcony. The father encouraged them to look because he said something extraordinary was going on. When someone had doubts, the religious fanatics would scare them. 'How can you not see that? You can't see that because you don't have faith!' In order not to be labeled sinners, people agreed that they did see something on the balcony.'' The article further described the miracle as a ''provocative happening'' that may have resulted from ''the fantastic imagination of Mr. and Mrs. Kizyn, who bow down to all the saints.'' At the least, it was a provocation, said the Communists, of us ''extremists.'' The article also accused a monk, Alexander Kowalchuk from the Chmelmytskyj province, who had once been at the monastery at Pochaiv, as being one of the instigators. The monk sold icons, according to the newspaper, and again they hinted it was all a money-making scheme.

''Things are slowing down with the miracle, but this does not mean we should weaken our attention to religious extremism or happenings that occur because of those trying to take advantage of religion to destroy society,'' concluded the newspaper story. ''The owners of the local collective farm are disgusted. 'How can people during working hours rush to the so-called miracles? These are nothing but hooligans and this happens when each hour is critical to work in the fields.'" Lastly, the article raised the fear that sanitation in the area was a problem and that someone might even intentionally try to infect all the people with disease.

That newspaper and others seemed upset at how fast and far the news had spread "even with poor telephone service," as one article complained. The press was also concerned about Russian Orthodox priests who were converting to Catholicism because of the miracle.

Even political dissidents were cool to such supernatural events. Just because someone is a dissident (or refusenik) doesn't mean he is a believer. This is a confirmation that we're casting off sin very slowly in the world. We saw all forms of attack against Christianity and what are perceived as Western values. For instance, the Soviets spread rumors that the CIA caused the Chernobyl disaster. Meanwhile, they continued to conceal the extent of radioactive damage and the results of clinical evaluations. Yet, certain information got out, including accounts and photographs of genetically altered fish (so big their muscles could not sustain them), five-legged horses, and hogs born without eyes. Some of these photographs made their way into the American magazine *Time*. We also know that funds and medical supplies never reached the victims of Chernobyl.

I believe now that the Chernobyl accident is related to events of the apocalypse. Such matters unfold slowly. But the indications are such that they have even drawn the attention of agnostic newspapers such as *The New York Times*. As that newspaper pointed out, many prominent scholars in Russia and elsewhere in the USSR were nervous about the nuclear events. They began to read Revelation and especially 8:11, which says *"Then the third angel sounded: And a great star fell from heaven, burning like a torch, and it fell on a third of the rivers and on the springs of water; and the name of the star is Wormwood; and a third of the waters became wormwood; and many men died from the water, because it was made bitter."*

Wormwood is a bitter wild herb used as a tonic in rural areas. And the Ukrainian word for wormwood is *"chernobyl."*

What was the meaning of Chernobyl? Was the "great star"

which falls in Revelation a symbol for nuclear missiles, which would spread "wormwood" across our planet? First of all, I believe in one form or another, there will be more Chernobyls. We are now witnessing the fulfillment of certain admonishments. People think we'll be punished by only one atomic war and that will be it, or that it will take place in only one part of the earth, but perhaps it has to do with the relationship of people and technology to our planet.

Technology has replaced spirituality, and we may reap grim results.

We must always think back to Fatima. The miracle of the sun—when it seemed to come crashing toward the earth—may have been a warning of nuclear warfare. The bombs dropped in Japan were later described as flashing with the force of the sun.

It also brings to mind the prophet Elija, who called down fire from Heaven to consume the pagan altar and end drought and idolatry. Elijah lived in the Mount Carmel region of Israel, and at Fatima, the Mother of God appeared as Our Lady of Mount Carmel.

What was the date America tested its atomic bomb? The test was on July 16, 1945, the feast day of Our Lady of Mount Carmel.

The bomb was later dropped, looking like the falling sun, and on August 15—the Feast of the Assumption—Japan surrendered. I believe we are all a part of a cosmic plan. When I look back at it now, I see the long series of coincidences, not only in our lives but in events of the world. For example, on October 13, 1960, there was an all-night vigil for peace at Fatima, and just days later, a secret super-missile under manufacture by the Soviets was destroyed in an accidental blast.

People often ask me if it is true that Satan resides in the Soviet Union. This is absurd. Satan is everywhere. Satan is where you find abortion, violence, pornography, egoism, rancor, lying, materialism, pollution, arrogant intellectualism, and a lack of faith. Satan is in rock albums, in bookstores, on television, in popular magazines. Is there not a glazed look in the eyes of satanists, criminals, and certain rock stars? Satan is in corporations, in government, and in the doctor's office. He is certainly in the clinics where young mothers deliberately murder their own unborn children. Abortion, like war, is one of Satan's greatest accomplishments—a blood sacrifice

But there is no doubt that Satan has been especially blatant in Russia, and the effect of his actions may soon be more noticeable. The way things are developing, evil is everywhere and people who do not understand their actions are destroying life in many forms. I am speaking again of environmental contamination. On May 16, at Hrushiv, I saw the whole planet and initially I saw each country like a map. Then I saw villages and towns and in some places petroleum tanks with spreading flames. I also saw sand moving. Was the sand a symbol of encroaching deserts from a change in climate?

We are being punished but we see none of this. We are oblivious. At Hrushiv I asked the Mother of God if the coming chastisements could be averted and she answered that without this punishment there will be no repentance. And God is punishing us not because he doesn't love us, but because sin *must* be punished. People go to church, but often they do so only as an ecstatic experience. We must stand in defense of our faith. The Mother of God said that until we recognize our sins and do penance, we will not come to Christ the King. The West bears guilt in spreading impure culture and technologies to other parts of the world and should immediately halt this. Only when the Western Christians cast off their own sin and constantly ask the Lord God for the conversion of Russia will the world be safe.

I believe everything I saw at Hrushiv, and I don't care if people call me a psychopath. I have been labeled as insane before. Everything is happening exactly as I heard, exactly as the Virgin said it would. Each and every one of us must come to God through continuous purification, so that we may begin to work for the conversion of Russians. And then we will attain our goal.

In 1987, I continued collecting signatures for causes such as the legalization of our Church, full disclosures about the Chernobyl disaster, and the freedom of Wallenberg. Through dissident groups in Moscow, I approached certain correspondents for foreign newspapers and with the help of a reporter at the Spanish publication *El Pais,* I made contact with officials (including Ambassador Pietros Buwalda) at the Dutch embassy. I also established connections at the American embassy, including a man named Richard Stevenson. Among other issues, we discussed the possibility that Wallenberg was still languishing in prison and the possibility of arranging a press conference for a man I had met who had been a translator at Wallenberg's initial interrogations. The former translator was willing to go public with what he knew, but there was worry that the Soviets would eliminate him. We wanted to bring the former translator to an interview with representatives from *The Baltimore Sun, The Christian Science Monitor,* and *The Washington Post,* along with a number of others. But later we severed some of these contacts, fearful that word would leak back to Soviet authorities.

For my own part, there were further indications that I was going to be thrown out of the USSR for "anti-Soviet" activities. Colonel Dziamko, a KGB agent from Carpathia, came to my home in a fit of anger. "What's this with Wallenberg?" he asked. "Why are you spreading these lies? Wallenberg was dead a long time ago. You're spreading these lies that Wallenberg is still alive. What translator is still alive?"

I said I didn't know anything about Wallenberg or the interrogation. It had been mentioned in the *Chronicles* and I told him I didn't know everything that went into the *Chronicles*. I was told that my fate was sealed and I would shortly be with the Americans. I was also warned that if I uttered one more word about Wallenberg, they wouldn't play any more games with me.

The atmosphere was getting very tense. But we had thousands of people publicly declaring their Catholicism and we were emboldened by that. Finally we were coming out of the catacombs. We gathered signatures and instructed the petitioners on what to do in the event of arrest. Bishop Sterniuk was initially cool to the idea because many priests were against publicly coming out. But on August 4, 1987, a declaration signed by two other bishops, Pavlo Vasyluk and Ivan Semedi, along with 24 priests, a number of monastics, and 720 lay activists, was sent to Pope John Paul II. Due to increasingly favorable conditions in the USSR, it said, "we therefore ask Your holiness to do all that is possible for the legalization of the Ukrainian Catholic Church in the USSR. Simultaneously, we turn, through Your Holiness, to the government of the USSR with our declaration that a significant portion of the Ukrainian Catholic Church [has] come out of the underground."

The night of August 12, from a diplomat's home, I read the declaration to contacts in Munich and Rome. The next day, August 13, at 10 a.m., I personally took the declaration to the Soviet Presidium. "Terelya from Carpathia," is how I identified myself. KGB agents dressed in civilian clothes had been following me and they watched as I registered the letter, received a confirmation, and left the room. When I did, 15 to 20 KGB agents surrounded me and began to search me. Then they took me to a room on the second floor. "What did you come here for?" they asked angrily. "Isn't Carpathia enough for you? We have enough problems with our own dissidents. Why did you come?"

I told them that our Church had come out of the underground. We were demanding our legalization. "We've decided," I said, "that we're not going to pray in the woods anymore. We're going to pray publicly."

They laughed and left me alone in the room. But to them it was really no laughing matter. The issue of our legalization was being discussed over radio stations in Spain, Canada, and the United States, as well as over Radio Free Europe.

The agents had taken my shoelaces and belt, which meant that I was about to be arrested again. I sat there for five hours not knowing what would happen next. One thing I did know: that if I were arrested I might never return. We had cut the Gordian knot.

I waited for them to sentence me to another 15 years. But instead of arresting me, they returned acting unusually courteous. They didn't know what to do with me. They asked when I was leaving Moscow and said I was misbehaving. But they let me go with just that slight slap on my wrist.

On August 15, the KGB came to the Moscow apartment where I was staying. They told me the "chief" wanted to talk to me. I refused, thinking they were talking about some ranking KGB official. They were not. They were referring to Yegor Kuzmich Ligachev, who at the time was the second most powerful man in the Soviet Union.

As a matter of protocol I had written an official letter on behalf of our Church asking for an audience with Ligachev, and that's what I got. Until he was demoted, Yegor Ligachev was a secretary of the Central Committee and in charge of Soviet ideology. Although he was later stripped of his central role, he remains a member of the Congress of People's Deputies. At the time I met him, Ligachev's power was second only to Gorbachev's. The first meeting was set for August 17. It was a rather positive meeting, and we had another encounter on August 21.

Ligachev knew very little about our Church. He thought we were just some other sect. I must say that while Ligachev is a Communist, he is a man of certain principles. I got the feeling that had he been in total charge, our Church would have been rehabilitated. I don't feel the same way about Gorbachev. I don't think he is as principled as Ligachev, who is a simple Russian peasant. But Ligachev is very pro-Soviet and despises everything that isn't. "Josyp, you're the son of a Communist," he said. "What the devil has made you believe in all these gods? There are no gods. What kind of Church is this?" He called me "son of Michael."

I had to explain what the Ukrainian Catholic Church was. Then I said, "We'll observe all the laws, but we want official recognition and we want our churches back."

I told him we were attached to the Vatican, and Ligachev wanted to know if something could be done about that. He asked if we would agree to separate from Rome, as the Chinese Catholics did.

I stood firm and told him that we would maintain our ties with the Vatican. He sort of sighed and indicated that it wasn't such a major point, since the government itself was starting to have relations with Rome. The Soviets would sign a document bringing us towards legalization, he promised, if we would agree to behave.

I asked what would happen if Gorbachev didn't agree. Ligachev made a remark to the effect that he didn't give a damn about *perestroika,* that the people needed something to eat and drink.

At the August 21 meeting, Borys Kashlev, who was with the ministry for affairs of religion and cults, attended the session, along with a representative of the Presidium named Myhajlov. Kashlev had a whole dossier on me and the Church. He presented it to Ligachev and made it seem like we Catholics were bourgeois nationalists using the Church as a cover. Ligachev turned to me. "Look at what all the newspapers are writing. You're a Banderite. Why are you deceiving me?"

I answered, "It's not true. They've blackened my name."

Ligachev said the issue would be delayed because he didn't know who to believe.

I said, "I'm telling you like it is. I gave you my word. And I'm not going to step back from what we've started."

During the conversation Ligachev told me that he had been baptized.

"If you're baptized, why are you a Communist?" I asked.

"Your father too was baptized and was a Communist," he responded accurately.

That aside, we discussed the possibilities of compromise. Ligachev said that by December he would personally preside over a subcommittee of the Central Committee that would hear from me and a few bishops. I explained that we had some internal problems but that what we all wanted was a decree to separate us from the Russian Orthodox Church.

Ligachev was an honorable man, and I also secretly met with the former general secretary of the Ukrainian Communist Party, as well as other leaders. We approached some through their parents and other relatives. But the Ligachev meetings were the most memorable and I took notes on what was said. We met in a reception area run by the Communist Party in the Kremlin complex, and though he was cordial, Ligachev had also been apprehensive. "The Russian Orthodox Church, it will not like the idea of legalization of the Ukrainian Catholic Church," he fretted. "The Orthodox authorities will be hostile to us."

I answered, "The Russian Orthodox Church is fully cooperative with the KGB and is the official government Church. The Church is completely under your control. This Church shows no real opposition to the Soviet government. And the

[handwritten margin note, rotated:] Russian Orthodox church not tied to Rome (the Pope)

hierarchy of the Orthodox Church fulfills the role assigned it by the Communist Party. At the same time, the Orthodox Church is important as an instrument of Russification of Ukraine as well as Moldavia and the Byelorussians.''

Ligachev wrote a comment and asked, ''The immigrant hierarchy of Ukrainian Catholic Church, it is hostile to the government of the USSR, is it not?''

''That's absurd, because the Ukrainian Catholic Episcopacy is composed of people who are citizens of their own countries. They never lived in the Soviet Union. How can they be hostile to you? They don't know you. Show them your true democratic face.''

Then Ligachev asked secretary Myhajlov to bring him a red dossier. ''The very name 'Ukrainian Catholic Church' contradicts the principality and suppositions of the USSR,'' he said. ''It says in the socialist system there can be no organization, the membership of which would be limited to belonging to some other nation.''

He was hung up on the word ''Ukrainian.''

I wasn't expecting that question. I wasn't prepared for it. Playing for time, I said, ''The Ukrainian Catholic Church is not an organization. It's a link in the chain of the universal Catholic Church.'' By this time, God had inspired me and I continued, ''In the USSR, you have the Georgian Orthodox Church and the Armenian Orthodox churches. Does their existence contradict the principles of the USSR? We see from this that what Moscow wants is simply that we Ukrainians not have our own Church.''

There was a long give-and-take. We reviewed the circumstances of 1946, when the infamous ''synod'' in L'viv falsely declared that the Eastern Rite Catholic Church was liquidating itself. I indicated that the Church should be separate from the state, but that in the USSR, the state controls the churches. This, I reminded him, was an infraction not only of the Soviet constitution, but also of all the international agreements concerning rights and freedom.

I gave Ligachev nine demands and he replied negatively. ''You've expressed nine points established by the initiatory group, nine points which are unacceptable to the Soviet government. We'll never be able to attain compromise on these nine points.''

I replied, "The Ukrainian Catholic Church and hierarchy, the central committee of Catholics, and the initiatory group will remove all nine points if the authorities will extend to us the same rights enjoyed by other organizations in the USSR, and if the Presidium of the Supreme Soviet will issue an act by which it will declare the Ukrainian Catholic Church legalized and rehabilitated."

"The circumstances do not allow us to invalidate the decision of the council of 1946," Ligachev responded.

But there were hopeful signs. It appeared that these were serious questions and that the Communists were looking for ways to legalize the Church. "The Soviet Union is undergoing *perestroika* and in this environment we can correct the errors of Stalin," I said, nudging him along. "Everybody who seeks to justify the actions of Stalin is aligning himself with Stalin."

I mentioned the provision in Paragraph 52 of the Constitution that guarantees religious freedom. "The Constitution is not for you," Ligachev responded. He missed few opportunities at contradicting my views. At that time, only two bishops had come out of the catacombs and he latched onto that fact. "The underground Ukrainian Catholic Church does not want to come out from the underground and request registration," he argued.

I was ready for that one. I mentioned that the majority of bishops wanted legalization. "There's a big difference between legalization and registration."

Ligachev had a book of official nomenclature and found the word "registration" in it.

Registration is the entry into the registry of certain books, persons, organizations, documents, or other entities, while "legalization" is the permissibility or the suitability of something to existing laws established by the appropriate authorities of a given party.

"We're not talking about registration but about the *legalization* of the Church in the USSR, with the participation of representatives from the Vatican and the Ukrainian archbishop. At the same time we want an apology by the government for crimes inflicted on our Church by Stalin, and remuneration for damages we suffered, as well as damages suffered by the Ukrainian Orthodox. We do not come out of the catacombs until then," I continued, adding: "The problems are created not by Ukrainian Catholics but by Gorbachev and an administration that does not want to solve the problem of our existence."

We left it at that. The first meeting was more cordial than the second. Soon the Soviets would promise our Church legalization, but I wouldn't be around to see it. Just a month after my last session with Ligachev, the Soviets sent me into exile.

Chapter 22

BEYOND
THE BORDERS

While Gorbachev was telling all the world about *peres-troika* and *glasnost,* local Communists continued their "investigation" of Hrushiv. They would enter a village, knock on dozens of doors, and ask, "Did you happen to go to Hrushiv? What is your relation to the Catholic Church? Do you really believe the Mother of God appeared?"

They told the people that Catholics were Polish traitors.

The health ministry issued a questionnaire to ascertain whether people who held jobs in its offices and hospitals were true atheists. It was a form to be filled out. There were questions that related to renewal of the Catholic Church and the events at Hrushiv.

It was the Communists' paranoid opinion that the Pope had declared a Marian Year to activate an anti-Soviet campaign. At the same time, certain elements of the Russian Orthodox Church nurtured the rumor that Americans had dynamited Chernobyl. Again, it diverted talk away from Hrushiv.

The atheistic press continued its propaganda and harangue. They were quite inventive in trying to debunk the Hrushiv miracle. They attacked the Basilians (referring to them as "the black army"), called the sites where apparitions had been reported "centers of Jesuit fanaticism," or carried headlines in such newspapers as *Leninska Molod*

that described the situation as an "illusion of sight."
These weren't just ordinary articles. They summoned
university professors to help dispel any thoughts of the
supernatural—a task that professors around the world are
adept at doing. A philosophy professor named Andrew
Biskup, who taught scientific communism at L'viv University, generously lent his "expertise" to dispel the supernatural, and other authoritative, "scientific" voices could be
heard over radio and television.

It was obvious that Hrushiv and the other apparitions had
taken the Soviets completely by surprise. They were initially at a loss for how they should respond. There was no
way they could readily explain this phenomenon.

The L'viv *Pravda*, the *Moscow News*—all tried to make
light of it. How could anyone believe in God when, after
all, the cosmonauts had been in the heavens and they hadn't
spotted Him?

While the struggle continued, and a strong undercurrent
of spirituality was developing, the Soviet economy, based
as it is on Marxism, continued to deteriorate. Socialism was
a failure to everyone but those who held cozy positions at
the top. The authorities went so far as to imply that the
Uniates were responsible for bread shortages. The Soviets
are always bold in perpetrating the "Big Lie."

Why was the Soviet media so disturbed? Consider a few
basic facts about the Soviet system. Throughout the USSR
regional party bosses are afraid of local problems because
the power or authority is totally centralized. Everything is
directed by the general director of the Central Party through
the republican, national, provinical, regional, and local parties. This system of immediate control is, in its turn, directed
by the fearsome and omnipotent KGB. There is collusion
everywhere. Anything uncomfortable is eliminated by local
and provincial authorities through the lies of propaganda.
The higher echelons falsify this information still more, until
it is totally whitewashed. And Gorbachev receives information that can be harmful to no one. This is called "wiping
one's eye." Deception. Wishful thinking. Telling the boss
only what he wants to hear. Up until Hrushiv, the deception worked almost perfectly. But now the press was freer
to write about such happenings, and even if the tone was

negative, it was better than completely ignoring supernatural events.

By simply covering the issue, television reports presented tantalizing hints that something inexplicable was occurring behind the Iron Curtain.

While Hrushiv is still relatively unknown to the West, I believe this will change and that one day pilgrims from afar will converge again around the historic chapel. That may not come, however, until the hard-liners are thrown out of power. From time to time the apparitions continue. There are those who claimed that when the chapel in Hrushiv was temporarily handed over to the Orthodox in 1988 the apparitions halted. This is not true. To say the Mother of God appears only to Catholics is not correct. The Mother of God is for everyone.

What had upset the authorities more than anything was their impotence in the face of a large crowd. By 1990 there were only 17 million members of the Soviet Communist Party, but 70 million Russian Christians. The Communists had to resort to bullying techniques to control the larger numbers, and they complained as if we in the majority were a pain in the neck. The atheists make a religion out of a non-religion and would rather people drink alcohol than pray. As one commentator noted: "Wouldn't it be better for our men to sit in a cafe in L'viv than to come out [to Hrushiv] for this hard work? Rain or shine, they have to be with the people to see if there's anyone doing something grave or evil, because the Uniates are distributing leaflets, prayers, religious literature and are even preaching. The officers of the KGB have a lot of problems. They are not strong enough to chase away these masses even with the help of militia because this will evoke a reaction. How can we tolerate such gatherings?"

The commentator further noted that detachments had to be called in not just from L'viv, but also from Ternopil, Carpathia, and Ivano-Frankivske—three other provinces.

How dare the Virgin prevent these fine young cadets from guzzling vodka in a cafe!

And they issued what amounted to rather stern warnings about making the other shrines centers of pilgrimage. (The press estimates that about a million and a half people have visited Hrushiv.)

Meanwhile, that "common criminal" and "religious fanatic" named Josyp Terelya had received his travel documents. I had accepted the offer of a visa because I wanted to go to Holland and Switzerland. The Soviets were being so kind! The travel papers were issued to me on July 28, 1987, and it was then, at the *ovir* office in Uzhhorod, that I saw another little vision materialize. Remember my dream about the man with the gray suit with the violet button and chain? I ended up meeting precisely such a man at the *ovir* office. I recognized him immediately. But there was no chain from his violet button, as in my dream. I mentioned this to him and he gave me a befuddled look. "My daughter tore off that chain," he admitted.

The parting was very warm. He gave us suggestions on how to behave, and I prepared myself for what seemed like a temporary little exile. I even embraced it. I was not ready to face another trial and head off to the labor camps for an additional 10 or 15 years. The Soviets thought I was ready to leave, but not quite yet. I had resigned myself to leaving my beloved homeland for a while—wanting to go to Switzerland for medical treatment—but there was still some unfinished business in the Ukraine. Fast approaching was the Feast of the Assumption (according to the Eastern calendar). I planned to spend that day at Zarvanystya.

Thousands of people were gathering at Zarvanystya for the important holy day. Dignitaries such as Bishop Vasyluk were present. We prayed and celebrated the Moleben service. There were faithful from all seven provinces of the Ukraine and even from Moldavia and Eastern Ukraine. A whole host of people were there to celebrate a final liturgy with me. There was also Chancellor Symkajlo, Fathers Senkiw, Volodymyr Wityshyn, Mykhailo Havryliw, and Yurchyshyn.

The KGB was observing everyone and fined the bishop and priests seventy rubles each when they went to Buchach. The basis for the fines was that they were outside the territory of their legal domicile. Meanwhile, the chancellor was fined fifty rubles. The militia came along with army soldiers and dogs. They declared the area a "forbidden zone." The people prayed fervently, ignoring both the KGB and the barking dogs.

There had been quite a few scenes at Zarvanystya. The militia beat people, pulled their hair, kicked them, and let the dogs have a go at them. The next day I was there when a black Volga pulled up with three people who made their way toward us. It was Sister Irene who ran to me and said the authorities had come. The people surrounded me so they couldn't get to me. We fell to our knees saying the Rosary.

Then I went to see the officials and greeted them with the words, "Glory be to Jesus Christ." Captain Alexander Stupyn asked why I was there, and the secretary of the Communist cell on the local collective farm said that we were in the forbidden zone. "You're a stranger," he said. "I don't know you and I have the right to arrest you."

"Why bother talking to him," the captain cried out.

I began demanding their documents. "You're a drunk," I said. "And I'll protest that the Russians are forbidding me to pray."

"Did you bring these people here? Do you know this is forbidden?"

I said, "These people came to say goodbye to me and to pray."

The third official refused to show his documents. Other KGB and militia surrounded a wooded area with billies in hand. Then I was spoken to in Ukrainian. "Why did you come from Carpathia all the way here?"

"In other words, you know who I am," I said.

They asked for my passport and I showed them my foreign one. I told the people that I was leaving the country and would let the world know how the Russians prevent people from praying, despite the lie of *glasnost.* The officers weren't anxious for me to know their specific names. "What can we do with you?" one fretted. The officials in Kiev had directed them to chase me away.

They decided to let the people pray and then quietly leave. "Josyp, call the people in from the glens and take them deep into the woods," one agent told me. The KGB wanted us to disappear during daytime so they could file a clean report. But there were people wounded from the previous day. We tried to bring them to a local hospital for treatment.

At midnight, someone came to us and said two men from the mayor's office had been sent by the KGB to observe us.

They couldn't recognize me because I had shaved my tell-tale beard. In the morning we celebrated the last liturgy. It was August 30. I left to see Bishop Dmyterko in Kolomaya and then went back to Moscow, where a press conference was planned with reporters from *El Pais, El Figaro,* and American papers such as *The Chicago Tribune.* I spoke of Chernobyl but very little ended up in print.

The officials were frightened about the events in Hrushiv and confused as to what to do with the "hostile" Ukrainian Catholic Church. Everything the Mother of God told me in 1972 was materializing.

I would like to say that I haven't even told my wife everything that I foresaw. I don't want to tell everything. People are not yet ready to hear about the colossal harm that is to come.

My date for our departure from the Soviet Union was September 18. We left from Moscow—me, Olena, and the three children, Marianna, Kalyna, and Paul. That evening we were in Amsterdam. Holland was the first to grant us entrance visas. There we were tended to by both Dutch and Canadian officials.

I issued a statement over the Ukrainian Press Service on September 24. "Was it difficult to get me and my family out of the USSR?" I said. "For now let it suffice to say yes! But everything was in God's hands."

Then I announced that Stalin had not destroyed us, and that the reason could be found in the words of Christ, in Matthew 16:18: *"And I also say to you that you are Peter, and on this rock I will build my Church, and the gates of Hell shall not prevail against it."*

Not only had we survived, I said, but we were growing in number.

I reminded everyone that there were nearly 15 million Ukrainian and Roman Catholics throughout the USSR. "In our underground, we have functioning seminaries which prepare candidates for the priesthood. In Transcarpathia we have an underground school for the catechetization of children." I also made a distinction between the official Russian Orthodox Church and the underground Synodal Russian Orthodox Church. While expressing the expectation that I would soon return to the Ukraine, I said that much change needed to take place and that only when Moscow changes its attitude toward Christians will we no longer be threatened by nuclear war. "Peace will come but only when the USSR finds in itself the strength to accept the ideas and words of Jesus. Further, as a spokesman for the faithful of the Church in Ukraine, I solemnly profess that we are all faithful to the Apostolic See of Rome with His Holiness John Paul II as its head. . . ."

A deal had been struck to send us to Canada, where there is a large Ukrainian population—part of the diaspora, including many old nationalists. A number of transcontinental organizations were assisting us, including International Solidarity of Switzerland. While final arrangements were being made, they put us in a safehouse far outside the city. We were surrounded by a wall, fence, and security police. One day we went swimming and returned to find a whole room overturned by intruders searching for something—or just trying to let us know that the KGB could get around fences and was still watching me. I speculated that they were looking for diaries and address books that— unfortunately for them—I always keep with me.

On September 30 we left for Toronto and were received by Bishop Isidore Borecky and representatives of the St. Sophia Religious Association of Ukrainian Catholics. Initially we settled in the city of St. Catherines, which is not far from Niagara Falls and the border of the USA. We drew support from the diocese and the Ukrainian Catholic community.

On October 22, 1987, I appeared in Washington, D.C. before the *Congressional Commission on Security and Cooperation in Europe.* In attendance were such luminaries as Senator Alfonse D'Amato of New York State, Senator Frank Lautenberg of New Jersey, and Rochester Congresswoman Louise Slaughter.

There I was, in the nation of the magnificent Statue of Liberty. I believe America has many spiritual problems, but she, like the statue, is the beacon of freedom. A militarily strong United States is essential to all the world. There is no telling what would have happened had America not been there to counter the spread of Communism.

The hearing was held at 10 a.m. in Committee Room 138

of the Dirksen Senate Office Building. The chairman of the commission, Congressman Steny H. Hoyer, introduced four of us refugees. Besides me there was a Ukrainian named Danylo Shumuk and two Georgians I had known and converted, Eduard and Tenghiz Gudava. "Their persistence despite the KGB's most tenacious efforts is a testament to their courage and devotion to ideals embodied in the Helsinki Final Act," said Congressman Hoyer, who was overly generous with his praise. "Mr. Josyp Terelya is the best-known leader of the Ukrainian Catholic Church, the largest banned religious denomination in the Soviet Union."

The co-chairman, Senator Dennis DeConcini, added that my biographical sketch "reads like a chilling resumé of one whose career has been based on how to survive in the Soviet gulag. His 'crimes' center around his leadership in the Ukrainian Catholic Church. According to a recent State Department report, the 'Communist Party has sought to eliminate religion,' and no religion has suffered more than the Ukrainian Catholic Church."

I began my opening statement. Out of my mouth came the frustrations and agonies of four decades. To be a Ukrainian Catholic, I explained, "is to be no less than a non-entity. Non-entities are disregarded; we are pursued, punished, persecuted, even murdered, or perhaps worse, allowed to endure endless years of inhumane treatment in the Soviet camps, prisons, and so-called psychiatric hospitals. Ukrainian Catholics form at least one-tenth of the population of the Ukrainian Republic, but not one church is open, not one of our monasteries functions, not one of our institutions can open its doors. To participate in church services the faithful must gather in the middle of the night, they must gather in private homes, in the forest, and always fearing arrest, searches, punishment. The children must learn not to use Christian greetings in public even though they do so in private. The children must learn to be silent when the issue of faith and religion is raised in school."

I explained that the underground Eastern Rite Church had five million members in the Ukraine and 1.9 million in other regions of the Soviet Union, along with 1,200 sisters and a thousand priests. It was a considerable number, and yet before the crackdown in the 1940s, we had 6,390 priests and monastics. In my written statement I mentioned the casualties: the Basilian monk, Peter Oros, murdered in 1953; the exiled lay activist Ivan Markiv, killed in 1957; the Basilian Oleksa Zarytskyj, tortured to death by the KGB; and Bishop Hoydych of Pryashiv, who died in a Czech camp in 1960.

"Our Church asks Mr. Gorbachev, 'If there is democratization, why do you not legalize the Ukrainian Catholic Church?'" I testified. "'If there is *perestroika* why are our churches still being destroyed, our crosses demolished, our people persecuted?'" I presented evidence on the most recent desecrations. From May 1986 to August 1987 there had been any number of such occurrences, including an iconostasis that was destroyed in Dornbratovo at the orders of a local Russian Orthodox bishop, a cross in Ardanovo destroyed by village Communists, and the complete ruin of a chapel in Bilky, where Communists refused to allow villagers to rebuild it. On Good Friday in 1987 authorities broke up a prayer session at a cemetery in Borzhavske and two people lost their jobs.

"Thousands of Evangelical Christian Pentecostals wish to freely emigrate if there is openness," I said. "Let them go. Hundreds of thousands of prisoners still languish in Soviet prisons, camps, and hospitals for their faith and for the principles which our Church upholds. I say let them go. If there is to be democratization then the Perm special regime camp in Kuchino, Number 36-1, should be closed and men of principle who languish there should be released."

Among my major concerns was the current chairman of the initiatory group, Vasyl Kobryn, who was still incarcerated.

"In the captivated world and the subjugated world, we know that the United States bears the torch of freedom," I said under questioning. "This is a country which built its state based on the Bible, and therefore it is very important how the government of the United States relates itself to atheist governments in its external affairs." I emphasized that the USSR, on the other hand, "is the first state in the world which openly stated its hatred of God."

"I was brought up among very leading Communists, in a family of leading Communists," I continued. "Mr. Shelest came to our home. I remember the conversations there. The Soviet Union is in a dilemma today, in technology, and it needs American bread. And, all of today's *glasnost* is a camouflage for the West, and they are demanding and need at any price the West to back off its principle.'' It was essential, I added, for the Soviet Union to present an angelic face to the West. Yet, between December 1986 and July 1987, more than 150 churches and chapels had been demolished. What we needed was a planned and constant policy from the West in its relations with the Empire of Satan.

Congressman Chris Smith then began questioning me about the apparitions. He described himself as ''a very strong believer'' in the miracle of Fatima. ''Now, we hear that there appear to be apparitions occurring in Ukraine,'' he said. ''I was wondering if you could tell us how seriously you regard those apparitions, and from a political point of view, what impact is that having upon people in terms of resurgence of faith and a belief that the Church, the Ukrainian Catholic Church, ought to be recognized by the Soviet Union? What impact are those apparitions having on the people?''

It was a weighty question. And I gave him my weightiest response. I told him it was my feeling that the prophecies of Fatima are a signpost for how Christians should conduct themselves in the USSR. ''Apparitions of the Mother of God in Medjugorje support the Fatima apparitions, and in a short while after, the apparitions in Hrushiv in Ukraine,'' I said. ''I was in Hrushiv soon after the apparitions began. What did I see? Above the church there was a light that shined 250, 300 meters high. In that light I saw a photogenic face of a woman, who was garbed—as if in flames. The sister servants that were there right beside me said that they saw the woman in white garb. It was like that for three weeks. In a day, 100,000 people would pass through Hrushiv. Over those three weeks, the way the woman would appear would change, it would be different. There were even prophecies.''

Although I did not reveal the prophecies, I continued to give the American politicians a sense of the miracle. I told them how the people cried with joy; I mentioned how it bolstered feelings about our Ukraine. Then I answered the question that Smith had specifically posed. ''The events in Hrushiv have definitely changed the political situation in

Ukraine," I said. "Non-Christians come to the apparitions. I was a witness to how a Russian officer, a captain, said, 'There is a God.' People are coming not just from the Ukraine but from elsewhere, and they accepted faith in God. Before my eyes a militia officer who was supposed to be there guarding the church—the head of the KGB from Drohobych, he was yelling at them: 'Why are you allowing these people to go and see the apparition?' The officer took off his cap, took off his epaulets, and said, 'What can I do if I have seen the Mother of God?' In two weeks the militiaman was sent to a psychiatric hospital, and we believe that the apparitions in Hrushiv are not for us Christians [only]. It is a sign for all politicians that times of change are coming."

Next I added some words of advice: "Approach these matters, this change, very, very carefully and cautiously."

Congressman Smith again spoke up. "I'm a great believer that it's often the hidden spiritual dimension that makes all the difference in the world," he said. "In this case, based on what you told us, and from other readings that I have done, it seems very clear that the revival in Christianity, and specifically in Catholicism, is directly linked to both the apparitions and the longsuffering of the Church and the fruit that has borne in terms of people who have been martyrs for their faith. I am moved by what you say. I think we ought to do further research into this to bring more of this information to light. I know that there are a great number of skeptics, but it seems that those skeptics are often convinced when they really look into the facts. In the case of some of those who have gone to Medjugorje, there has been a real change of heart, even from the most hardened skeptic."

I was happy the congressman expressed favorable inclinations towards the famous Marian apparitions. What Lucia communicated at Fatima was an absolute prophecy concerning Russia. And she also emphasized the importance of First Saturday devotions to save souls, reverse errors, and forestall some of the punishments. The fate of Russia—and of the world—hinges upon Russia's conversion to God. Perhaps we can mitigate and even prevent certain catastrophes if we respond to Our Lady's call. The danger of nuclear annihilation will continue until the USSR is changed from within—converted to God. Political events depend upon spiritual ones. Peace will reign when we obey Our Lady. All that Our Lady of Fatima predicted has come true, except for "Russia's conversion," which we are still awaiting. Let us always remember what the Mother of God told Lucia: *"In order to prevent God's punishment of the world for its crimes, I shall come to ask for the consecration of Russia to my Immaculate Heart, and the communion of reparation on the first Saturdays. If my wishes are fulfilled, Russia will be converted and there will be a period of peace. If not, Russia will spread her errors throughout the world, promoting wars and persecution of the Church."*

In Washington there was also a reception in the White House and a press release. In my statement to the press, issued through the St. Sophia society, my emotions were apparent. "I am overjoyed to be able to say, without worrying about the KGB, 'Be vigilant, strengthen Christian solidarity.'" I also expressed my gratitude to Canadian Prime Minister Brian Mulroney and Canadian Foreign Minister Joe Clark. "With joy and sincerity I would also like to thank the government of Queen Beatrice of the Netherlands and the Christian communities of that country for their many efforts on my behalf and ultimately for their granting me my initial visa for travel to the West."

I said that no one will *ever know* the number of martyrs in the Soviet Union. "But we must remember that in the Soviet gulag, more Christians may have died than for the entire period from Christ to 1917," I said.

President Reagan was supposed to attend the reception but was diverted to a local hospital, where his wife Nancy was recuperating from a mastectomy. After the reception, I was escorted to a small room where Americans who spoke Ukrainian and Russian debriefed me. I had hardly the time to collect my thoughts when another trip was in order: a visit to Rome. On the morning of November 7, I was escorted by an archbishop for a meeting with Pope John Paul II.

They asked me what languages I spoke and I told them Russian and Polish. The archbishop briefed me on etiquette in the papal court. Then I was escorted to the papal apartments. Pope John Paul, his face so solemn and yet bright, was seated behind a desk and I was brought to the left of him. I bowed down and the Holy Father blessed me.

The Pope was especially interested in my family and how they had endured my years in prison. The Holy Father said I should have come with my wife and children. We spoke about the family for about 15 minutes. After that I got down to business, presenting him documents and photographs pertaining to the underground Church. He stopped me when I got to Zarvanystya, his eyes beaming; he had visited that shrine. He asked about it in detail. I showed him pictures of people praying in the woods; then the Pope said, "What is the status of the religious question in the Ukraine? I'm not asking about the priests and religious but the faith of the simple people."

I began to describe the condition of the people and the issue of legalization. It was evident the Pope had never seen photographs of our underground Masses. We had been sending material to the Vatican for ten years, but apparently it had never gotten to him. I don't know why. He was under the impression that our Church was just a few thousand diehards—not five-million strong. The Pope showed special interest in the Russian Greek Catholic Church. I explained there were people detained in prison for their involvement with it. The Pope was also interested in my future and how I would support myself. I made mention of Hrushiv but did not have time to go into it at any length. The meeting flew by, lasting 43 minutes.

Afterwards I was taken to lunch by Archbishop Silvestrini and Cardinal Cassaroli and then the next day had dinner with Cardinal Ratzinger, the prefect of Congregation for the Doctrine of the Faith, and other notables. Ratzinger had ordered boiled veal for me. I mentioned to someone that I hadn't eaten ice cream in twenty years, and so they also had that for me. I discussed the Hrushiv apparitions with Ratzinger and he seemed very open to them. The U.S. ambassador to the Vatican invited me to a reception the next day. Then I was taken for another reception, at the home of the Italian ambassador to the Vatican.

This first visit to Rome was also when I met the cardinal whose face I had seen on the "screen" at Hrushiv. We spoke for five hours and he began to weep when I discussed the wrongful way he had conducted himself with the Communists. The Virgin told me not to mention names and I prefer not to go into further details.

Ratzinger had suggested that I speak in Venice at an upcoming conference on Church persecution, and I did. But I arrived there with bodyguards. I believe it was in January of 1988. The Soviet delegation protested my appearance but I stood firm and distributed literature to back my case.

How disconcerted was a leader of the Russian Orthodox Church to find himself seated next to me!

I had a couple other encounters with the Pope, including at celebrations in 1988 marking the millennium of Ukrainian Christianity. I was privileged to receive Communion from John Paul's own hands. Olena was also there, seated at the front in St. Peter's Church. But there are still some issues I wish to discuss with the Pope. We need to talk more about Hrushiv and we need to speak more about the consecration of Russia to the Immaculate Heart of Mary, which I don't believe has been fully done. Many priests and bishops should come to Rome and the consecration should be loudly announced.

I also wanted to discuss such issues with Sister Lucia, the visionary of Fatima. I obtained papal permission to meet with her in Portugal. The appointment was set for May 13, 1989. But for some strange reason they refused me a visa at the last minute. My concern is that people do not know the truth and do not know God's will. I am saying this now, and if Sister Lucia can hear me, I feel she knows what I am saying. I'm saying the truth. There is a place prepared for her, she knows where she will be, she will be with the Mother of God.

Sister Lucia is suffering due to the fact that there is not a public announcement of Russia's consecration. Lucia will live to see the beginning of the chastisement. After the Pope publicly announces the consecration of Russia to the Immaculate Heart of Mary, Sister Lucia will pass to her eternal reward.

Chapter 23

OUR
JESUS

So here I sit in Canada, spending my days in a house on the edge of Toronto, where we moved after St. Catherines. My children attend Ukrainian Catholic school, my wife attends classes to learn English, and I remain at home nursing various illnesses—and mailing letters, medical supplies, bibles, and rosaries back to the Soviet Union. Anyone reading this who wishes to donate holy pictures or religious items should contact me through the Riehle Foundation.

I've tried to get back to the Ukraine but they will not issue me the necessary travel documents. Three months after I left Moscow, on January 18, 1988, the consulate in Ottawa called me in and made me return my Soviet passport. The Russians were stripping me of Soviet citizenship! The decree formalizing this was issued on January 21. I didn't know what to do then and I still don't know what to do. I had gone to Canada to speak in front of Ukrainian groups—not to spend the rest of my life here. So it wasn't just a trip they were letting me take; it was permanent exile.

Life in exile can be as trying as life in a camp. I feel isolated from the world and am truly a man without a country—stripped of Soviet citizenship and with no status other than that of "visitor" in Canada. The Soviet commandants weren't fooling when they said that I would spend the rest of my life paying for medicine. I have heart trouble, liver problems, severe headaches, an ulcer, and very bad rheumatism. At age 47 I sometimes feel like a cripple; when the weather changes my joints give me trouble.

But I remain grateful to God for all the miracles he has worked in my life and for the spiritual consolations. The mysticism? It's not like before. I don't have quite as much time to pray as I once did. I am too involved with politics and writing essays and books, including one about Masons. When I speak about the apparitions, I feel this pulsating sensation like electricity come through me, as if ants are crawling on my hands, which become numb. I dream vivid dreams. And while talking of Hrushiv uplifts me, afterwards I am drained of all energy and feel out of sorts.

I also dream strange dreams. While I haven't seen the Virgin Mary since Hrushiv, I still have dreams in which certain messages are conveyed to me, and I experience inner wellings that feed my intuition. These are personal revelations. In one dream I was flying above a devastated earth. It was all gray. But I do not know from what. Then there are the little "coincidences." For example in 1988 an American woman came to our home and asked if I lived there. She gave me photo cards of Mother Teresa—ten of them. I immediately got the inkling that I would be meeting Mother Teresa in ten weeks. But how could that be possible? I was in Canada and she was in India.

Yet we did meet in 1988, and it was ten weeks after I got those cards from the stranger. I was invited to the 12th Congress of the Christian Family in Vienna and there I met the famous nun.

You may recall my dream of seeing Jesus in a celestial city. The dream sort of repeated itself when I was in freedom in 1987. Jesus was standing. I knew it was Jesus now, but there were no longer 12 apostles but 72. I was apprehensive and confused. *"Don't be surprised at any of this,"* Jesus said. What I felt when I was there was that it wasn't an environment anything like what we are accustomed to here. It was very beautiful but it wasn't living nature—no animals or trees. I felt this sorrow or regret: This is very beautiful but nothing around us is alive, I thought. I was afraid to express these feelings to Jesus. He was very young and all the others were so old. One had a very good but severe face. It was like they were judges, and yet I'm not sure they were judges. I didn't want to leave but neither did I want Jesus to think I would run away from my tasks on earth. Jesus smiled and said, *"You have to go back. It's not your time to come here yet. No one wants to return from here and go back there."* I felt a cold shivering go through me and soon found myself on earth waking up in a bed.

Events in the USSR continued to captivate my attention. I talked about such issues at a panel in Pittsburgh that included the journalist William F. Buckley. What was the extent of repression? Before World War I, there were nearly 5,000 Orthodox churches, 25,000 mosques, and tens of thousands of synagogues, Protestant churches, and Buddhist temples, according to one former KGB agent. By the 1980s, there were less than 4,000 places of worship for all religions and sects combined in the USSR. On the surface it looks like some progress is being made. On October 5, 1989, the Pope called on Soviet authorities to recognize our religious rights. Although not adequately, the Soviets did respond to such calls. We have all seen photographs of the historic meeting on December 1, 1989, between Gorbachev and the Pope. It was very dramatic. And our Church won partial, superficial liberty. As *The New York Times* reported, "Officials in the Ukraine have announced that they will register congregations of the Ukrainian Catholic Church, ending more than four decades in which the church's status was illegal, church members said today."

Still, many issues remain to be resolved. We had also demanded that the government rescind the Stalin-sponsored synod or "sobor" of March 1946 that merged us with the Russian Orthodox Church. This needs to be done, and we must wait and see if true religious freedom has come to the USSR. Most pressing of all is the matter of our 4,000 churches that were turned over to the Orthodox or used for secular purposes—warehouses, museums, funeral parlors. The congregation of Transfiguration Cathedral in L'viv voted to transfer its allegiance to the Eastern Rite Catholic Church, and many other churches, encouraged by the papal meeting, declared themselves Catholic. Immediately, more than a hundred churches in Western Ukraine alone announced that they were turning back to Catholicism and many more were sure to follow. By January of 1990, 600 churches in the larger cities and towns of the Ukraine were functioning as Eastern Rite Catholic, 700 others had applied for registration, and an estimated 350 priests who formerly served in the Russian Orthodox Church asked to be accepted by Catholic bishops. The smaller villages had not yet been tallied. They will account for many more.

But the Kremlin and Russian Orthodox leaders actively oppose such changes. The Orthodox opposition is for an obvious reason: a quarter of its churches are in the heavily Catholic Western Ukraine and may be reconsecrated to Catholicism. Orthodox officials in Moscow claimed that Transfiguration Cathedral was forcibly seized, and faced with threats from the government, parishioners had to maintain a 24-hour vigil at the cathedral.

In L'viv there has been confrontation and the threat of serious violence as Ukrainian Catholics seek to regain St. George's, our most precious cathedral. On August 12, 1990, 30,000 Ukrainian Catholics marched from the Church of the Transfiguration to the Cathedral of St. George for an outdoor prayer service. There were reports that the church's doors were forced open by Catholics who also hurled stones through the windows, but many such reports have been exaggerated to make us look bad. By August 19, the baroque cathedral was back in Catholic hands. Hundreds of thousands came to celebrate. "This day," said Bishop Sterniuk, "was prepared by God and we rejoice that God has allowed us to reclaim this temple, which up to now has been in enemy hands."

In L'viv, by the beginning of 1990, only four of 19 churches remained in Orthodox possession.

At times it has nearly sounded like a holy war is in the offing. That would be terrible. We shouldn't fight the Orthodox, but neither should we capitulate. The Orthodox leaders in Moscow are opposed to our new legal status because of ecclesiastical differences and because of the inevitable battle to take back what was once ours. Our demand is simple and unassailable: we want our churches, chapels, and monasteries back.

There are also major philosophical differences. The Orthodox often go along with Kremlin hard-liners. In December of 1990, as the issue of independence for Soviet republics began gathering steam, Patriarch Aleksy II, the Orthodox primate, joined a galaxy of top military officers in urging Gorbachev to assert more direct rule in rebellious territories—in other words, to crack down on moves for independence in such places as Latvia, Lithuania, Byelorussia, Georgia, and the Ukraine. By 1991 Gorbachev, showing his true side, had done just that.

The Orthodox are very vicious and vituperative against the Catholics. Is it any wonder that they strongly disliked and tried to debunk apparitions that occurred at Catholic chapels?

I continue to receive letters relating experiences at places like Hrushiv. The message remains the same: pray and repent. Sacrifice. After original sin, sacrifice is the principle law for mankind. Remember that sin is forbidden pleasure. Make public demonstrations of your faith. Fear not, pray constantly, and publicly acknowledge Jesus. Raise your hat, bow your head or make the sign of the cross on streets and in buses when you pass a church. At Mass, kneel to express your obedience. It is not essential to repeat every word at Mass; it is okay to recite the Rosary. But kneel and give visible witness. Only under the leadership of the Catholic Church will the world find peace. If we give mass witness, the world will take note and convert. We must give witness. We must give witness and react against unchristian events. A Christian has no right to remain silent. If we give witness we will have more personal peace.

And we must work. We all wait for God to put everything in order, but that's our job! The conversion of sinners? That's our job! Some of the happiest moments in my life were in prison because it was there that I converted many people.

I would also like to say that, in the end, true freedom is not something that a politician can give us. Freedom comes from within. Freedom is an internal feeling and for it to grow one must listen to and love God.

There was a flare up in apparitions from April to July of 1988. The Orthodox are very negative and skeptical of the apparitions and this has infected many of the people. That's why I'm doing everything in my power to return to the Ukraine: to help my Church in its continuing evolution and to establish Hrushiv as a place of pilgrimage. The pilgrim numbers are getting small and unless it increases, none of the bishops will accept it. I must go back. I'm demanding that they return my citizenship so I can return home. People tell me that I could still be killed there, that I could be put into prison again. I want to say that it's better to be in prison than stay in exile not knowing. And I believe that if I were in prison, this would raise the morale of the Catholic Church to a higher degree than can be done here in the West.

One day the enemy will throw the might of his armies against us and we shall overcome them with banners and crosses, which are more powerful than tanks or missiles. I will be back in the Ukraine for this. I believe that with my heart. There will be mass conversions. I believe the Ukraine will become one of the stronger nations of Europe and that through it a great conversion of the world will take place. When the Ukraine is free, peace will be established. If there is conversion, we will have an independent Georgia, an independent Armenia, an independent Lithuania.

And if the Ukraine is not freed, there may be a revolution that provokes a global war. The Ukraine would rather have it come through peaceful means but we will do what it takes.

In the meantime the atheists have started new attacks against the Church. Unfortunately, there are Protestants who are using their new religious liberty to likewise circulate anti-Catholic attacks. Such propaganda is hurtful because the Catholics have very little literature of their own. Bibles aren't enough; they need a systematic presentation of Catholic doctrine.

There is too little assistance from the West. Here in North America, everyone is taken up by Gorbachev-mania. There are still more monuments to Lenin that need to be taken down. There are still thousands in the camps and prisons.

Now it is 1991. What will happen before the turn of this chaotic and calamitous century? While I'm not predicting world war as such, I remain apprehensive. No matter how they act in public, I am still very skeptical of Gorbachev and for that matter, any Communist. Remain strong and vig-

ilant, America! I believe Gorbachev may be the last leader
before the great chastisements begin. And I don't believe
he's any different from his predecessors. While there have
been gains in religious freedom, much of it has been for
show and much remains to be done.

As Europe begins a new transformation, there are countless scenarios that could play out. There is the new Germany, there are the new leaders in Eastern Europe, there
is civil strife in Yugoslavia, there is China acting very quietly,
and then there is the monstrous state called the USSR. How
many have the Soviets killed? Counting the Bolshevik
takeover, the famines, and those who died in camps, more
than 50 million Soviet citizens have died as a result of their
government's repression. Yes, at least 50 million. Hard-liners
are gaining power in Moscow while in the Ukraine nationalists are gathering steam, setting the stage for conflict. Once
again, the tinderbox is the Ukraine. But even the republic
of Russia itself is distancing itself from the central powers
of the Soviet Union.

If the USSR is truly becoming an open society, why is
the KGB still fully in place, and if Gorbachev is so humane,
why do we still not know the fate of Raoul Wallenberg?

America, remain vigilant, but America, also look at the
plank in your own eye. Purify yourself. Stop killing unborn
babies. Halt the filth that comes out of Hollywood. I have
now been in the West long enough to know that its brand
of evil is different than in the Soviet Union, but evil nonetheless. Purge yourselves of lewdness, erotica, obsessive sensuality and aberrant sex. Purge yourselves of materialism,
ego, and the rampant vanity. Take a second look at the rock
star who, like a cosmic trick, is called "Madonna" while
she gallivants across television screens lewdly and blasphe-
mously. Purge yourselves of addiction and sloth. Elect only
politicians with solid morality. Stop polluting the
atmosphere. *Feel* the words of God at Mass. Pray. Fast. And
always search your souls for proper humility.

Love and humility. Forgiveness. With those three things
we achieve all our goals. By now you have seen the terrible
strength of Communist force, but the Rosary renders even
the KGB impotent. I am a living witness before you. If we
call out to move a mountain and do so in faith, the moun-

tain will truly move. Human love imbued with Divine love gives us immense possibilities. We must direct our attention to our youth.

Have I been able to forgive the Russians? I'm human like you. It's difficult even now for me. When I begin to recount the losses in just my own family, I'm filled with remorse and sadness and anger. But I seek to overcome myself. So likewise with you: overcome yourselves. We must live in the humility of God. Humility before God, to God, and opposition to Satan. Our life is short. We want to obtain everything immediately. But most of us want to obtain this without God. We can not. And we must forgive. If we learn to forgive, then even the enemies who see us forgiving with sincerity will join in solidarity with us. There is much to be done. But remember, we are not alone. God is with us.

In the West, young people are quick to unite in marriage and just as quick to depart. The sacrament of marriage is violated. And the offspring are aborted. Even mafia criminals have more legal rights than the unborn. And we Catholics can not passively accept this. A small group of atheists has imposed its views on the entire population. Why do authorities disallow crucifixes in the schools at the same time they permit drugs, pornography, lewd music, and symbols of Satan? Is this really democracy? There are more Christians in the world than atheists, and yet we let atheists design our systems of law, communication, and education.

They will persecute us but it will not last for long. All the atheists' fancy tools cannot stand up to the tools of Christ—two pieces of wood forming the cross.

Two thousand years have passed since that birth which was so different from anything else in history. Who is this man? Of whence did he come? He never traveled far, and only once in His life, as an infant, did He cross the boundaries of His own country. He lived poorly, had no wealth, no gold, no political influence. His parents were simple people, and He Himself never completed higher studies, but from early childhood, people marveled at His understanding and wisdom. He submitted to the laws of nature but at will could rise above them. He walked across the stormy surfaces of the waters, and the wind listened to Him and obeyed His commands. He healed people, seeking no remuneration. He never wrote a book, but the libraries and bookstores of the world are filled with books written about Him. He never wrote letters, but the greatest writers and composers have written of Him. He was never a painter or artist but representations of Him are more widespread than any others. He established no learned institutions or societies, but no school or university can boast of the number of students or disciples that He has. He was never a commander of armies and never took up arms, but the world knows of no leader with as many followers. He never practiced psychiatry, but he healed the broken hearts of many people. Proud emperors, kings, and political leaders are forgotten but the name of this man is more and more known among the nations of the world. He died on the cross almost 2,000 years ago but He remains alive and always will. He resides now in the infinite glory of Heaven as Man and God.

Our own Jesus.

Our Lady's apparitions are the precursor for the Second Coming of Him.

The intellectual skeptics laugh at the supernatural, but the days of such mockery are coming to an end. Atheistic humanism, like Communism, will not dominate us for much longer. Nor will the spiritual blindness that so badly narrows the vision of scientists. Soon science will no longer proclaim itself as the new religion, and at the opposite end of the spectrum the occult and New Age movement will be recognized for what it is: a device of Satan.

There will be ups and downs. Sometimes it will look like we are losing again. At times it will seem as if the materialists, occultists, and atheists are again winning. But in the end they cannot dominate the world, and in the end they will receive a clear rebuke. I don't know exactly what the Eternal One will send in the way of chastisement, but the scales of Divine justice must be brought into balance and the way must be cleared for the return of Christ as King.

OTHER RECENT TITLES AVAILABLE
THROUGH THE RIEHLE FOUNDATION

NINE YEARS OF APPARITIONS: By Fr. René Laurentin.
An update book for the years 1989-1990 of the events in Medjugorje, Yugoslavia. Contains 250 pages of witnesses, testimonies and interviews with the seers, the fruits of the apparitions, and 32 color photos. One of Fr. Laurentin's finest. $7.00

AN APPEAL FROM MARY IN ARGENTINA: By Fr. René Laurentin.
An exciting account of the incredible events taking place in San Nicolas, Argentina. The complete story of the apparitions to Gladys Quiroga de Motta. 156 pages. Color photos. $6.00

POWER OF THE ROSARY: By Fr. Albert Shamon.
A modern, complete and factual account of the power of this traditional prayer form. Provides the basis for its use and a history of its results. 64 pages. $2.00

SPIRITUAL WARFARE: By Fr. George Kosicki CSB.
The author provides us with some straight-forward, "tell it like it is" facts concerning the existence of Satan and his all-out-warfare being waged against this age. 156 pages. $5.00

UNICORN IN THE SANCTUARY:By Randy England.
A complete book-length study of the impact of the New Age on Catholicism. In clear, down-to-earth style, the author tells readers what's wrong, where it came from, and what to do about it. 176 pages. $7.00

WHY PRAYER? By Fr. René Laurentin.
Through this small book, Fr. Laurentin provides a brilliant response. He gives us the "theology" of prayer and some clear insight to some forgotten truths concerning our relationship with our Creator. 96 pages. $4.00

THE RIEHLE FOUNDATION
P. O. BOX 7
MILFORD, OHIO 45150

Donations are accepted for materials, though not required. Suggested values are indicated.

THE
RIEHLE
FOUNDATION...

The Riehle Foundation is a non-profit, tax-exempt, charitable organization that exists to produce and/or distribute Catholic material to anyone, anywhere.

The Foundation is dedicated to the Mother of God and her role in the salvation of mankind. We believe that this role has not diminished in our time, but, on the contrary has become all the more apparent in this the era of Mary as recognized by Pope John Paul II, whom we strongly support.

During the past four years the foundation has distributed over two million books, films, rosaries, bibles, etc. to individuals, parishes, and organizations all over the world. Additionally, the foundation sends materials to missions and parishes in a dozen foreign countries.

Donations forwarded to The Riehle Foundation for the materials distributed provide our sole support. We appreciate your assistance, and request your prayers.

IN THE SERVICE OF JESUS AND MARY
All for the honor and glory of God!

The Riehle Foundation
P.O. Box 7
Milford, OH 45150

Faith Publishing Company

Faith Publishing Company has been organized as a service for the publishing and distribution of materials that reflect Christian values, and in particular the teachings of the Catholic Church.

It is dedicated to publication of only those materials that reflect such values.

Faith Publishing Company also publishes books for The Riehle Foundation. The Foundation is a non-profit, tax-exempt producer and distributor of Catholic books and materials worldwide, and also supplies hospital and prison ministries, churches and mission organizations.

For more information on the publications of Faith Publishing Company, contact:

Faith Publishing Company
P.O. BOX 237
MILFORD, OHIO 45150

Apparition of Our Lady in Cell 21,
    pg. 121

Pg 278: Our Lady's words to the people
    of the Ukraine: "I love the Ukraine
    and the Ukrainian people for their
    suffering and faithfulness to Christ the
    King. And I shall protect the Ukraine for
    the Glory and the future of the kingdom of
    God on earth, which will last a 1,000 yrs.

Pg 279: further visions on this page

An Anti-Christ is simply a person who stands
up against God.

Pg 282 Vision of America.